The Balance of Power in
International Relations

The balance of power has been a central concept in the theory and practice of international relations for the past five hundred years. It has also played a key role in some of the most important attempts to develop a theory of international politics in the contemporary study of international relations. In this book, Richard Little establishes a framework that treats the balance of power as a metaphor, a myth and a model. He then uses this framework to reassess four major texts that use the balance of power to promote a theoretical understanding of international relations: Hans J. Morgenthau's *Politics Among Nations* (1948), Hedley Bull's *The Anarchical Society* (1977), Kenneth N. Waltz's *Theory of International Politics* (1979) and John J. Mearsheimer's *The Tragedy of Great Power Politics* (2001). These reassessments allow the author to develop a more comprehensive model of the balance of power.

Richard Little is Professor of International Politics at the University of Bristol. He is a former Chair and President of the British International Studies Association and the author of *International Systems in World History* (with Barry Buzan, 2000).

D1475564

The Balance of Power in International Relations: Metaphors, Myths and Models

RICHARD LITTLE

CAMBRIDGE
UNIVERSITY PRESS

CAMBRIDGE UNIVERSITY PRESS
Cambridge, New York, Melbourne, Madrid, Cape Town, Singapore, São Paulo

Cambridge University Press
The Edinburgh Building, Cambridge CB2 8RU, UK

Published in the United States of America by Cambridge University Press, New York

www.cambridge.org
Information on this title: www.cambridge.org/9780521697606

First published 2007

Printed in the United Kingdom at the University Press, Cambridge

A catalogue record for this publication is available from the British Library

ISBN   978-0-521-87488-5 hardback
ISBN   978-0-521-69760-6 paperback

For Christine

Contents

List of figures

Acknowledgements

This book was written while I was holding a Major Research Fellowship from the Leverhulme Trust. It was a huge privilege to be awarded one of these fellowships and I am extremely grateful to the Trust for providing me with the opportunity to read and write without the normal daily pressures associated with academic life in the twenty-first century. By the same token, I am also very grateful to all my colleagues in the Department of Politics at the University of Bristol for making it possible for me to take up the fellowship.

My main debt of gratitude, however, is to my wife Christine who has lived with this book as long as I have. She was always my first port of call when I got stuck and although I did not always appreciate her insistence that I try to articulate clearly why I was running into a problem, the book would never have been completed without her steadying influence and her unwavering conviction that I could finish the manuscript. I dedicate the book to her.

PART I

Introduction

1 | Reassessing the balance of power

THIS BOOK REASSESSES the important but also highly controversial role that the balance of power plays in the contemporary theory and practice of international relations.[1] Attempts to understand international relations in terms of the balance of power can be traced back for more than five hundred years and no other theoretical concept can boast this length of provenance. But not only is the balance of power one of the most enduring concepts in the field, it also persists, by some considerable distance, as the most widely cited theory in contemporary literature.[2] Jervis (1997: 131) concludes, moreover, that it is not only the best known, but also, arguably, the most effective theory available to account for the fundamental character of international relations. This is because, according to its advocates, the balance of power provides the ingredients needed to explain the resilience of the modern international system of states. It is no surprise, therefore, that ever since the end of the Second World War a succession of key theorists in iconic texts have attempted to demonstrate that the balance of power provides the foundations on which any overall understanding of international relations must start to build. This book focuses on four texts written during the era since the end of the Second World War that have all made significant albeit contentious theoretical contributions to the field. The texts are Hans J. Morgenthau's *Politics Among Nations* (1948), Hedley Bull's *The Anarchical Society* (1977), Kenneth N. Waltz's *Theory of International Politics* (1979) and John J. Mearsheimer's *The Tragedy of Great Power Politics* (2001).

[1] I use upper case to identify International Relations as an academic field and lower case to identify international relations as the subject matter of this field.

[2] For example, according to Bennett and Stam (2004), between 1991 and 2001 citations of the chief contributions to the balance of power literature dwarfed those concerning all the other major propositions in conflict studies, including those related to democratic peace.

The sheer longevity of the balance of power idea is unchallengeable. If the essence of the balance of power theory is encapsulated by the idea of counterbalancing hegemony, then it is possible to trace the theory back to the work of contemporary historians and political theorists who described and analyzed the relations that existed among the Italian city states in the fifteenth and sixteenth centuries (Nelson, 1943; Vagts, 1948; Haslam, 2002).[3] Ever since that time it has remained a widely held assumption that when a great power shows signs of attempting to dominate the international system, then other great powers will ally in order to preserve their own security by establishing an unequivocal counterweight to the aspiring hegemon. Since all great powers are seen to be aware that this is the probable response to any hegemonic venture, there is little incentive to try to establish hegemony within the system. In this event, the balance of power theory can be viewed as a self-fulfilling prophecy. But it is clearly a prophecy that has sometimes been disconfirmed by events. Over the last two hundred years, there have obviously been leaders like Napoleon and Hitler who have attempted to establish a Eurasian hegemony, although in line with the balance of power theory, they were eventually confronted and defeated by an overwhelming anti-hegemonic coalition.

The balance of power, however, is not only associated with the idea of anti-hegemonic alliances. It is also linked to the idea that states have habitually attempted to maintain their security and promote their interests by joining forces with other states. If one group of states ally in an attempt to promote their common interests, then the balance of power thesis presupposes that other states, observing this development, and fearing that they might be the potential victims of this alliance, will combine and form a counter-alliance. In this case, instead of an overwhelming alliance forming against an aspiring hegemon, there will be two sets of competing alliances that establish a balance of power.

---

[3] Hume famously argued that the idea, although not the phrase, goes back to the ancient Greeks and Haslam (2002: 89–90) agrees with him. By contrast, Butterfield (1966: 133) insists that the balance of power 'did not exist in the ancient world' and that 'more than most of our basic political formulas, this one seems to come from the modern world's reflections on its own experience'. Wight (1977: 66) makes the same point. As becomes clear later, Hume and Haslam are relying on a different conception of the balance of power to Butterfield and Wight.

Although most theories in the contemporary study of international relations can trace their provenance some way back into the past, there is no other theory that has the extended pedigree of the balance of power. However, the theorists examined in this book, who came to the fore after the end of the Second World War, were well aware that they were confronting a very different environment to the one that had confronted European theorists and practitioners from the Renaissance through to the twentieth century.[4] At the start of this period, Europe was situated on the edge of Eurasia, at the end of trading routes that extended across the hemisphere to societies that were richer and more powerful than any that existed in Europe. Yet by the twentieth century, there were few if any areas of the world where the Europeans had not had some impact. As we move into the twenty-first century, moreover, there is a substantial and growing debate about whether or not this impact was more malign than benign. But either way, by the end of the Second World War the future of Europe no longer lay solely in European hands. The centre of global power had shifted to the United States and it was thinking about international politics within this polity that began to count in the future.

Three key factors almost immediately began to differentiate the American experience from the European experience and all three had crucial consequences for a balance of power perspective on international politics. The first was that the United States had the power to shape a new world order and, indeed, they wanted to establish an order that was very different from the order that had prevailed in Europe. The thinking is very evident in a statement made in 1943 by Francis Sayre, an influential State Department official, concerning the prospects for a post-war peace settlement. He argued that 'if we are to build for lasting peace, we must abandon the nineteenth-century conception that the road to peace lies through a nicely poised balance of power. Again and again world experience has told us that no peace dependent upon a balance of power lasts' (cited in Graham, 1948: 271). The second difference was that the United States had to contend with the Soviet Union, another state that also had pretensions to establish a new global order but an order that was radically opposed to the one that

---

[4] Haslam (2002) provides a comprehensive survey of how thinking about the balance of power evolved across this period. See also Sheehan (1996) and Wright (1975).

the United States had in mind. The third difference was that the United States had developed a weapons system that was immediately seen to have the potential for global destruction and it was quickly apparent that the Soviet Union had the technological capability to follow suit.

Establishing a balance of power framework to accommodate these radical changes was not straightforward for the Americans. They had, after all, operated from a very different international perspective from the Europeans for more than a century. In the eighteenth century, North America was still very much influenced by European ideas and there was an extensive debate before the United States gained independence about how this development would affect the European balance of power, and there was a concern that the Europeans might attempt to partition the new state as they had done with Poland (Hutson, 1980: 13–14). Nevertheless, the idea of a balance of power continued to influence thinking in the post-revolutionary era (Lang, 1985), but during the course of the nineteenth century the Americans began to insist that thinking about the balance of power must not be allowed to affect the consolidation of the United States. In 1840, for example, when the United States was in the process of annexing Texas, Guizot, the French Prime Minister, announced to the Chamber of Deputies that North America was a divided continent and that it was in France's interest 'that the independent states should retain their independence – that the balance of the Great Powers among which America is divided should continue, and that no one should become preponderant'. President Polk responded with asperity that the balance of power was an undesirable European practice and that it 'cannot be permitted to have any application on the North American continent' (cited in Sellers, 1966: 342).[5]

By the start of the twentieth century, American hostility to the balance of power began to have a direct impact on Europe. When the United States entered the First World War, President Wilson wanted to ensure that a new system of security was introduced at the end of the

---

[5] Merk (1966, Ch. 3) argues that Guizot did not use the French equivalent of a balance of power in America (équilibre américain) and that Polk's hostile reference to the balance of power was another attempt by an American President to warn Europeans not to intervene in North America.

war and that the balance of power would then become 'the great game, now for ever discredited' (cited in Claude, 1962: 82).[6] He favoured a system of collective security established under the auspices of the League of Nations. But the system failed and with the onset of the Cold War US policy-makers quickly began to think in terms of a global balance of power and so, unsurprisingly, the concept became a central focus of attention in the study of international relations. It is the attempt to theorize the balance of power in the era after the Second World War that provides the focal point for this book.

For several decades after the Second World War it was generally accepted that the first attempts to establish International Relations as an independent field of study were made in the wake of the First World War by idealists who, appalled by the horrors of that war, wished to transform international relations by promoting ideas and institutions that would help to eliminate the kind of balance of power politics that had dominated Europe in previous centuries. According to this conventional account, therefore, it was only during the course of the 1930s, and more especially when the policy of appeasement was reassessed during and after the Second World War, that a new breed of realists succeeded in hijacking this agenda, sidelining the idealists, and locating the balance of power at the centre of thinking about international relations, thereby ensuring that the concept would play a crucial role in the future development of the nascent discipline.[7]

In line with this argument, Guzzini (1998) suggests that the European *émigré*, Hans J. Morgenthau, came forward after 1945 with the express intention of acquainting US leaders with the maxims of nineteenth-century diplomatic practice. These self-identified realists assumed that the US diplomatic tradition was innocent of the frequently brutal ways of power politics and also lacked a sufficiently sophisticated understanding of the complexities of international politics. One of Guzzini's assumptions is that the new breed of realists recognized that to achieve their goal of making European diplomatic

---

[6] Claude (1962) provides an excellent discussion of debates surrounding the balance of power.

[7] This account has been swept aside by Schmidt (1998) who traces the US study of international relations back to the nineteenth century and an elaborate debate about the nature of anarchy and the nature of the state that persisted throughout the twentieth century.

practice, and in particular the balance of power, palatable to American decision-makers they would have to translate the practical and political maxims associated with European diplomacy into scientific truths. In the process they effectively brought into existence and simultaneously defined the boundaries of an independent discipline of International Relations.

Guzzini then draws on this initial insight to provide a complex historiographical account of how International Relations has developed since the Second World War and, more specifically, how realists have responded during this period to the changes that have occurred both in International Relations theory as well as the real world. In essence, Guzzini argues that with the onset of the cold war, realist thinking coincided with American foreign policy practice, and, as a consequence, realists occupied a hegemonic position within the discipline. He then argues that realism lost its hegemonic status within International Relations as the result of the formation of alternative schools of thought and a changing international reality. Guzzini focuses, in particular, on the way that realists have shifted their methodological stance in an attempt to maintain the scientific credibility of their well-worn diplomatic maxims, but he insists that this has not enabled them to recover their lost hegemony.

Nevertheless, Guzzini, wearing his constructivist hat, acknowledges that realism still needs to be taken seriously because he accepts that there are circumstances when policy-makers do operate from a realist perspective. On such occasions, he argues, realist theory might appear to be valid, but the validity is coincidental and, in truth, the realists have a spurious understanding of the situation because their theoretical framework does not allow them to identify, much less understand the significance of this coincidence. By the same token, he argues that the balance of power also requires investigation, but only because there are occasions when diplomats deploy the concept (Guzzini, 1998: 231). The close analysis of the four texts in Chapters 4 to 7 challenges much of this analysis, in particular, the idea that realist theory neatly mapped on to US practice and that their thinking simply transported ideas from European diplomatic practice to provide an erroneous understanding of the contemporary international arena. The analysis suggests, in particular, that Morgenthau has a much more sophisticated understanding of the role of ideas in balance of power thinking than is often acknowledged.

Even the most casual survey of the literature on the balance of power quickly confirms, however, that while the concept is long established and deeply entrenched so too is the criticism directed at the concept.[8] In 1836, for example, Richard Cobden, the nineteenth-century advocate of free trade, acknowledged the importance attached to the balance of power when he surveyed a range of attempts by theorists and practitioners from the eighteenth and early nineteenth centuries to define the concept. But he reached the conclusion that the inconsistencies surrounding the term demonstrated that the phrase represents 'mere words, conveying to the mind not ideas, but sounds like those equally barren syllables which our ancestors put together for the purpose of puzzling themselves about words, in the shape of *Prester John*, or the *philosopher's stone*!' (cited in Wright, 1975: 110).[9] From Cobden's perspective, then, just as Prester John and the philosopher's stone represent familiar myths from the medieval era, so the balance of power needs to be seen as a myth of the European Enlightenment.[10]

Cobden, moreover, was certainly not the first person to voice such a fundamental critique of the balance of power. Frederick the Great acknowledged in his *Confessions* that although 'balance is a word that has subdued the whole world' it has to be accepted that 'in truth this same balance is no more than a bare word, an empty sound' (cited

---

[8] Haslam (2002: 89) argues, however, that criticism of the concept only started about 250 years ago and that this suggests that for the previous 250 years 'the consensus was under a sustained misapprehension, or that circumstances so changed by the time criticism arose that the notion had become suddenly redundant, or that conditions unknown and unconnected with the merits of the concept prompted criticism with other purposes in mind'.

[9] *Prester John* (or 'Priest John') was the mythical ruler of an idyllic Christian kingdom, located initially in the twelfth century in Asia and then by the fourteenth century in Africa, that was under siege by infidels. Over the centuries, more than 100 letters allegedly from Prester John requesting assistance circulated around Europe and precipitated a series of expeditions to locate the kingdom. The *philosopher's stone* was believed by alchemists to be a common but unrecognized substance containing a property that would transmute base metal into gold.

[10] Elsewhere, however, Cobden argues that the balance of power successfully 'preserves the integrity of the Austrian Empire' (cited in Holbraad, 1970: 154), suggesting that Cobden could have had 'other purposes' in mind when he identified the balance of power as a meaningless concept (see footnote 8).

in Schuman, 1948: 80). Reassessing the role played by the balance of power in the eighteenth century, Anderson concluded that it must be viewed as a meaningless concept that served to 'inhibit thought' (Anderson, 1970: 184). Holsti (2004: 26) extends the criticism into the twenty-first century when he insists that there are 'so many theories and renditions of the concept that it ends up essentially meaningless'.

There are few if any theoretical concepts in the social sciences where such polarized reactions are so entrenched and so enduring. The polarization is even more surprising if it is acknowledged that the balance of power is an expression that regularly occurs throughout political and popular discourse as well as across the social sciences, without precipitating any comparable controversy. There are ubiquitous references to the balance of power throughout the media and popular culture where the concept is conventionally appealed to as a way of characterizing developments not only in the international arena but in almost every conceivable social and political setting from the nuclear family to a sports team. On a Google search I came up with 75 million references to the balance of power on one occasion and 186 million on another. No doubt my approach to searching is primitive in the extreme (Sherman, 2005), nevertheless, a quick perusal indicates that the balance of power is, on the one hand, an expression that is firmly embedded in the way that international relations is discussed in popular culture and, on the other, a term that clearly resonates in a huge number of different settings.

So, for example, Google identifies a BBC report from its Pentagon correspondent who observes that the United States is calculating how to respond to the emergence of China as a strategic power. The correspondent notes that 'By steps big and small, China is changing the balance of power in the world' (Brookes, 2005). There is a clear presumption that the correspondent sees this as an uncontroversial sentence and that its meaning is unambiguous and unproblematic. But the balance of power is not a term that is restricted to the analysis of international relations. Sports writers, it appears, also habitually refer to the balance of power. Insert cricket and balance of power into Google and you can get well over a million hits.

References to the balance of power extend into every sphere of social and political life. In 2002, for example, the Department of Health in Britain published a report with the title *Shifting the Balance of Power* which discusses how patients and staff are to be located 'absolutely at the heart' of the National Health System.[11] The point of the report is that as patient power increases, so the power of doctors and senior management will diminish. By referring to the balance of power in the title, however, it is evident that the authors of the report assume that they are employing a meaningful and uncontroversial concept that will elicit a positive response from its audience.

It is indisputable that the balance of power is a concept that is routinely drawn upon in attempts to characterize ongoing social and political relations. But whereas references to the balance of power in general discourse presuppose that the concept is relatively commonplace and uncontroversial, within the study of international relations the concept is regarded as crucial by some theorists as well as highly contentious by others. There is, therefore, a striking contrast to be drawn between the position occupied by the balance of power in the study of international relations and the role that the concept plays in all other contexts.

A key aim of this book is to illuminate the central, complex and yet contentious role that the balance of power plays in the theory and practice of international relations. An important aspect of the complexity associated with the balance of power, however, is often not acknowledged or even registered in the contemporary field because of the dominance of American realists who ostensibly adhere to a strictly materialist approach to theory-building. From their perspective, the balance of power is a product of the insecurity experienced by states operating in an anarchic international system.[12] Although there are significant areas of disagreement among these realists, it is generally accepted that the great powers monitor the material power possessed by all the other states in the international system and endeavour to manipulate the resulting distribution of power in their own favour as a means of enhancing their chances of survival. I associate this approach with an *adversarial* view of the balance of power.

By contrast, although this alternative line of thinking is not widely acknowledged, English school theorists (and as I show in Chapter 4, classical realists such as Morgenthau) also link the balance of power

---

[11] www.dh.gov.uk/assetRoot/04/07/35/54/04073554.pdf downloaded 2 December 2005.

[12] As a consequence, the balance of power is closely related to the idea of a security dilemma. For a comprehensive overview of competing approaches to the security dilemma, see Booth and Wheeler (2007).

to the existence of an international society and their approach requires them to take account of ideational as well as material factors. One of the crucial ideational factors is the recognition by great powers that they have a collective responsibility to maintain order in the international society and that as a consequence they are required to establish and maintain the balance of power. English school theorists argue that it is the institutionalization of this idea that has preserved the contemporary international society and that the impact of this idea distinguishes this society from previous international societies that have emerged across world history. I link this approach with an *associational* view of the balance of power.

From either of these perspectives, however, events since the end of the cold war create a potential anomaly for the resulting theory because the fragmentation of the Soviet Union is seen to have left the United States as the sole super power in a unipolar world. Unsurprisingly, therefore, debates about the balance of power have become even more vociferous in the post-cold war era. For critics, the balance of power looks increasingly anachronistic and unhelpful as a tool for understanding international relations. By contrast, unipolarity has acted as a spur for advocates of the balance of power who have endeavoured to refine their theories to make sense of the reputedly unipolar world that has persisted since the end of the cold war. Many American realists argued, initially, that unipolarity is a very unstable structure and the other great powers in the system would soon begin to balance against the United States. When this did not happen, alternative explanations developed, with, for example, some theorists arguing that unipolarity is likely to be an enduring and stable structure, and others postulating the idea of soft balancing or even arguing that the nature of the international system has undergone fundamental changes that render hard balancing (in the form of arms races and military alliances) redundant. But unreformed balance of power theorists continue to insist either that the United States is restrained by the potential that still exists for balancing, or that balancing is already beginning to come back into play. During the post-cold war era, therefore, American realism provides an increasingly pluralized approach to the balance of power.

I aim, however, to locate this latest development within a much broader framework that identifies and accounts for the important and remarkably distinctive role that the balance of power plays in international relations. To appreciate just how very distinctive this role is, it is necessary to embrace a wider perspective and account for the fact that despite ubiquitous references to the balance of power in every conceivable social setting, from hospitals to cricket, it is only in the field of international relations that it is treated as both a defining feature by some theorists and practitioners and a meaningless concept by others. Elsewhere, the concept is almost invariably regarded as both commonplace and uncontroversial.

Two main moves are made to achieve this end. With the first move, the balance of power is identified as a simple but extremely effective and universally applicable metaphor that transforms an agency-based concept of power, where one actor has control over another, into a structural concept, where power is a product of the system and the overall distribution of power must be constantly reconfigured. The metaphor is employed promiscuously, and yet only in the field of international relations has the metaphor also been transmuted into a long-established myth that narrates how the balance of power ensured the survival of Europe as a system of independent states. This mythification of the balance of power, unique to the field of international relations, is deeply contentious, however, and has generated widespread controversy.

My second, much longer and more elaborate, move explains why, in contrast to other areas in the social sciences, the balance of power has emerged and persists as a central and complex concept in the study of international relations despite the surrounding controversy. In making this move, I associate the concept with a model but suggest that attempts to model the balance of power directly or indirectly draw on its metaphorical and mythical status. I then suggest that these models of the balance of power lie at the heart of some of the most important attempts made since the end of the Second World War to develop a theoretical understanding of international relations. I focus on four key texts written across this period that are all considered to have made lasting albeit controversial theoretical contributions to the field.

The first text, Hans J. Morgenthau's *Politics Among Nations* was initially published in 1948 in the wake of the Second World War, and the eighth edition was published in 2005, twenty-five years after Morgenthau's death. It is often, albeit erroneously, seen to have spearheaded the study of international relations in the United States and it is now widely viewed as providing an exemplar of classical realism. I rely on the 1973 edition which is the last one revised by Morgenthau himself. The second text, Hedley Bull's *The Anarchical Society* was first published in 1977 at a time when the so-called era of *détente* was beginning to peter out. It has been republished twice since Bull's death and is often considered to provide a seminal account of the English school approach to the study of international relations. The third text, Kenneth N. Waltz's *Theory of International Politics* appeared in 1979 at the onset of what Fred Halliday (1986) identified as the Second Cold War, although it can be viewed as a clarion call to *détente*. In the past it was seen to have articulated a neorealist or structural realist approach to international politics although more recently it has been associated, problematically, with a defensive realist approach. Finally, the most recent text is John J. Mearsheimer's *The Tragedy of Great Power Politics*, published in 2001, and so the only one of the four books that is able to take account of the collapse of communism and the end of the cold war. It is also seen to provide the definitive account of an offensive realist approach to international politics. Of course, because this book has been published relatively recently, it is difficult to know whether it will acquire the iconic status possessed by the other three books. But at the very least it has been hailed by its supporters as offering a distinctively new statement on international politics.

Given how familiar and widely cited these books are in the literature, it is legitimate to ask what purpose is served by returning to them and rehearsing their arguments yet again. There are two fundamental reasons for doing so. In the first place, these are all broad-ranging books and the aim here is to focus on what the four theorists specifically have to say about the balance of power and, by doing so, to show how central the concept is to their thinking and to their overall assessment of international politics. By concentrating on what they have to say about the balance of power, moreover, it becomes much more apparent than would otherwise be the case that each author approaches the concept from a very different angle. As a consequence, it emerges that the balance of power is a more complex and multifaceted concept than is often recognized.

In the second place, it is argued that, partly because of their iconic status and the fact that their basic themes get repeated *ad nauseam*, there are now stereotyped images and accounts of these books that distort the actual content. On the one hand, the essence of these books is often distilled down to a single sentence, while on the other, well-worn phrases and arguments from the texts are constantly repeated, but without any attempt to locate them within the context in which they originally appear. Perhaps even more important, there is no attempt to see how the authors were influenced by the climate of the times when the books were originally written. As a result, the prevailing view of all these books is over-simplified and distorted. One key intention here, therefore, is to recover what the authors actually say about the balance of power and how the concept relates to their overall thinking about international politics. A second is to show how the balance of power can become the central focus of very different models of international politics. A third intention is to reveal how the approach to the balance of power has shifted across the last fifty years as successive theorists have endeavoured to come to terms with a complex and changing environment. So while International Relations theorists often endeavour to adjust to a changing environment by formulating new concepts, what we observe here is the way that theorists can also adapt long-established concepts, like the balance of power, to the new circumstances.

There is also an important methodological and historiographical point to be made on the basis of the four books that are investigated here. The survey reveals that there is a very poor understanding of how thinking about the balance of power has evolved in the field because there is a persistent tendency for new developments in thinking about the balance of power to take place at the expense of existing approaches. None of the four theorists engages in a sympathetic reading of what their predecessors had to say about the balance of power and there is not the faintest suggestion that they might be standing on the shoulders of giants.[13] On the contrary, there is a tendency to ignore or to over-simplify if not distort what previous theorists have had to say in the process of accentuating the originality of their own contribution. The irony is that each theorist soon finds that after consolidating his own position, it too then starts to be over-simplified by the next generation of theorists. Very far from these theorists helping knowledge and understanding to accumulate, they each adopt an approach that

---

[13] For a discussion of this familiar phrase originally popularized in medieval times, see Merton (1993).

inhibits accumulation. If this is the common practice among theorists drawing on a common concept and working from a broadly similar perspective, then it does not give much hope for a more general process of accumulation. Nevertheless, by looking collectively as well as in depth at the work of these four theorists, the balance of power does then start to emerge as a more comprehensive and intriguing concept than when the models of any of the theorists are examined in isolation.

PART II

Metaphors, myths and models

2 | *Metaphors and the balance of power*

THE NEXT TWO CHAPTERS establish a multifaceted framework that treats the balance of power in terms of metaphors, myths and models. The primary aim of these chapters is to account for the very distinctive role that the balance of power plays in the field of international relations. Although references to the balance of power occur habitually in every conceivable social setting, the concept has never been regarded as particularly significant or controversial in the social sciences. By contrast, the balance of power has been treated as a central but highly contentious concept in the theory and practice of international relations for several centuries and it still continues to generate substantial controversy. By making provision for metaphors, myths and models, the framework established in Chapters 2 and 3 reveals that the balance of power is a more interesting concept than is generally recognized in social science and a more complex concept than is often acknowledged in International Relations.

This chapter argues that the concept becomes more interesting when it is accepted that the balance of power is a metaphor and that important implications then follow if it is also accepted that metaphors have the capacity to transform the established meaning of a concept. It surveys the debate that has taken place about the significance that can be attached to metaphors and in doing so it demonstrates that very little importance has been ascribed to the metaphorical status of the balance of power in either the social sciences in general or International Relations in particular. But when the metaphorical status of the concept is taken seriously, then the effect is dramatic because the source of the metaphor (balance) has the ability to transform the accepted meaning of the target of the concept (power). Standard approaches to the conceptualization of power in the social sciences have failed to note the importance of this move or to take account of it. This chapter aims to identify the existence of a generic metaphor that is employed ubiquitously to transform the conventional conception of power.

Chapter 3 then goes on to argue that if we want to understand why the balance of power has become such a central and yet contentious concept in the theory and practice of international relations it is necessary to develop a framework that not only allows us to identify the balance of power as a metaphor, a myth, and a model, but also to acknowledge that positivists and postpositivists view the relationship between metaphors, myths and models in rather different ways. The balance of power is shown, moreover, to be a more complex concept in International Relations than in other areas of the social sciences because it is associated with divergent metaphorical sources. One source promotes the image of the balance of power as an adversarial phenomenon and the other as an associational phenomenon. These competing metaphorical sources begin to open up areas of disagreement about the nature and role of the balance of power in the international arena. The competition, however, has been exacerbated by the roles that these different metaphors play in the establishment of opposing ideological narratives or myths about how the international arena should be organized. These myths play a significant role in both the theory and practice of international relations. In the final section of Chapter 3 it is then argued that these divergent metaphors and myths underpin the various competing models of the balance of power that have been constructed by International Relations theorists in the era since the end of the Second World War.

The framework established in Chapters 2 and 3 not only helps us to understand the very distinctive role that the balance of power plays in the theory and practice of international relations but it also provides a map on which to plot the debates about the balance of power in the contemporary discipline and to identify where exactly the four models of the balance of power examined in Chapters 4 to 7 are located. This chapter, however, focuses specifically on metaphors and it is divided into three sections. The first examines the debate about the nature and role of metaphors and it distinguishes between substitution (negative) and interaction (positive) views of metaphors. Both approaches to metaphors are shown to have had an impact on the debate about the balance of power in International Relations. The second section then shows how metaphors have had a substantial and wide-ranging impact on our conception of power. Finally, the third section focuses specifically on the balance of power and argues that there is a generic metaphor that provides a pervasive structural meaning for power in both social science and popular discourse.

Debating the significance of metaphors

This chapter starts from the premise that the balance of power is a metaphorical expression that, on the face of it, takes the same linguistic form as figures of speech like a pillar of respectability and a tissue of lies. The implications of viewing the balance of power as a metaphor, however, very much depend on the position that is taken on deep-seated debates about the role of metaphors in language and the significance of language in the construction of social reality. Although the study of metaphors can be traced back to Aristotle, contemporary analysis was profoundly affected by the linguistic turn in twentieth-century philosophy when it was insisted that all philosophical problems are ultimately problems of language.[1] Interest in metaphors increased exponentially as a result of this turn and extended from philosophy to cognitive linguistics and literary theory and the interest now stretches across the social sciences. A massive literature on metaphors has accumulated and this chapter draws on only a tiny fraction of it.[2]

It is not possible to survey this literature here but, very broadly speaking, from a social science point of view metaphors are assessed from either a positive or a negative perspective. When viewed from a negative perspective, metaphors are simply treated as figures of speech that add nothing of substance to our understanding of the world.[3] So, in the case of a pillar of respectability, the metaphor encourages us to visualize respectability as an upright pillar and respectability is thereby

---

[1] The origins of this linguistic turn go back to the eighteenth-century Italian philosopher, Giambattista Vico, if not before. For a survey of the twentieth-century literature, see Rorty (1992).

[2] Murray (1931) identified very few studies on metaphor at the start of the twentieth century, whereas Black (1990) says that the study of metaphors is now inexhaustible. Shibles (1971) provides a bibliography of around 4,000 entries. Noppen (1985) identifies 4,000 items published between 1970 and 1985; and another 3,000 items appeared over the next five years (Noppen and Hols, 1990).

[3] As we will see in the next chapter, however, positivists have identified what they see as a much more significant problem with the role played by metaphors in scientific analysis.

associated with being upright. But upright and respectable are synonymous terms and so the metaphor becomes almost a tautology. By the
same token, a tissue of lies presents us with the image a piece of woven
cloth and the metaphor thereby encourages us to think of lies as the
tightly interwoven threads that form the piece of fabric. In this case,
there is no question of the metaphor forming a tautology. But, as it
happens, this meaning of tissue is archaic and largely forgotten; yet it
seems that we can use the figure of speech without even fully understanding its metaphorical significance. From this negative perspective,
however, it really does not matter whether or not we comprehend the
metaphor because, it is argued, such figures of speech add nothing of
substance to our overall understanding of the world; metaphors are
only depicted as verbal ornaments that represent potentially diverting
but ultimately unnecessary additions to our language. On the other
hand, it is also argued that because metaphors can become a source
of ambiguity and confusion we should avoid using them. Certainly
this criticism has often been extended to the international balance of
power because as we will see the concept is frequently considered to
be ambiguous to the point of being meaningless.

There is, however, a second and much more positive perspective
on metaphors, which insists that they have a crucial role to play in
the way that we understand the world. The amount of literature on
metaphors, however, reflects a lack of agreement on how to characterize this role. This negative assessment lies at one end of a spectrum and
the study of metaphors in cognitive linguistics lies at the other end.[4]
From this latter perspective, far from being ornaments, metaphors are
seen to have an integral role to play in our use of language. Kövecses
(2002: 4) indicates that in cognitive linguistics a 'metaphor is defined as
understanding one conceptual domain in terms of another conceptual
domain'. At first sight, this definition does not seem to be incompatible with the negative perspective on metaphors. So, in the case of
a tissue of lies, the conceptual domain associated with cloth is used
to understand the conceptual domain of lies. In cognitive linguistics,
however, the implications of this definition of metaphors are extremely
far-reaching, because it is argued that we can *only* understand one
conceptual domain in terms of another conceptual domain. The cognitive linguistic position is extended to suggest that the meaning of

[4] See, in particular, Lakoff and Johnson (2003).

every concept is determined on a metaphorical basis because language is inherently metaphorical. There are important philosophical consequences that flow from this cognitive linguistic position on language and metaphors although they are certainly not going to be pursued in this chapter.[5] Instead, a more limited assessment of metaphors is employed here in the process of articulating a favourable assessment of them.

From this positive perspective, metaphors have the ability to transform the meaning of an established concept and they also play an essential role in comprehending aspects of the world that are new or that we do not understand. It is unsurprising, as a consequence, that the concept of the balance of power emerged at the time of the renaissance when the medieval era was slowly giving way to the modern era. Long-established ways of understanding how the world operated were being questioned and it became necessary to formulate new ways of thinking about the world; and it was at that juncture that the conceptual domain of power began to be understood in terms of the conceptual domain of a balance. The effect of the metaphor was to transform the established hierarchical meaning of power; it reframed or reconfigured how power was conventionally understood. The origins of the metaphor, however, are examined in the next chapter and attention is focused here on the two competing views of metaphors.

The substitution view of metaphors

Metaphors are intriguing from a philosophical point of view because although we use them on a habitual basis they fail to make logical sense. The most trivial example illustrates the point. Announcing that your new car is a peach indicates or certainly implies that the car is a piece of fruit. The announcement, however, is unlikely to cause any surprise because it is instantly recognized that the reference to a peach is not intended to be taken literally. There is no doubt that if we lack or lose this capacity to make sense of a metaphor, then it certainly becomes extraordinarily difficult to communicate. It is very revealing that people with Asperger's syndrome have fundamental problems with metaphorical language. The young narrator in Mark Haddon's novel

---

[5] For an attempt to follow through these philosophical implications, see Lakoff and Johnson (1999).

The Curious Incident of the Dog in the Night-time, who suffers from Asperger's syndrome, is well aware that a metaphor involves 'using a word for something it isn't'. But he thinks that a metaphor should be called a lie. He ponders on the metaphor 'he is the apple of her eye' but concludes that 'when I try and make a picture of the phrase in my head it just confuses me because imagining an apple in someone's eye doesn't have anything to do with liking someone a lot and it makes you forget what someone is talking about' (Haddon, 2003: 20). There have always been theorists who have had a good deal of sympathy with this position and see metaphors as a source of ambiguity and confusion. Nevertheless, this symptom of Asperger's syndrome suggests that the cognitive capacity to recognize that metaphors must not be taken literally is a crucial feature of communication and is based on the ability to draw a distinction between a literal and a figurative use of language.

According to the negative or (less pejoratively) ornamental assessment, metaphors are no more than verbal or (more positively) poetic flourishes and so, as a consequence, nothing of substance is lost by substituting the metaphorical peach with the literal statement that you are pleased with the new car, or the metaphorical apple in the eye with the literal statement that you like someone a great deal. In a widely cited philosophical discussion of metaphors Black (1962: 32) argues that with this *substitution* approach, interpreting a metaphor is like 'deciphering a code or unravelling a riddle'.[6] Once deciphered and a literal expression inserted, then the metaphorical riddle is solved without any residual meaning left un-deciphered.

The view that metaphors are designed to entertain rather than to instruct is widely accepted and gives rise to the stylistic rule that good writers must always strive for new metaphors because when metaphors are used too frequently they dull the palate and lose their ability to divert the reader. On the other hand, it is possible with the passage of time for a familiar metaphor to slip its own metaphorical moorings and become a literal expression with its own dictionary definition.[7] This process is seen to be an important source of new words. For example, in *Collins English Dictionary* the fourth, admittedly informal, meaning

---

[6] Black, however, goes on to defend an 'interaction view' of metaphors, as we will see below.

[7] In this event, according to Ricoeur (1978) the metaphor has been lexicalized and it can be questioned whether it still constitutes a metaphor.

given for a peach is 'a person or thing that is especially pleasing'. What this definition illustrates is that metaphors can lose their original poetic force and become 'dead' metaphors. Substitution is no longer necessary because the metaphor has acquired a literal meaning.[8]

The balance of power has arguably reached this stage. Although the concept is not listed in the *Shorter Oxford English Dictionary*, it is defined in the *Collins English Dictionary* as the 'distribution of power among countries so that no one nation can seriously threaten the fundamental interests of another'.[9] So has the balance of power lost its metaphorical status? Is the metaphor now acting as a symbol for the literal definition given in the dictionary? Oakeshott (1962: 235) observes that metaphors of this kind are like 'counters which may carry an attractive design upon their face but it is a design which merely indicates (and does not constitute) their value: for "son of Adam" read "man", for "golden meadow" read "sunlit field of grass", for "plum blossom" read "chastity".' And, by the same token, for 'balance of power' read 'distribution of power among countries so that no one nation can seriously threaten the fundamental interests of another'.

There are two reasons to question this conclusion. First, the balance of power is referred to ubiquitously in every conceivable social setting. Even if the meaning is fixed in international relations (and it is not), the dictionary definition certainly makes no literal sense when, for example, the family is discussed in terms of a balance of power. It has been reported, for example, that contemporary teenagers in the United States have precipitated a shift in the balance of power within families by regularly having their advice accepted on issues that in the past would have been the sole prerogative of the parents.[10] But a second reason for questioning whether the balance of power has

---

[8] Miller (1979: 157) notes other metaphors – fossilized, hidden and latent – that have been used to characterize this process. He argues that hidden or dead metaphors occur in all languages and cites Asch (1955) who provides evidence to suggest that there is consistency in the way that they are used – for example, straight and crooked for honesty and dishonesty.

[9] This definition comes closer to what I am calling an associational balance of power than to an adversarial balance of power, often linked to two competitive but evenly balanced alliance systems.

[10] Debra Pickett and Janet Rausa Fuller, 'Teens Shifting Balance of Power', *Chicago Sun-Times*, 27 April 2003 www.suntimes.com/special_sections/teen/cst-nws-teenmain27. html, downloaded 20 April 2006.

lost its metaphorical status is that its meaning is certainly not fixed in the international context. On the contrary, one of the main criticisms levelled at the international balance of power relates to its protean or polysemic character; it is criticized for having too many meanings.

The wholesale criticism of metaphors is generally associated with social scientists who insist that language must perform a neutral role and provide us with an accurate representation of the real world. They argue that there are clear and unambiguous rules of correspondence between the real world and the language that we use to describe it. Because metaphors involve an erroneous designation, as in 'my car is a peach', they are seen to challenge a fundamental rule of correspondence; and so they need to be eliminated from social scientific discourse. This is certainly not a new assessment of metaphors. In the seventeenth century, Hobbes stressed the importance of observing the 'settled signification' of words and he argued that the use of metaphors must be avoided because they give rise to 'innumerable absurdities'.[11] But, as is often noted, despite his disavowal of metaphors, Hobbes relied very heavily on them to develop his own arguments.

Although it is acknowledged in contemporary International Relations that the balance of power is a metaphor, a common criticism levelled at the concept is that, in practice, it is extraordinarily difficult to decipher what the term means and the problem is then almost always related to the ambiguity surrounding the idea of a balance. Rather than exploring in more depth the implications that follow from treating the balance of power as a metaphor, the usual solution to the problem is to provide a definition. But this response fails to provide a universal answer to what is meant by the balance of power because it quickly emerges that there is a large number of definitions available. In a survey of the concept, Sheehan (1996: 2–4) advances ten definitions that have been established over the past 300 years. The first is:

'An equal distribution of power among the Princes of Europe as makes it impractical for the one to disturb the repose of the other.' (Anonymous, *Europe's Catechism, 1741*)

---

[11] Hobbes, *Leviathan* Part 1, chapters v and vi. See Miller's (1979: 155) assessment of Hobbes on metaphors. Williams (2005: 23), however, depicts Hobbes as a sceptic rather than a proto-positivist and argues that for Hobbes, 'Words and concepts are not pale reflections of an "objective" reality – they are fundamental constituents of the reality of the agents that use them to make sense of their worlds'.

Although some of the definitions are very similar, there are also significant variations. So, for example, on the one hand, the balance of power is sometimes defined in terms of a set of states where each state possesses approximately the same amount of power through to the situation where a group of states ally in order to overwhelm a potential hegemon. None of the definitions correspond exactly with the dictionary definition given above. Sheehan acknowledges the variation in the meanings ascribed to the balance of power and he follows the route charted by Wight (1966: 151), who identifies nine different ways in which the concept has been used.[12]

1. An even distribution of power.
2. The principle that power ought to be evenly distributed.
3. The existing distribution of power. Hence, any possible distribution of power.
4. The principle of equal aggrandizement of the great powers at the expense of the weak.
5. The principle that our side ought to have a margin of strength in order to avert the danger of power becoming unevenly distributed.
6. (When governed by the verb 'to hold':) A special role in maintaining an even distribution of power.
7. (Ditto:) A special advantage in the existing distribution of power.
8. Predominance.
9. An inherent tendency of international politics to produce an even distribution of power.

It is frequently argued that these lists of definitions invariably reveal that the balance of power is sometimes used to define an even distribution of power and on other occasions an uneven distribution of power. This level of ambiguity is regarded as intolerable, which is why it is argued that the term should be dispensed with, or linked to one meaning. These variations in meaning, moreover, are seen to arise from ambiguities associated with 'balance', the source of the metaphor. As a consequence, for critics it is often the metaphorical status of the balance of power that lies at the root of the problem.

In the case of the balance of power, therefore, far from representing a harmless verbal flourish, the metaphor is seen to be the cause of major confusion. The most persistent and fundamental criticism

---

[12] Sheehan (1996: 141) later in the book refers to Schroeder (1989: 137) who argues that policy-makers in the nineteenth century used balance of power in eleven different ways.

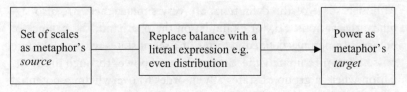

Figure 2.1 The substitution view of the balance of power metaphor[13]

levelled at the balance of power for over fifty years from within the contemporary field of International Relations relates to its polysemic character because it is seen to provide an endless source of ambiguity.[14] In literary theory, the polysemy often displayed by metaphors is regarded as a virtue.[15] But many social scientists have tended to be deeply sceptical about the putative merits of this characteristic. One well-known critic of the concept notes, for example, that A. J. P. Taylor (1954), in his classic diplomatic history of Europe, relied heavily on the idea of the balance of power but failed to define the term and, as a consequence, he 'profits from the principle that it is difficult to prove anything against a concept which slips so easily from one meaning to another' (Claude, 1962: 24).[16] So rather than treating the balance of power as a metaphor, one of the major responses in the contemporary field has been to drain the concept of its metaphorical associations and to leave the concept with an unambiguous or univocal meaning. So if we associate the source of the metaphor with a set of scales, then by replacing the source with a literal expression such as 'an even distribution of power', the danger of ambiguity can be dispensed with (see Figure 2.1).

However, not everyone has seen the ambiguity associated with the balance of power as a disadvantage. Wight develops the argument that the international system is inherently ambiguous and so we need metaphors that capture that ambiguity. Although he does not discuss the nature of metaphors, it is clear that he is taking metaphors seriously and is suggesting that they provide a distinctive and important tool of

---

[13] The set of scales is identified in the final section of the chapter as a generic source for the balance of power.

[14] See the classic critiques offered by Haas (1953) and Claude (1962).

[15] For one of the most important statements on the role of metaphors in literary theory, see the series of lectures given by Wheelwright (1962) at the University of Bristol.

[16] But see Schroeder (2001) for a very different assessment of Taylor.

analysis. Wight (1966: 150) points to the 'equivocalness and plasticity of the metaphor of "balance"'. But he sees this as an advantage. He suggests that part of the fascination of the balance of power lies with the difficulty of pinning down its meaning. We resort to balance of power terminology, he argues, because it is 'flexible and elastic enough to cover all the complexities and contradictions' encountered in the international system (Wight, 1978: 173).

Wight, of course, is moving away from a negative assessment of metaphors. But even he fails to grapple with the full significance of treating the balance of power as a metaphor. From the positive perspective on metaphors developed in cognitive linguistics, the aim is to draw on the source of the metaphor in order to transform the meaning of the target of the metaphor. So in the case of the balance of power, therefore, the purpose of the metaphor is to re-view power through the lens associated with the idea of a balance.

But, in practice, almost all discussions of the balance of power assume that the meaning attached to power – the target of the metaphor – is unproblematic and attention is focused instead on the ambiguity that is seen to be generated by the idea of a balance – the source of the metaphor. The failure to focus more specifically on the meaning of power is effectively the consequence of adopting a negative or ornamental view of metaphors. A very different perspective on the balance of power emerges if metaphors are given a more positive evaluation. It is then argued that the effect of treating the balance of power as a metaphor is to transform the established assessment of power and this gives rise to a very different view of how the world operates.

The interaction view of metaphors

There is now an extensive literature that questions the negative or substitution view of metaphors and it is widely accepted that metaphors can play a crucial role in the way that human beings understand and interact in the world. Metaphors, it is argued, are not a linguistic aberration but represent an important dimension of cognition and can tell us a great deal about how we think. For some theorists working within this frame of reference, the very ubiquity of metaphors helps to confirm that language and thinking is inherently metaphorical. It is often noted, for example, that attempts to provide an understanding of metaphors invariably require the theorists to use metaphors to explain how metaphors work. So Black, for example, discusses the substitution approach to metaphors in terms of deciphering a riddle. Indeed, within cognitive linguistics, metaphors are seen to be 'pervasive in everyday life, not just in language but in thought and action. Our ordinary conceptual system, in terms of which we both think and act, is fundamentally metaphorical in nature' (Lakoff and Johnson, 2003: 3). There are echoes from Nietzsche here, because he also believed that 'Tropes are not something that can be added or abstracted from language at will; they are its truest nature'; and elsewhere he argued that there is '*no real knowing apart from metaphor*'.[17]

Although the international balance of power is often identified as a metaphor, the implications that flow from this identification are rarely explored in any depth. Indeed, the general importance of metaphors until very recently has simply not been taken on board in International Relations.[18] However, a radical assessment of metaphors is beginning to impinge on the study of international relations. Chilton (1996), for example, has developed a cognitive linguistic understanding of security. Thinking metaphorically, he argues, is part of our mental apparatus and it plays a particularly important role in the process of concept formation.[19] Metaphorical processes are depicted as a key element in the formation of the mental image that provides us with an understanding of a concept like security. Political scientists run into problems with the concept, according to Chilton, because they fail to acknowledge the cognitive complexity underlying the concept.[20] Following a similar route, and also drawing on the approach pioneered by Lakoff and Johnson (2003), Beer and Landtsheer (2004b: 19–21) provide a list

---

[17] Cited in Cantor (1982: 71–2).

[18] There is, however, a growing interest. Fry and O'Hagan (2000: 10) have edited an introductory textbook on international relations that builds on the contention that 'images or metaphors that are deployed to understand world politics should also be seen to be contributing to the constitution of world politics'. See also Medhurst, ed. (1997), Eubanks (2000), Pemberton (2001), Marks (2003), Beer and de Lantsheer (2004a), Musolff (2004), and Hirschbein (2005).

[19] Chilton argues that his approach is reflected in the work of the contributors to Medhurst, ed. (1997).

[20] Buzan's attempt to deal with the concept of security fails according to Chilton (1996: 22) because he does not expose the way that the meaning of the concept is 'entangled with a whole system of political concepts, the depth and ramifications of which can only be understood if their metaphorical dimension is taken into account'.

of over two hundred metaphors ascribed to politics, that range from politics as cooking through to politics as dentistry. They then classify the metaphors into thirteen preconceptual schemas, such as politics as spectacle (drawing on metaphors like the circus and soap operas) and politics as nature (with rainbows and the weather acting as metaphors). Like Chilton, Beer and Landtsheer presuppose that these intersecting metaphors demonstrate the existence of a much more complex conception of politics than is often acknowledged.

A very different response to the ubiquity of metaphors, however, is to meet the substitution interpretation half way and acknowledge that many metaphors perform a purely ornamental and symbolic function but then accept that there are other metaphors that can have a significant impact on the way that we look at the world. Although it is easy to make this distinction in theory, it is much more difficult to do so in practice. So, for example, if we say that the evidence presented in court was a tissue of lies does this figure of speech have the same connotations as when we say that the witness presented a pack of lies? In terms of the substitution theory, the key question is whether a tissue and a pack – the two very different metaphorical sources – can be replaced with the same literal expression. In essence, both metaphors indicate that the evidence consists of nothing more than a lot of lies. More to the point, neither figure of speech affects in any significant way what is meant by a lie. The main aim here is to demonstrate, by contrast, that the effect of the balance of power metaphor is to transform the usual meaning ascribed to power. So although a tissue of lies and a balance of power both take the same linguistic form, the impact of the metaphors is quite different in these two cases.

The difference is clarified by Black (1979), who thought long and hard about metaphors, and eventually reached the conclusion that it was necessary to establish two categories of metaphors. After initially rejecting the substitution theory of metaphors, and attempting to establish a universal theory for how metaphors operate, he did subsequently accept that the substitution rule can be applied to many metaphors without any significant loss of meaning, but he also insisted that there is an important class of metaphors that has the effect of transforming the meaning that we attach to the target of the metaphor. He discussed the transformation in terms of an *interaction* theory that now represents an extremely influential account of how metaphors operate.

Transformative metaphors are used to understand complex, abstract or unstructured domains with the assistance of concepts from domains that are more familiar and concrete. Given the complexity of international relations, it would be very surprising if theorists and practitioners did not resort to metaphors in order to make sense of what is going on. Slater (1987: 105) argues, for example, that during the cold war, American decision-makers drew on a rich menu of metaphorical sources to justify and bolster their policy in Central America but he also argues that 'whether the metaphor is falling dominos, rotten apples, spreading disease, or the weakest link in the chain, the nature of the argument is the same'.[21] Each of these metaphors helped to promote the idea that if one state succumbed to communism, then it was more likely that the other states would also become communist. More than twenty years ago, Larson (1985: 55) acknowledged that practitioners frequently invoke metaphors in public and private to analyse events in international politics. But she went on to observe that the role of metaphors in foreign policy-making remains unexplored. According to Shimko (1994; 2004) there has been little change in the intervening period.

One possible reason for this surprising lack of interest in metaphors is the existence of broad support for a negative or substitution interpretation of metaphors.[22] But, in fact, the significance of metaphors

[21] Indeed, this argument can be traced back to the origins of the cold war, in 1917, when the Bolsheviks took control in Russia. Winston Churchill said to the members of the House of Commons 'I dare say honourable members recall the sinking of the Titanic. The state of Europe seems to me to have many points of sinister comparison with that event. The great vessel had compartment after compartment invaded by the sea. She remained almost motionless upon the water . . . Finally, when the decisive compartments which regulated flotation of the ship filled, the whole brilliant structure of science and civilization foundered in the ocean, leaving those on board . . . swimming in the icy water of the sea.' 3 March 1919 *Parliamentary Debates* CXIII, p. 84.

[22] It is also possible that Shimko overlooks a growing postpositivist interest in metaphors. Weldes (1999: 99–100), for example, sees metaphors as part of the linguistic repertoire used by the United States to define and promote the national interest. Part of the problem with trying to understand the role played by metaphors, as we discuss in the next chapter, is that it is not sufficient to discuss metaphors in isolation and we need to develop a more comprehensive view of metaphors to understand their importance. In particular, it is necessary to acknowledge a very close link between metaphors, myths and models.

has always been recognized in the social sciences. Indeed, some theorists have described the cognitive process associated with transformative metaphors in almost mystical terms. For example, Nisbet (1969: 4) argues that metaphors make it possible to move from the known to the unknown because 'the identifying qualities of one thing are transferred in an instantaneous, almost unconscious flash of insight to some other thing that is, by remoteness or complexity unknown to us'. Using more mundane language, Geertz (1993: 211) describes the same process, arguing that the power of a metaphor derives from 'the interplay between the discordant meanings it symbolically coerces into a unitary conceptual framework; while the success of the metaphor is determined by its ability to overcome the psychic resistance such semantic tension inevitably generates.' For example, it might seem at first sight that a set of scales (a balance) has nothing to do with power, but the resulting semantic tension represents a necessary feature of any effective metaphor and by harnessing these two dissimilar concepts, the metaphor then makes it possible to re-view the target concept of power.

Black (1962: 44) argues that the source of any transformative metaphor acts as a cognitive prism that then 'selects, emphasizes, suppresses, and organizes' how the target of the metaphor is characterized. But it has been noted that Black's prism metaphor fails to capture fully his overall view of how metaphors operate.[23] The prism presupposes that metaphors establish a one-way street, with the source of the metaphor determining how the target of the metaphor is interpreted. Although Black accepts that the main impact of the metaphorical process affects the target domain, he also insists that it has some effect on how we view the source domain as the result of interaction between the two domains (see Figure 2.2). In other words, when a transformative metaphor is established, there is a two-way or *interaction* process between the source and the target, with the source primarily determining how the target is viewed, but the target is also seen to have some effect on how the source is viewed. So it follows that in the context of the balance of power, the overall meaning is heavily determined by the effects of thinking about power from the perspective of a balance. But

---

[23] As a consequence, even supporters of Black's interaction view acknowledge that his account is inadequate. See, for example, Rothbart (1997: 25) and Zashin and Chapman (1974: 299–300).

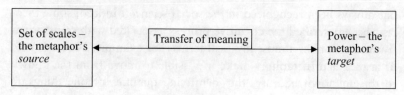

Figure 2.2 The interaction view of metaphors

how we think about a balance is to some extent also affected by our view of power. We need to come back and expand on this point later.

This *interaction* view of metaphors is now deeply entrenched in the theoretical literature on metaphors and it has also been used in the history of science, to chart, for example, how our understanding of memory has evolved in terms of a succession of metaphors. Draaisma (2000) relates, for instance, how in 1677 Robert Hooke observed a demonstration of the newly discovered phosphorus at the Royal Society and then, five years later, used phosphorus as a metaphor to explain how the mind retains visual images. Schön (1979: 257–60; Schön and Rein, 1994), an organizational and public policy theorist, develops a similar position to Black. Referring to generative metaphors, he shows how they can have very practical consequences. He cites the example of researchers trying to improve on the performance of a new paintbrush with synthetic bristles. They made the metaphorical leap that a paintbrush is a pump, but it was only after establishing the metaphor that the researchers came to recognize that the space between natural bristles forms channels along which paint flows as the brush is pressed against a surface. The spaces between the bristles effectively form a pump. When the more rigid synthetic bristles were pressed against a surface, however, they bent at an acute angle and effectively shut off the pump. Schon, like Black, acknowledges, however, that the metaphor had the effect of determining how the researchers thought about both paintbrushes and pumps.

New metaphors necessarily get pressed into service in the social arena when developments can no longer be understood in terms of existing language resources. Steiner (1975: 21) suggests, moreover, that under these circumstances the consequences of retaining established metaphors is substantial because when words 'go dead under the weight of sanctified use' language can create paralysis by acting as a barrier to new experiences. He talks of the 'sclerotic force' of unexamined similes and worn tropes and notes how a civilization can become 'imprisoned in a linguistic contour that no longer matches or matches only at certain ritual, arbitrary points, the changing landscape of fact'. It is often argued in the current era that decision-makers and theorists who continue to think in balance of power terms are 'imprisoned in a linguistic contour' that is preventing them from coming to terms with globalization.[24] Far from opening up new ways of understanding the world, metaphors can close down the potential for understanding or bringing about change. However, it would be a mistake to think that these metaphors are dead because as Kövecses (2002: ix) notes, this assessment misses the important point that 'what is deeply entrenched, hardly noticed, and thus effortlessly used is most active in our thought'.

Transforming how we view the world, as a consequence, can be an extraordinarily difficult exercise. Although influential metaphors may be resistant to change, it remains the case that new metaphors can play a significant role in reinvigorating political language. A number of political theorists have discussed this development in terms of the need to employ a poetic idiom. Dallmayr (1984b: 201, 222) observes that while at first sight, the poetic idiom seems to be a 'stranger to political life' it has to be acknowledged that its role is 'neither negligible nor marginal'. He accepts Heidegger's argument that the poetic idiom is required to sustain and renew language.[25] In particular, Dallmayr argues that what is distinctive about the poetic idiom is its 'openness to strangeness and unfamiliarity'. He goes on to suggest that periods of crisis or profound reorientation 'are liable to have an ear for the voice of unfamiliarity and innovation'. And along the same lines, Rorty (1979: 360) describes poetic activity in terms of 'the attempt to reinterpret our familiar surroundings in the unfamiliar terms of our

---

[24] See, for example, Paul (2004: 2), Buzan (2004a: 232) and Chilton (1996: 409). Pemberton (2001), however, pushes the argument the other way and insists that much of the appeal of globalization rhetoric relies on technological fantasies about the future and that a comparison of the metaphors applied to globalization reveals that the current debate is in effect a rerun of the same debate from 1920s and 1930s.

[25] Heidegger (1971) is cited as saying that everyday language is 'a forgotten and therefore used-up poem'. Emerson (1903: 329) made the same point: 'The etymologist finds the deadest words to have been once a brilliant picture. Language is fossil poetry', cited in Sarbin (1972: 337).

new inventions'.[26] Similarly Geertz (1993: 220) argues that political ideologies rely on poetic language because they emerge in periods of political instability and provide 'maps of problematic social reality'. These ideologies are seen to rely, in particular, on metaphors to extend language and help to provide 'novel symbolic frames against which to match the myriad "unfamiliar somethings" that, like a journey in a strange country, are produced by a transformation in political life'. In the same vein, Chilton (1996: 413) argues that metaphors appear 'to play a particular role at moments when the international environment has to be reconceptualized'. What all these analysts accept is that when confronted by change, transformational metaphors can play an important role in generating new concepts that can help to make sense of the newly emerging reality. As we see in the next chapter, moreover, metaphors are also closely related to ideological narratives or myths that are often developed in the attempt to shape the emerging reality.

Before extending the discussion of how the idea of a balance affects the concept of power, however, it is necessary to focus first, albeit briefly, on how the concept of power itself has evolved.

Metaphors and the conceptualization of power

Lukes (2004), who has written one of the classic texts on power, argues that it is a primitive and essentially contested concept.[27] It is *'primitive* in the specific sense that its meaning cannot be elucidated by reference to other notions whose meanings is less controversial than its own', and it is *essentially contested* because any assessment of power 'cannot be disconnected from what we commonly call the "value assumptions" of the person making the judgement' (Lukes, 2005: 477). Krieger (1968: 3–8) accepts that power is a primitive concept but not essentially contested; and he considers power to be 'invisible and intangible not by abstraction but by direct reference to realities that are themselves

---

[26] However, Rorty (1987) develops Davidson's (1979) position on metaphors and insists that they do not change how we represent the world, rather they cause us to change our desires and beliefs about the world. Barnes (1996) applies Rorty's thinking to geography.

[27] The first edition was published in 1974. For a range of interesting assessments of Lukes' conception of power see the 'Review Symposium on Steven Lukes' Power: A Radical View' in *Political Studies Review*, 2006, 4 (2).

metaphysical'.[28] Because dictionaries invariably 'devitalize' concepts, Krieger thinks that their generic, undifferentiated, and unqualified definition of power as 'the capacity to act' is unsurprising, but he insists that the definitions of power offered by philosophers and political theorists display the 'same formal vacuity'.[29] As a consequence, Krieger (1968: 4) concludes that an 'elemental attitude towards unqualified power' has been a persistent feature of the dominant culture in the western world. There is a good reason to think, therefore, that metaphors will inevitably play an essential role in any attempt to come to terms with a more concrete assessment of power. However, although it is widely accepted that power is a complex and multifaceted concept, there have been very few attempts to show how metaphors help to maintain the coherence of the divergent approaches to power that have developed across time.

The importance of metaphors becomes very evident, nevertheless, when a theorist tries to move away from the conventional meanings of power. Vail (2004), for example, who wants to re-conceive the role of power in society, contrasts the long-established metaphor of 'power is a hierarchy' with his preferred metaphor of 'power is a rhizome'. He borrows the metaphor from Deleuze and Guattari (1987) and notes that a rhizome takes its name from the structures of plants such as bamboo and other grasses. It is a web-like structure of connected but independent nodes. Each node is autonomous from the larger structure, but the nodes work together in a network that extends benefits to each node without creating dependence. In contrast to hierarchy, therefore, rhizomes cannot suffer exploitation from within because the structure is incompatible with the centralization of power. Vail (2005) argues that after invading Iraq in 2003, the US military had difficulty dealing with the subsequent insurgency because of its non-hierarchical composition and he suggests that the tactical blindness can be accounted for by its failure to understand the differences in information processing that take place in a hierarchy and a rhizome.

Conceptualizing power as a hierarchy is an easy move for theorists in International Relations to make because they habitually juxtapose

---

[28] Leonard Krieger was a leading twentieth-century historian of ideas. See Hacohen (1996).

[29] He illustrates this point by referring to Hobbes who defines power as 'a present means to provide some future good' and Bertrand Russell who defines power as the 'production of intended effects'.

hierarchy with balance, but to conceive of power as a rhizome is more difficult because the metaphor is much less familiar.[30] Nevertheless, it contains elements of other approaches to power that social theorists have been coming to terms with for several decades. Having assumed, in the past, that power is an agency-based concept because it is conceptualized as something that is possessed and exercised by an actor or agent, a growing number of theorists now acknowledge a conception of power that stresses its 'relational, networked, distributed, or immanent nature' (Sayer, 2004: 255). Sayer is here reviewing the attempt by Allen (2003), a geographer, to accommodate a spatial or structural dimension of power.

Although Allen unquestionably makes a significant contribution to attempts to give power a spatial and structural dimension, he revealingly makes no provision for balance of power theorists who place the spatial and structural dimension of power at the very heart of their theories.[31] Moreover, from the perspective of International Relations, it seems odd to treat the ideas of relational or distributed power as a new development because in International Relations, power has traditionally been conceived in this way; both characteristics are absolutely central when power is conceptualized as a balance. It is delusional to imply, however, that conventional theory in International Relations has somehow stolen a march on Foucault, Deleuze, and other social theorists, who want to re-conceptualize power in this way. Indeed, what a cognitive approach to metaphors can help to illustrate is that the notions of power distribution and relational power take very different forms depending upon the metaphors that are brought into play.[32] But while it is unquestionably the case that the French philosophers have developed a distinctive approach to power, it needs to be recognized

---

[30] The metaphor, however, is now becoming much more familiar and Smith (2006, 328–31), the Deputy Supreme Commander Allied Powers Europe from 1998 to 2001, has written about the 'rhizomatic command system' of modern guerrilla and terrorist networks, and distinguished it from the hierarchical structure of conventional military forces. The role of power in a hierarchy is discussed in more detail in Chapter 3.

[31] See also Haywood (2000) for another interesting attempt to re-orient traditional ways of thinking about power.

[32] Any metaphysical concept such as power or cause is defined in many different ways. The argument developed in this chapter is that metaphors necessarily play a crucial role in determining and stabilizing the specific meaning of the concept in any given context.

that whereas social theorists acknowledge the originality of the French contribution, they invariably fail to observe how the meaning of power is also transformed in rather different ways by the balance metaphor. Indeed, the balance of power sits rather uneasily between the long-established and agency-based idea of power as a possession and the nascent and structural idea of power as a network.

Drawing fruitfully on the work of political theorists, Clegg (1989), an organizational theorist who has noted the importance of metaphors for understanding and conceptualizing power, observes that while the established behavioural and agency-based approach to power can be traced to Hobbes, the nascent network approach can be traced further back to Machiavelli.[33] He then argues that with the consolidation of the state and the emergence of 'new science' in the seventeenth century, political theorists lost sight of Machiavelli's fluid notion of power and, as a consequence, his military metaphors that associate power with strategy and manoeuvres were superseded by Hobbesian metaphors that depict power in mechanical, causal and atomistic terms.[34]

In his broad-ranging discussion of power and metaphors however, Clegg makes no attempt to accommodate the balance of power that emerged when Machiavelli was writing, but which then persisted through to the twenty-first century. He also fails to accommodate Krieger's (1968: 11) argument that in western culture it has always been recognized that power operates in two diametrically different ways: one is instrumental, political and negative in character and the other is teleological, ethical and positive, and so it is necessary to accommodate 'two constant and fundamental ideas of power'. Krieger's central thesis is that prior to the sixteenth century these divergent attitudes to power proceeded along separate tramlines, but as political theorists began to confront the implications of the world that was overtaking the medieval era, the two attitudes began to converge and produce 'a

---

[33] Foucault also acknowledges the link. More surprisingly, Foucault's approach has also been linked to the approach to power developed by the American sociologist, Talcott Parsons. See Kroker (1984).

[34] Organizational theorists have proved more receptive to the cognitive function of metaphors than most other social scientists. See Morgan (1997: 4) who, in one of the standard textbooks, argues that 'all theories of organization and management are based on implicit images or metaphors that lead us to see, understand and manage organizations in distinctive yet partial ways'.

single, unstable and ambiguous scheme of power' (Krieger, 1968: 16). Duverger (1972: 18–19) develops a similar line of argument and insists that, in the context of the modern state, power (and, as a consequence, politics) is inherently ambivalent and, as a consequence, the 'two-faced god Janus is the true image of power and expresses the most profound political truth'. So, on the one hand, power 'is essentially a struggle, a battle' whereas, on the other, power is associated with 'an attempt to establish order and justice'. From Duverger's (1972: 19) perspective, because the two elements 'continually coexist' the essence of power (and politics) is 'always ambivalent'.

In the next chapter, which examines the relationship between metaphors and myths, it becomes clear that the international balance of power embraces both of these faces of power. But before taking account of this complication, it is necessary in the final section of this chapter to focus in more detail on the image of a set of scales, which provides us with a generic metaphorical source for the balance of power. The metaphorical source is generic because it is applied across a wide spectrum of relationships from relations among the members of a family through to the relations among states in the international system. Although the metaphorical source was originally used to analyse relations among the Italian city states, it is now employed ubiquitously and applies to any setting where there is a set of interconnected actors.

Metaphors and the balance of power

So far in this chapter it has been taken for granted that the balance of power is a metaphor. In this final section the implications of treating the balance of power as a metaphor, and specifically as a set of scales, are examined in more depth. The aim of this section is to demonstrate that by drawing on the interaction theory of metaphors we can see how the use of a set of scales as the metaphorical source has the effect of transforming the meaning of power.

One problem with treating the balance of power as a metaphor is that the source, like the target, is an elemental or primitive concept. In contrast to the metaphorical source in a 'pillar of respectability', the idea of 'balance' does not immediately bring forward a visual image and so it is unclear what conceptual domain power should be linked to. This can be illustrated with visual representations of the balance of power from the past. The French nineteenth-century

Figure 2.3 The European Balance of Power: L'Équilibre Européen by Honoré Daumier from *Le Charivari*, 1 December 1866 DR 3540 © www.daumier-register.org[35]

lithographer, Honoré Daumier (1808–1879), produced at least two lithographs of the European balance of power (see Figures 2.3 and 2.4). One depicts a globe resting (or balancing) on top of a circle of bayonets held by a motley crowd of soldiers and citizens. A second

[35] Image available on http://homepage.mac.com/dmhart/WarArt/Study Guides/Daumier.html.

Figure 2.4 The European Balance of Power: Équilibre Européen by Honoré Daumier from *Le Charivari*, 3 April 1867 DR 3566 © www.daumier-register.org[36]

depicts a woman, possibly Marianne, the French symbol for freedom, teetering (balanced) precariously on top of a large spherical smoking

[36] The image is used in a frontpiece in Friedrich's (1938) book on foreign policy. It is also used by Stamato (2000) to illustrate (presumably metaphorically, and presumably ironically) the difficulties that women can face in the workplace.

bomb.[37] Daumier was critical of the European balance of power and this comes through clearly in the lithographs. In both cases he is suggesting that the European balance of power rests on a very unstable basis. But Daumier is only providing symbols (or counters in Oakeshott's language) of the European balance of power, and so we say: for 'woman teetering on a bomb' read 'European balance of power'. But we are effectively dealing here with a substitution metaphor and not a transformation or interaction metaphor. As a consequence, the visual representation does not illuminate the conceptual domain that underpins the ubiquitous references to the balance of power in the contemporary world.

To identify the conceptual domain that defines the balance of power in terms of a generic and transformational metaphor, it is necessary to dig deeper. One possible route is to go back to the origins of the metaphor. Although there is no detailed genealogy of the balance of power available (but see Nelson, 1943 and Vagts, 1948), Anderson (1993: 151) suggests that the earliest clear reference is given in 1439 by Francesco Barbaro, who suggests that Venice was attempting to establish a balance of power in Italy at that time.[38] But a better known, more substantial and sustained discussion of the balance of power appears in the work of the diplomat and historian, Francesco Guicciardini, writing in the early decades of the sixteenth century, who not only draws very explicitly on the idea but has the balance of power playing a very significant role in his account of the events surrounding the French military intervention in 1494 onto the Italian Peninsula.[39]

Guicciardini makes reference to the Italian city states 'counterbalancing' each other, but there is a range of very different metaphorical sources from fifteenth-century Italy that are compatible with the idea of counterbalancing. Vagts (1948) notes, in particular, that the term *bilancio* was associated with double-entry book-keeping, which developed in Italy at the end of the Middle Ages, and *punctus contra punctum*

---

[37] The claim that the woman is Marianne is made by Max Kohnstamm (1992).

[38] Haslam (2002: 92), however, does not accept that the idea can be traced this far back.

[39] The references appear in Guicciardini (1984 [1561]). Because there is a significant myth-making dimension to Guicciardini's use of the balance of power, I reserve a more detailed discussion of his work for the next chapter.

was related to the theory of harmony in music.[40] Vagts also refers to weighing scales, traditionally regarded as the symbol of justice. Beyond Italy, he identifies two German woodcuts, one from the fifteenth and the other from the sixteenth century and they not only reveal the Pope and the Emperor balanced insecurely on the top of a ship's mast, but the Pope is also holding a set of scales in one hand, while grasping the Emperor with the other.[41]

Guicciardini, however, never makes it explicit which of these metaphorical sources he is relying on. From Vagts' (1948: 94) perspective, this may not matter, because he suggests that 'mixing metaphors' was characteristic of the 'cocktail language of politics in the Renaissance'.[42] And this position is reinforced by Slater's (1987) argument, discussed earlier, that metaphors as different as falling dominos and rotten apples can generate a common structural point of view. But as we will see in the next chapter when exploring the links between metaphors and myths, although superficially the metaphorical sources identified by Vagts seem to take an identical form, on closer investigation, even the scales metaphor can be refined in radically different ways with very different mythopoeic consequences.[43]

Certainly the set of scales now represents a generic metaphorical source. There are also good grounds for thinking that while the metaphorical source for Guicciardini's idea of counterbalancing may not have been made explicit, it was very quickly interpreted in terms of a set of scales. So, for example, Geffray Fenton's dedication in 1579 to Queen Elizabeth in the first English translation (albeit from a French translation of the original Italian) of Guicciardini's *History of Italy* renders the metaphorical source for the balance of power crystal clear. It states 'God has put in your hands the balance of power and justice to poise and counterpoise at your will the actions and counsels of all the Christian kings of your time' (cited in Vagts, 1948: 97). The set of scales is brought to mind, first, by the reference to 'justice', which is

---

[40] 'Counterpoint is a moderate and reasonable concord which arises when one tone is placed opposite another, from which also *contrapunctus*, that is "note against note", can be derived.' Johannes Tinctoris, *Liber de Arte Contrapuncti*, 1447 cited at www.contrapunctus.com/contrapunctus.htm, last downloaded on 6 December 2006.

[41] Reproductions of both these woodcuts appear in Vagts (1948).

[42] This assessment, however, now seems dated if it is accepted that language is inherently metaphorical.

[43] Mythopoeic means myth-making.

symbolized by scales, and second, by the assertion that the Queen can 'poise and counterpoise' the other European monarchs; these are terms that refer to weight.

The conceptual domain associated with weighing scales has very deep historical roots as a metaphorical source. According to the Book of Daniel, for example, Belshazzar, the ruler of Babylon (in the sixth century BCE) held a feast where the sacred vessels taken from Solomon's Temple in Jerusalem were used for drinking by the king and his guests. During the course of the evening, unintelligible words appeared on the wall which were then interpreted by Daniel to mean 'Thou art weighed in the balances and art found wanting' (Daniel, V:27). That night, it is then related, Belshazzar was killed and his empire was divided between the Medes and the Persians. The metaphorical source is obviously a set of scales and the metaphor's target is the history of the king and his empire. What the metaphorical source does is to encourage us to recognize that the imperial record can be accurately measured and judged. It can also be suggested that there is a degree of interaction because the meaning attached to the metaphor's target draws attention to an important feature of the metaphorical source; scales not only determine the weight of a commodity but they also ensure that the outcome is absolutely impartial and is, for example, unaffected by the views of the parties who may be buying or selling the commodity on the scales.

Although balance of power and balance of justice can both rely on a set of scales for their metaphorical source, the impact of the metaphor is very different in the two cases. The balance of justice takes exactly the same form as a pillar of respectability. Here, the set of scales can be deciphered to mean impartiality and when the substitution has taken place, the substituted term becomes if not a synonym then certainly a necessary ingredient of justice. But interpreting what is meant by the balance of power is much less straightforward. In the first place, whereas the balance of justice is no longer a term in common usage (although the set of scales remains a familiar iconic image for justice) the balance of power remains a familiar, indeed, a colloquial expression. In the second place, as the Daumier lithographs illustrate, the balance of power is associated with a variety of very different images that generate competing meanings. Daumier's images, for example, associate the balance of power with danger and precariousness. These are unequivocally terms that critics have frequently linked to the international balance of power, but they are certainly not terms that necessarily come to mind when

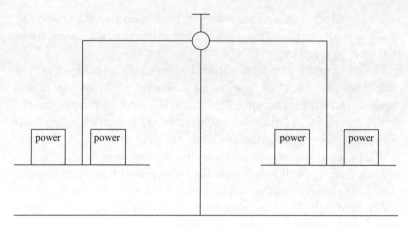

Figure 2.5 A set of scales as a generic metaphorical source for the balance of power

the term is drawn upon colloquially. As a consequence, they leave the meaning of the term underdetermined. By contrast, when a set of scales provides the metaphorical source for 'balance' it brings a very distinctive view of power into focus and my claim is that weighing scales now constitute the generic metaphorical source and conceptual domain for the balance of power in the contemporary world (see Figure 2.5).

This claim, however, can be no more than an assertion that is in practice impossible to validate because references to the balance of power are so ubiquitous. The problem of validation is made even more difficult because direct references to a set of scales are so rarely made when the balance of power is under discussion. Shimko (2004: 207), however, has come up with an intriguing response to this problem. He argues that the power of some metaphors does not depend on their 'explicit repetition' because the associated terminology immediately brings the metaphorical source to mind. He illustrates his argument with the familiar metaphor of falling dominos that was used by the Americans during the cold war. As it happens, there are remarkably few explicit references to dominos by policy-makers. But Shimko insists that speech formulas related to the image were pervasive during the cold war, as when 'nations "fall" or are "toppled," governments are "supported" or "propped up" and "chain reactions" are set off'. This argument can certainly be extended to the balance of power. There are constant references in the contemporary world to metaphorical

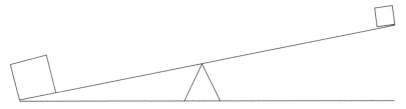

Figure 2.6 A see-saw as an equivalent conceptual domain for the generic balance of power

balances of power that 'tilt', 'tip', 'swing', 'shift', 'adjust' and 'change' as well as to situations where an actor 'holds', dictates', 'turns', 'controls' or 'regulates' the balance of power. All of these speech formulas help to summon up the image of a set of weighing scales (or an equivalent image and conceptual domain, such as a seesaw or a tug of war) and the perennial use made of these speech formulas certainly suggest that weighing scales at the very least provide a dominant conceptual domain for the balance of power (see Figure 2.6).[44]

But the point being made here is not just that scales provide a dominant image, but it is also a generic image. Just as Baldwin (1989: 1) notes that thinking about power is '*ubiquitous* in the sense that all social arenas of social life involve power' so it appears that all social arenas also involve a balance of power and that a set of weighing scales provides the generic metaphorical source for understanding the implications that follow from making this assessment. Moreover, if we accept a transformative role for metaphors, then the implications are significant because they require us to change our established conception of power. Baldwin (1989: 1) argues that power involves getting someone to do something they otherwise would not do. What impact does the scales metaphor have on this conception of power? In essence, it moves us away from an agency-based conception of power and towards a structural conception of power. It tells us less about the power possessed by the participants as agents and more about how the power possessed by the members of the system defines the structure of the social setting.

---

[44] Osgood (1962: 76), for example, depicts the cold war as a see-saw 'balanced on a point that juts over a bottomless abyss', and Schattschneider (1960) uses the conceptual domain of a tug of war to show how the balance of power can change.

The metaphor not only encourages us to think that we can measure power, but it also indicates, at the same time, that that measure only becomes significant when examined in the context of the power possessed by the other actors in the system. It discourages us from thinking that power is hierarchical, monopolized or concentrated in one location. But it also indicates that power is fluid rather than fixed and that the power possessed by the actors in the system has to be constantly recalibrated. Outcomes, moreover, are always unpredictable because actors can relocate their power at any point in time, thereby shifting the overall systemic distribution of power. Ironically, theorists who specialize in the concept of power do not always seem to recognize the impact that the metaphor has on the conceptualization of power. For example, Baldwin (2004: 182) argues in the context of international relations that 'No matter which version of balance of power one considers, the idea of power as a property rather than a relation is firmly embedded'. But this assessment ignores the transformative impact that the balance of power metaphor has on the concept of power.

When weighing scales are used as a symbol for justice the focus is on the impartiality displayed by an accurate set of scales. By contrast, when scales are used as the metaphorical source for the balance of power, the focus is on how the scales form a system and interest is centred on how the behaviour of the scales is determined by the distribution of the weights on the two pans; every slight adjustment in one pan has an equal and opposite effect on the other pan. As Black suggests, therefore, there is a degree of interaction between the source and the target of the balance of power. The metaphor has a transformative effect on what we mean by power, but the concept of power also has some effect on how we characterize the scales. Despite, or perhaps because of, the familiarity of the generic metaphorical source, it is extraordinarily effective at changing our assessment of power. Instead of focusing on how one party can control the behaviour of another party, the metaphor requires us to examine power from a structural perspective and view any situation in terms of the overall distribution of power. So, for example, relations between the United States and Vietnam in the late 1960s look very different if we think of China and Vietnam in one pan and the United States in the other, rather than simply looking at the relations between Vietnam and the United States. Once we bring the broader picture into focus, moreover, we can see how the distribution of power changes across time. If, at one point in time, for example, we have a mother and father in one pan and the children in the other, and then the father and the children in one pan and the mother in the other, at a different point in time, then the structure of the situation looks quite different and we can anticipate a new set of outcomes.

This generic use of weighing scales as a metaphorical source to transform us from an agency-based to a structural-based conception of power is an uncontroversial move and, indeed, the balance of power has failed to register as a significant concept in the social sciences. It has not even been highlighted in attempts such as Lukes' (2005) to provide a comprehensive account of how power can be conceptualized. The lack of interest displayed by social scientists in the balance of power can be accounted for in part by the general failure to appreciate how significant and effective metaphors like the balance of power are in determining how we look at the world. On the other hand, the response to the balance of power in the field of international relations has been very different. For several centuries the balance of power has provided not only a central but also an extremely contentious element in the analysis of international relations. In the next chapter, therefore, we extend the assessment of the balance of power in order to accommodate and account for both the importance attached to the concept in international relations and the controversy surrounding the concept in this field.

3 | *The balance of power: from metaphors to myths and models*

I N THE PREVIOUS CHAPTER I argue that metaphors are not only a surprisingly complex phenomenon but also that any assessment of the balance of power is profoundly affected by whether we regard the concept as a substitution or an interaction metaphor. If we treat the balance of power as an interaction metaphor, then the effect is to reconstitute the meaning of power and we move from an agency-based concept to a structurally based concept and I suggest that a set of weighing scales provides a generic metaphorical source that promotes this conceptual transformation. The ubiquitous use made of the generic balance of power reveals that the transformation is an easy and uncontroversial step to take. However, despite the promiscuous use that is made of the generic source, it has proved insufficient to elevate the balance of power into a key concept across the social sciences.[1] Only in the area of international politics has the balance of power come to be regarded as a central or indispensable concept. Yet, ironically, international politics is also the only area where the concept is regarded as highly contentious.

The aim of this chapter, therefore, is to account for the centrality and significance of the balance of power in the theory and practice of international politics as well as the controversy that surrounds the concept. But to do this, it is necessary to establish a broader analytical framework for examining the concept and view the balance of power not only as a metaphor but also as a myth and a model. These approaches to the analysis of the balance of power, however, are not unrelated; indeed, the overall framework reveals that metaphors, myths and models are potentially all very closely linked.

There are, however, two very different ways of viewing the relationship between metaphors, myths and models: one draws on a positivist approach to social science and the other on a postpositivist approach.

---

[1] Moreover, the huge swathe of literature on the balance of power is simply ignored in most discussions of power.

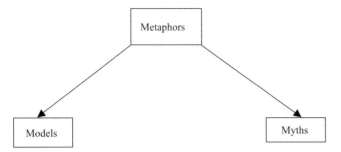

Figure 3.1 A positivist view of relations between metaphors, myths and models

These approaches provide very different accounts of the centrality and the controversy surrounding the balance of power. Moreover, the meaning attached to myths changes dramatically when we move from one approach to the other. From a positivist perspective, myth is used in a colloquial sense and is associated with a fundamental error of some kind, whereas postpositivism associates myths with ideological narratives that draw on deep-seated beliefs about the nature of reality.

The first section of this chapter examines the relationship between metaphors, models and myths from a positivist perspective. It shows, on the one hand, how metaphors are regarded as an important source for models, but, on the other hand, it is also recognized that if the metaphor is reified and is treated as a real phenomenon, then it is effectively transformed into a myth and promotes an erroneous view of reality. Instead of illuminating reality, it becomes a source of distortion. From this perspective, therefore, the balance of power metaphor has the potential to transform the concept into either a model or a myth (see Figure 3.1). From a positivist perspective, the balance of power can be seen to be a central but simultaneously controversial concept throughout the contemporary study of international relations because although a wide range of significant theorists have chosen to place the concept at the centre of their attempts to theorize international relations, these attempts have all invariably run into fundamental and persistent criticism. At no time in the contemporary era, therefore, has the balance of power operated as an uncontested concept.

The remainder of the chapter focuses on how postpositivists view the relationship between metaphors, myths and models. Positivists presuppose that, in principle, there is no difference between the way social scientists observe social reality and natural scientists observe the natural world. Postpositivists insist that although this may be true in principle, the nature of social and natural reality is so fundamentally different that, in practice, social and natural scientists do employ radically different ways of observing the two realities. The problem with the positivist perspective in the social sciences, according to postpositivists, is that it assumes that there is a material reality and fails to recognize that even the most physical aspects of that reality, such as an ocean, can only be understood in terms of the ideas that define the significance of the ocean for a society (Steinberg, 2000). In the case of the balance of power, therefore, it becomes essential to explore the balance of power as an idea.

For postpositivists, therefore, the balance of power is seen to be a central concept in the study of international relations because it has played such a crucial role in the way that theorists and practitioners have thought about international relations from the early modern era through to the present day. For the same reason, however, the balance of power must be regarded as a controversial concept, because it has also come under continuous criticism since the eighteenth century. It follows that metaphors are significant, not because they provide an important source of models as positivists indicate, but because they are habitually used by social actors and they provide a vital insight into how these actors understand the nature of reality. Balance of power metaphors emerged in Renaissance Italy and so it can be inferred that there was a change at that juncture in how people thought about the world in which they operated. More specifically, it can be inferred that there was a change in how they thought about power.

It was indicated in the previous chapter that Krieger argued that power emerged as a very unstable and ambiguous concept at this time, embracing both negative and positive connotations. If this is the case, then it can be anticipated that the balance of power should also reflect a similar ambiguity and it should be possible to identify divergent sets of metaphors. The second section in the chapter demonstrates that in addition to the metaphors that generate an adversarial view of the balance of power, there is also a different set of metaphors that promote an associational view of the balance of power, so that instead of an equilibrium emerging as the result of actors pulling against each other, it is also possible to conceive of an equilibrium emerging as the result of independent actors cooperating to construct a stable balance of power.

The identification of the balance of power with different points of equilibrium has always been a fundamental feature of the concept, because in the context of international politics the balance of power has never simply been a metaphor that allows us to rethink an agency-based conception of power, it has also been a source of political myths that are instantiated in the form of ideological narratives about how a system of independent states has been maintained in the past and can be maintained in the future. There has been relatively little attention paid to political myths and myth-making in the field of international relations, and the remainder of the second section explores the idea in the context of the balance of power.[2] The third section then illustrates the role of the balance of power in the mythopoeic process by looking initially at Guicciardini's *History of Italy*, written at the start of the sixteenth century, which reveals a good deal about the origins of balance of power myth-making. The section goes on to explore the mythopoeic role of the balance of power in the contemporary era, focusing on Churchill's 1946 Iron Curtain speech and Bush's Introduction to the 2002 *National Security Strategy*.

The final section explores the relationship between metaphors, myths and models from a postpositivist perspective. According to postpositivists, it is a mistake to postulate a divide that cannot be breached between the analyst and the topic of analysis because social scientists are inevitably part of the social reality that they are analysing. It follows that it is no more than a convenient fiction to identify contemporary attempts to understand the balance of power as models and to establish a categorical distinction between them and earlier attempts to analyse the balance of power. When contemporary social scientists draw on the balance of power to develop models that are designed to account for the survival of the modern state system, therefore, there will inevitably be a myth-making or mythopoeic dimension to this activity. It follows that models, metaphors and myths are all seen to be closely inter-related (see Figure 3.2). As a consequence, this section concludes by establishing

---

[2] But myths were sometimes seen to be important in the context of the cold war. See, for example, Wheeler (1960), Kautsky (1965) and Freedman (1981). More recently, Weber (2001) associates myths with 'unconscious ideologies' that are seen to underpin all International Relations theories. Weber relies on a postmodern reading of myths, most closely associated with Barthes (1972; 1974). For an alternative reading of Barthes, see Flood (2002: 61–6).

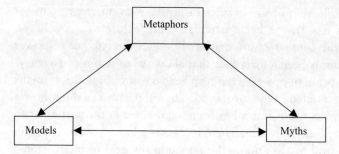

Figure 3.2 A postpositivist view of relations between metaphors, myths and models

a framework that shows how the adversarial and associational balance of power metaphors have generated a limited number of ideological narratives about how a stable state system can be maintained. Anticipating and at the same time establishing a path into Part III, it is then shown how the models of the four contemporary theorists examined in the next part – Morgenthau, Bull, Waltz and Mearsheimer – tap into different aspects of these myth-making narratives.

Positivism, metaphors, models and myths

The Chinese view crises as the source of both opportunity and danger and positivists view metaphors in exactly the same light. They broadly accept the interaction view that metaphors create the opportunity for viewing reality in a new way or allowing the scientist to express an abstract theory or idea in concrete terms that can be visualized. But there is, at the same time, a constant danger that the scientist will start to treat the metaphor literally and mistake the metaphor for concrete reality. When this danger materialises, it has been suggested that we get a metaphor-to-myth transformation. In this context, myth is being treated as a mistake or a methodological error. In this section, I first briefly review the positivist literature that examines the relationship between metaphors and models and then I discuss the relationship in the context of the balance of power. This is followed by a discussion of the danger of metaphors transforming into myths and I use Waltz's criticism of the way Morgenthau employs the balance of power metaphor to illustrate how positivists in International Relations conceive of the danger. Both Waltz and Mearsheimer can be regarded as positivists in the sense that they assume that there is a material reality that constrains the way that states act. Morgenthau and Bull accept the importance of material constraints on states as well but they also recognize the crucial importance of an ideational dimension in the international realm. None of these theorists, however, goes as far as contemporary constructivists want to take this ideational dimension.

From metaphors to models

A very tight connection between metaphors and models is often established in positivist literature discussing how theory is developed in the natural and social sciences. This literature focuses on the positive role that metaphors can play in the scientific process. Black (1979: 31), for example, comes to the conclusion that 'Every metaphor is the tip of a submerged model'. The task of the theorist then becomes to expose and test this model. Metaphors, therefore, provide an essential first step in coming to terms with aspects of the world that are not amenable to direct observation. As Zashin and Chapman (1974: 310–11) argue, metaphors are a 'tactic of immediate expression' which 'burst upon the audience without warning' and are designed to 'stimulate and even manipulate the imagination' by inducing 'an unusual picture or combination of images in their minds'. Miller (1979: 166) also observes that a metaphor 'gives us some insight into its subject at the moment that we understand it' but while he acknowledges that for some 'this sense of illumination is sufficient in itself to verify the metaphor' he insists that political inquiry cannot be satisfied with this solution. In the same vein, Barnes (1996: 150) argues that metaphors provide a 'bridge' that we need to cross before we can start to develop and formulate theory.[3]

Any standard definition of a theoretical model immediately reveals this proximity to a metaphor. Barbour (1974: 30), for example, defines theoretical models as 'imaginative mental constructs invented to account for some observed phenomena. Such a model is usually an imagined mechanism or process, which is postulated by analogy with familiar mechanisms or processes.'[4] He illustrates this definition

---

[3] Along the same lines, Brown (1976: 16) views model-building in terms of a 'spelled out metaphor'.

[4] More basic texts are prone to stress that models are simplified versions of reality. Lave and March (1975: 3), for example, define a model as 'a

with the well-known example of a gas being conceptualized as tiny elastic spheres constantly coming into contact with each other. If these hypothetical spheres are then assumed to act in a similar way to the familiar behaviour of billiard balls colliding into each other, then it becomes possible to use the model to formulate the kinetic theory of gases. Of course, it is much more unusual for models in the social sciences to be transformed into formal theories expressed in the form of equations and, as a consequence, theories and models tend to get used synonymously.

Although Barbour makes reference to analogies rather than metaphors, the two terms are often considered to be closely related. However, Zashin and Chapman (1974: 310–11) argue that analogies occur at a more abstract and deliberative phase in the thought process. Whereas metaphors induce a spontaneous change, an analogy generates a much more self-conscious process, with the analyst moving backwards and forwards looking for similarities and differences.[5] But if this assessment is accepted, then it follows that any metaphor can be turned into and treated as an analogy. So the metaphor 'power is a rhizome' can be changed to the analogy 'power is like a rhizome'. Indeed, Schön (1979: 255–60) postulates the existence of a metaphor life cycle or development process that embraces this change. He argues that the potential always exists to 'spell out the metaphor, elaborate the assumptions which flow from it, and examine their appropriateness'. In the early stages of the life cycle, we 'notice or feel that A and B are similar'. This feeling opens the way to restructuring one's perception of A and B, making it possible to identify the elements that precipitated the initial intuition. It then becomes possible to 'formulate an *analogy* between A and B'. Later still it becomes possible 'to formulate a general model for which a redescribed A and a redescribed B can be identified as instances'.[6]

---

simplified picture of part of the real world. It has some of the characteristics of the real world but not all of them. It is a set of interrelated guesses about the real world. Like all pictures it is simpler than the phenomena it is supposed to represent or explain.'

[5] See also Barbour (1974: 16) who argues that 'a metaphor is used momentarily, whereas a model is used in a sustained and systematic fashion'.

[6] See also Schön (1963). This approach to metaphors extends the interaction view, although it is simply not the case that all productive metaphors lead to the kind of general model postulated by Schön.

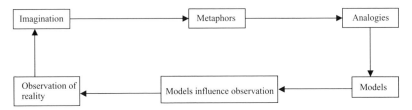

Figure 3.3 The role of metaphors and models in the logic of discovery (Adapted from Barbour 1998: 107 and Schön 1979: 260)

This approach to the scientific method acknowledges the importance of embracing metaphors and analogies within a logic of discovery. Indeed Landau (1972: 222) insists that in political science 'to employ a model is *always* to propose the existence of an analogy'. He also acknowledges an inextricable link between metaphors, analogies and models and concludes his discussion of metaphors by arguing that the choice is not 'between models and no models but between a critical consciousness of their use and an uncritical acceptance' of the 'hidden, implicit, and rigidified metaphors' that are frequently found in political science textbooks (Landau, 1972: 102). It follows that all significant metaphors must be made fully explicit and their implications spelled out and subjected to close empirical investigation (see Figure 3.3). The criticism often directed by positivists at metaphors is not that they are employed in analysis but rather that their implications are not spelled out. It follows that 'metaphors, when developed as clear and explicit models, can play a vital role in the search for political knowledge' (Miller, 1979: 158).[7]

Given the importance attached to metaphors in natural science methodology, it is unsurprising that positivists in the social sciences have also expressed an interest in metaphors. But although there are persistent attempts to formulate innovative metaphors across the social sciences, producing metaphors that provide real and enduring illumination is easier said than done. Nevertheless, despite the difficulty of establishing effective new metaphors, the enduring quality of the balance of power as well as its prolific and ubiquitous use is still extraordinary. The generic metaphor is now applied in every conceivable social setting and it shows no signs of waning. By contrast, attempts to

---

[7] Miller is here discussing the position on metaphors adopted by Landau (1972) and Deutsch (1963).

transform the metaphor into a model are very much more limited and, indeed, are largely confined to the field of international relations.

There are at least two possible reasons why weighing scales have proved to be such an effective and enduring metaphorical source. First, they provide the basis for what Barnes (1996: 149) calls a 'big' metaphor, and Luke (2004) refers to as a 'megametaphor'.[8] Metaphors of this kind enable us to see how a whole system is structured. The balance of power requires us to identify who is located on the pans of the scales and can thereby have an influence on where the pans will eventually come to rest. It follows that the balance of power metaphor presupposes a set of interacting parts and, as a consequence, presupposes or is synonymous with the existence of a system. Reference to a balance of power requires us to think in terms of a system even when there is no overt reference to weighing scales. This is unsurprising because, as Ball (1988: 86; see also Dallmayr, 1984a) notes, 'the rule of metaphor is most powerful when it is least recognized'.

A second reason for the metaphor's resilience is that it so easily and effectively reframes our conception of power. Instead of power emanating from one source, the weighing scales metaphor acts as a gestalt switch requiring us to identify the presence of power in the context of interacting units. The switch has profound consequences for our conception of how power operates because the metaphor allows us to move, almost without noticing, from an agency-based to a structurally based conception of power. Instead of seeing one party exercise power over another, power is seen to be a product of the system and no individual member of the system has power because outcomes are determined by the overall distribution of weights in the pan.

This 'switch' phenomenon has often been illustrated with the ambiguous duck/rabbit drawing which is now perhaps most closely associated with Wittgenstein. You first see either a duck or a rabbit (see Figure 3.4). If you are looking at a rabbit and then you are told that the rabbit is a duck, there is a gestalt switch and suddenly the two long ears are transformed into a beak and the rabbit does indeed

---

[8] These conceptions resonate with Pepper's (1972) notion that all philosophers operate within a limited number of 'root metaphors' as well as Nietzsche's notion of 'master' metaphors. Cantor (1982: 76) argues that 'One's choice of master metaphor will determine what one regards as literal and what as figurative.'

Figure 3.4 A diagrammatic illustration of Jastrow's Duck/Rabbit[9]

appear to be a duck. Thinking of power in terms of weighing scales precipitates an equally dramatic transformation.

Analyses of power, however, rarely, if ever, explore the conceptual implications that flow from treating the balance of power as a metaphor. This failure results in a significant gap in most of the major attempts to conceptualize power. So, for example, although Hindess (2006: 121) notes the inability of Lukes' (2005) classic text on power to accommodate the international dimension, which is depicted in terms of 'a regime of government with no controlling centre', Hindess then fails to recognize that the absence of a controlling centre can be treated as a generic condition, as the ubiquitous references to the balance of power highlight.

Although metaphors are often seen to lose their transformative capacity through overuse, this has not happened in the case of the balance of power. The metaphor retains its utility because power, the target of the metaphor, is a universally applicable and crucially important idea that also needs to be viewed in both agency and

---

[9] Although the figure is often attributed to Wittgenstein (1980; see his discussion in §515–17 of Volume II of *Remarks on the Philosophy of Psychology*) it was originally discussed by the American psychologist Joseph Jastrow in 1899. Other examples of the figure appear in Kihlstrom (2004). The figure is taken from http://philosophy.wisc.edu/forster/220/kuhn.htm, last downloaded 4 December 2006.

structural terms. The metaphor enables, indeed requires us, to reconfigure power as a structural concept. This is the primary function of the metaphor.

In Chapter 2, weighing scales are identified as the source for a generic metaphor of the balance of power that gets applied in every conceivable social setting. But the metaphor not only reveals the structural implications of competitive power, it also highlights the uncertainty and ambiguity that are inherent in any system where there is no controlling centre. A new development in a state may initially seem to tip the balance of power in its favour, but the development may also precipitate a reconfiguration in the positions adopted by the other members of the system and, as a consequence, the initial development may precipitate a very different and unintended consequence.

When establishing models, however, contemporary theorists in the social sciences have tended to shy away from the implications of a metaphor that stresses the indeterminate nature of a system. By the same token, power theorists have also been reluctant to open up an avenue of investigation that associates power with indeterminate outcomes. On the other hand, this is perhaps why the metaphor is such a familiar feature in everyday speech. But, in any event, the failure of the balance of power to become a significant concept in the social sciences raises the question of why, by contrast, the balance of power has been opened to such intense scrutiny by positivists in the field of international relations.

There are two possible answers. One is that although it is possible to think of a family or a football league as a balance of power system, it is not possible to conceive of either as an autonomous system. Both are nested in broader and highly controlling systems. As a consequence, there is no notion that the operation of the system is coping with existential threats. Murder may take place within a family, but it has never been suggested that this outcome can be understood by reference to a balance of power system. By contrast, it is generally assumed that the international balance of power generates the idea of a system that is completely autonomous and where the survival of the units is regarded as the focal point of the system. Moreover, and this supplies a second reason why positivists have attempted to build models by drawing on the balance of power metaphor, for the past five centuries the international balance of power has been inextricably linked to a political myth, that has become progressively more deeply rooted, that associates the concept with the stability and survival of a system of independent states. I will look in more detail at the implications of identifying the balance of power as a political myth in the next section, but at the moment, it is sufficient to note that a political myth will be defined in terms of ideological narratives that cannot be equated in any straightforward way with erroneous beliefs, which is how positivists think of myths. It is, moreover, only in the context of international politics that such myths have taken root.

The key point for positivists about the myth is that it moves us away from the idea that the scales are in constant motion and generate indeterminate outcomes, and towards the idea that there is a tendency for the scales to reach a natural resting point or equilibrium. The myth takes us beyond the generic metaphor because it only acts as a gestalt switch that transforms our conception of power from an agency base to a structural base. The mythopoeic dimension of the metaphor presupposes that the set of scales not only identifies the structural nature of power but also provides an account for the emergence of a point of equilibrium. So, according to one narrative, if two states ally, then the scales move in their favour, but this will alarm other states and they will then ally and the balance will be restored (see Figure 3.5ba). Alternatively, if a state starts to extend its military capabilities and display hegemonic tendencies, then the scales will move in its favour. However, allies, fearing for their security, will realign and the scales will return to a point of equilibrium (see Figure 3.5b). Narratives of this kind are deeply embedded in the way that Europeans have thought about international politics over the past five hundred years. But, from the perspective of positivists this is largely irrelevant; they are only interested in the narrative because it provides the basis for testable models that yield determinate outcomes.

The metaphor-to-myth transformation

At first sight, it might seem that the conceptions of myth as error and myth as ideological narrative are quite distinct and easily distinguishable. In practice, however, disentangling erroneous beliefs from normative or ideological beliefs about how we want to organize society is far from straightforward. Indeed, from a constructivist perspective, the distinction is problematic because so many aspects of the world that we treat as 'natural' turn out on closer inspection to be a reification

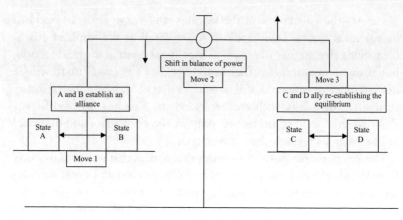

Figure 3.5a Political equilibrium and the balance of power

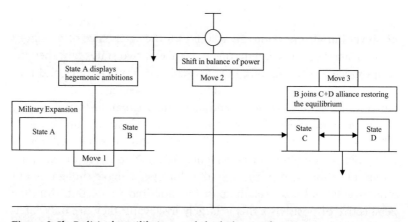

Figure 3.5b Political equilibrium and the balance of power

of ideas that are, in fact, tractable and amenable to change.[10] At the very least, the constructivist perspective problematizes the identification of a myth as an erroneous belief, because erroneous beliefs can

[10] This is not an entirely new insight because social scientists have long recognized the importance of self-fulfilling prophecies – a term originally coined by Merton (1957). During the cold war, Soviet beliefs were often identified in the West as myths, but there was less recognition that deep-seated western beliefs took exactly the same form. See Wheeler (1960) and Kautsky (1965).

play a vital role in sustaining structures and processes that reproduce our social world.

Moreover, although often reluctant to examine their own contribution to the establishment of social reality, positivists can be responsible for helping to promote beliefs that are later taken to be erroneous myths. Research by natural and social scientists during the nineteenth and twentieth centuries, for example, helped to reify the concept of race, thereby justifying and reinforcing extant racial beliefs and policies. Indeed, at the very end of the twentieth century the American Anthropological Society still considered it necessary to send a formal memorandum to the US Census Bureau arguing that 'racial myths' had significantly distorted 'the reality of human capabilities and behaviour' (Thomas, 2000: 111–12).

Because positivists are well aware that 'false' beliefs can create self-fulfilling prophecies, they often express concern about the use of metaphors in our language, because they are all too easily reified and transformed into myths. As Landau (1972: 83) insists, 'to take a metaphor literally is to create a myth, and the more conventional the myths become, the more difficult they are to dislodge'. Brown (1976) agrees that to 'unmask metaphors that have become myths requires negative insight and circumspection'. Reified metaphors, they both accept, have the capacity to distort analysis in a very significant way. Theorists, it is argued, fail to recognize either the 'hypothetical character' of their statements or indeed how their thoughts and observations are being unwittingly shaped by the metaphors. Rather than providing illumination, therefore, the metaphors present a picture of the world as viewed through a distorting mirror.

Sarbin (1964; 1972) argues that such reification is a relatively common phenomenon in psychology and that there is a constant need for 'demythification'.[11] Terms such as image, anxiety and mind established initially on the basis of metaphors have all, with the passage of time, become 'hypostatized' or reified entities as the result of a 'metaphor-to-myth transformation'. It follows, Sarbin (1972: 336) argues, that the metaphorical qualities of a term like 'imagination' have been 'so long submerged that its ontological status has been taken for granted'.

---

[11] Shortly before his death in 2005, aged 94, Sarbin (2003) extended the idea of 'metaphor to myth transformation' to the political realm and, specifically, to 'the war on terror' metaphor.

As a consequence, our understanding of how the mind operates is seriously inhibited. But, of course, this assessment itself presupposes that the mind/body distinction is valid.

There are theorists in International Relations who have adopted a similar line of argument, often in the context of denigrating the value of metaphors. Waltz, for example, criticizes Morgenthau's use of the balance of power because his analysis is seen to drift steadily towards a reification of the metaphor. Instead of treating the balance of power as a theoretical concept and viewing it, as Waltz (1979: 120) claims to, as the unintended outcome of states endeavouring to survive, Morgenthau is seen to give the concept an ontological status in the form of a set of rules that impact on how states behave, thereby transforming 'a possible effect into a necessary cause'. But as the detailed discussion of Morgenthau shows in Chapter 4, this account does not provide an accurate assessment of the role played by the balance of power in Morgenthau's approach to theory.[12]

Postpositivism, metaphors and myths

Ironically, constructivists argue that neorealists, indeed all realists, have fallen victim to a much more fundamental form of reification that extends far beyond metaphors.[13] In making this criticism, constructivists are seeking to undermine complacent certainties that, from their perspective, underpin all realist thought. What they wish to show is that the international structures that realists treat as material features of the world need to be re-viewed as intersubjective ideas that are shared by international decision-makers and then are subsequently reproduced uncritically by realist theorists. The realists, in other words, unwittingly form part of a dominant culture that promotes a distinctive view of international politics. The end of the cold war, however, created the opportunity to change the dominant ideas about international politics adhered to by international decision-makers and, in doing so, transform the prevailing culture. Given this assessment, it is unsurprising

---

[12] Schroeder (2001: 17) worries that historians are prone to reify the concept and notes how the balance of power can be treated as 'a self-sustaining, self-adjusting mechanism' operating independently of states, despite the fact that this is 'empirically speaking, nonsense'.

[13] See Wendt's (1992: 410) discussion of reification.

that realists have run into so many problems as they try to make sense of the newly emerging culture in terms of 'truths' that were derived from the previous culture (Williams, 2006). From Guzzini's (1998; 2004; 2005) perspective, what all realists have traditionally done is to reify a set of ideas about the balance of power, thereby rendering themselves incapable of understanding the concept.

Despite the common interest in reification, positivists and postpositivists view the relationship between metaphors, myths and models very differently because postpositivists are interested in telling stories from the inside as well as from the outside.[14] So from a postpositivist perspective it is necessary to accommodate the fact that the balance of power metaphor is often embedded in the way that international actors think about the world and so metaphors are not just a route to the formation of new models, they are also an integral element of the world under investigation. From this perspective, therefore, it becomes important to identify the range of metaphorical sources that have been associated with the balance of power over the past five centuries. Although there is no doubt that the generic metaphor has persistently been used to think about international politics, attention is also drawn in the first part of this section to a second set of metaphorical sources that promotes an associational rather than an adversarial view of the balance of power.

Attention is then turned to the postpositivist approach to myths. While it is not unusual to see the balance of power identified as a metaphor, it is rare, although not completely unprecedented, to see the concept portrayed as a myth. Liska (1977: 5), for example, describes the balance of power as 'the dominant myth and the fundamental law of interstate relations', although he then fails to amplify what he means by a myth and he also fails to identify the relationship that exists between the idea of the balance of power as a metaphor and as a myth. Political myths about the balance of power are associated here with ideological narratives that establish a link between the past, present and future and account for the emergence of stable points of political equilibrium that have the effect of ensuring that the system of sovereign states survives. For postpositivists, therefore, there is an intimate link between balance of power metaphors and myths.

---

[14] Hollis and Smith (1990) use this metaphor as a useful shorthand for distinguishing between the two modes of explanation often associated with positivism and postpositivism.

Postpositivism, metaphors and the balance of power

A close reading of Guicciardini's *History of Italy*, written at the start of
the sixteenth century, suggests that there was unquestionably a tension
in the way that he assessed the role of power in the relations among the
Italian city states. The tension arose because while he was interested
in providing an account of the adversarial relations among the Italian
city states, he also identified that the Italian city states needed to collaborate in order to secure their independence.[15] The existence of this
tension adds weight to the argument made in Chapter 2 that power
became a very ambivalent concept at the time when the metaphors
associated with the balance of power began to emerge in the sixteenth
century. But if we acknowledge that power embraces positive and negative connotations then the balance of power should display a similar
ambivalence.

It has already been established that the weighing scales associated
with the generic metaphor readily translate into the image of an adversarial balance of power, with the metaphor encouraging us to think
of the system splitting into two sides that are then locked into a competitive relationship with each other. In other words, the metaphor
encourages us to think that power relations are inherently adversarial.
However, there is an alternative and longstanding tradition of thought
that promotes a more cooperative perspective on the balance of power
and is linked to a different set of metaphors. The tradition extends back
to classical antiquity when the desirability of a constitution that established a mixed government was first advocated. Polybius (ca 203–120
BCE), argued, for example, that although there are virtues attached to
monarchy, aristocracy and democracy, if left unchecked, each promote
specific rather than general interests and so it is necessary to establish a
constitutional structure whereby the power possessed by the monarch,
the aristocrats and the people generates a political equilibrium and so
'by being accurately adjusted and in exact equilibrium, the whole might
remain long steady, like a ship sailing close to the wind' (cited in Fink,
1945: 4).[16] The metaphor promotes the image of a system that is built

---

[15] This line of argument is developed in greater length in the next section
where Guicciardini's history is examined in some detail.

[16] Plutarch drew on exactly the same metaphorical source. See Fink
(1945: 7).

in such as way as to promote the interests of everyone operating within the system.

From the Renaissance onwards, attempts were made to recapture this view of an *associational* balance of power from classical antiquity and apply it to both domestic and international politics. When applied to international politics, the central argument was that no state could be allowed to expand to the point where it threatened the independence of the other states of Europe, and so there needed to be a distribution of power that ensured that no state could overwhelm the system. A range of metaphorical sources was used to identify an associational balance of power. For example, in the sixteenth century, Gentili identified Europe as an arch and argued that 'if anyone should pluck out the keystone of an arch, on which all stones lean, the rest would follow and fall with it' (cited in Wright, 1975: 14). Using an identical metaphorical source, Fénelon argued in the eighteenth century that the European states had a mutual interest in common security because if 'one stone is taken out of an arch, the whole falls to the ground, because all the stones sustain each other in pushing against each other' (cited in Wright, 1975: 42). He insisted that just as every citizen has a duty to defend the nation against an invader, so 'common safety' requires neighbouring nations to unite against a potential hegemon, because any nation shares a common interest in the 'welfare and repose of that universal republic of which it is a member and in which are enclosed all the countries composed of private men'.

A related metaphorical source depicts Europe as a body. Vattel argued in the eighteenth century that 'Europe forms a political system in which nations inhabiting this part of the world are bound together by their relations and various interests into a single body. It is no longer as in former times, a confused heap of detached parts, each of which has but little concern for the lot of others' (cited in Hinsley, 1963: 166). Metternich used the same metaphor the following century, arguing that the European states formed 'a kind of social body' that reflected 'the application of the principle of solidarity and of the balance of power between states' (Gulick, 1967: 32). The practice that lay behind these metaphorical images of an associational balance of power emerged most clearly during the discussions of the major peace conferences from the 1713 Utrecht settlement onwards, when the territorial arrangements agreed at the settlement were legitimized in terms of establishing a 'just equilibrium'. At the heart of this notion of the balance of power, as Clark (2005: 83) makes clear, lies the concept of consensus and the idea of a just equilibrium was premised on the assumption that the balance of power was the product of an agreement amongst the major powers. It was an associational rather than an adversarial balance of power.

By the start of the twentieth century, however, the idea of an adversarial balance of power began to take precedence over any idea of an associational balance of power. Indeed, A. F. Pollard, an Oxford historian, insisted in the early 1920s that the meaning of the balance of power had been unwittingly transformed during the course of the nineteenth century. At the time of Lord Castlereagh, the British foreign secretary at the end of the Napoleonic Wars, the balance of power, according to Pollard (1922: 25–6), referred to the situation where states were 'co-operating to produce a general stability or equilibrium'. During the nineteenth century, however, the term was debased and had come to refer to a situation where two hostile alliances 'broke up the unity of the European system' by forming 'two weights or forces balanced one against the other'. Pollard (1922: 27) believed that the transformation was unwitting because diplomats in the British Foreign Office were surprised when it was pointed out to them that their use of the term 'was an entirely different balance from that of which Castlereagh had approved as a guarantee of peace'.[17]

From metaphors to myths

The contradictory images that Pollard presents in his despairing assessment of developments in the aftermath of the First World War leads him to conclude that the balance of power had become a thoroughly confused concept and, as a consequence, should be abandoned. Of course, this never happened. In making this recommendation, moreover, Pollard ignores the fact that from Guicciardini onwards there was a range of metaphors that makes it possible to draw a distinction between an associational and an adversarial balance of power. Moreover, as we will see in Part III, the idea that an associational balance of power gave way to an adversarial balance of power in the twentieth century provides a central theme in Morgenthau's account

[17] Schroeder (1989) makes a similar distinction, but argues that the adversarial eighteenth-century balance of power system gave way to an institutionalized political equilibrium after the Napoleonic Wars.

of the balance of power although, in contrast to Pollard, this does not surprise him, and instead he sees it as a product of broader historical forces.

Despite the fact that Pollard portrays the late nineteenth century balance of power as dividing Europe, he accepts, nevertheless, that the two sides counterbalance each other and establish a political equilibrium. The fact that the sides end up evenly balanced, however, is only a possible not a necessary outcome from the perspective of the scales metaphor. Indeed, the metaphor can just as easily embrace the power transition model (Tammen, 2000), which assumes that there is generally one dominant state in the system. Nevertheless, the idea that an adversarial balance of power can produce such an equilibrium reflects a longstanding political myth that can be traced back to Guicciardini.

In everyday speech, a myth is habitually associated with any proposition that is, or is believed to be, factually incorrect. When used in this sense, the assumption is that once a statement is shown to be empirically false, then any rational person will, in future, draw on the correct account of the facts. Nevertheless, when used in this way, the term is often also intended to draw attention to the fact that the erroneous view is systematically and widely adhered to.[18] At this juncture, then, the existence of the myth itself becomes an interesting sociological phenomenon that requires some explanation. The need for explanation becomes even more important, however, if the myth has the characteristic of a self-fulfilling prophecy that starts to have real and important consequences in the world. Effectively this is where constructivists are coming from. Power politics represents an erroneous but pervasive myth that realists have bought into. Constructivists want to expose the myth, but they are also interested in where the myth came from and how it has been perpetuated. Although they have not drawn on it, there is an expanding literature on the significance of myths in contemporary life and the importance of myths in political communication. Much of the early research on myths and myth-making was carried out in the social sciences by anthropologists working with pre-scientific communities. Cassirer (1946), one of the most important twentieth-century theorists in this field, initially drew a sharp distinction between the

[18] See, for example, Halliday's (2005) *100 Myths about the Middle East* or, coming from the opposite end of the political spectrum, Minter's (2005) *Disinformation: 22 Myths that Undermine the War on Terror*. But there are a huge number of books in international relations and elsewhere using this colloquial conception of myth in their titles.

mythical consciousness that prevails in pre-scientific communities and the scientific consciousness that exists in the modern world. In the aftermath of the Second World War, however, while still maintaining that mythical thought is necessarily non-rational and even 'demonic', Cassirer (1946: 280) accepted that myth-making is an important feature in the modern world. However, he associated it with the conscious process employed by leaders of totalitarian states who self-consciously propagate myths and instil them in entire populations by recourse to mass communications.

There is now a growing recognition, however, that myths and myth-making are an essential and normal feature of all societies and, since the end of the Second World War, the importance of political myths has been acknowledged by a range of political theorists including MacIver (1947), Lasswell and Kaplan (1950) and Friedrich (1980). From their perspective, political myths embody the fundamental, largely unconscious or assumed political values of a society. MacIver (1947: 4) argues that any society 'is held together by a myth-system, a complex of dominating thought-forms that determines and sustains all its activities'.

More recently, Flood (2002) notes that while the majority of the literature on myths relates to sacred myths (whose believers consider them divinely true), there is a growing interest in political myths. He depicts these myths as ideologically marked narratives that focus on how to maintain or change the political order, and because of the centrality of these accounts in any political system Flood insists that myth-making is an everyday practice that permeates the discourse of all political communicators. The process of myth-making involves 'the intricate, highly variable relationship between claims to validity, discursive construction, ideological marking, and reception of the account by a particular audience' (Flood, 2002: 7). As one of the most widely employed ways of making political events intelligible in the light of ideological beliefs, Flood (2002: 275) concludes, therefore, that 'the production and reproduction of mythopoeic narratives are constant features of political life.'

An ideology is defined by a belief system that underpins a preferred political order and it is made up of an image of this order alongside a political programme for how to bring about or preserve the order.[19]

---

[19] See Eccleshall (1984: 7). There is an enormous literature not only on the content of competing ideologies but also on how to conceptualize

Myths are seen to play an integral role in the process of producing or preserving a political order because they provide a persuasive account of how this is going to happen. As a consequence, they represent a 'neglected but common type of political argument' (Tudor, 1972: 110) and a 'form of ideological discourse' (Flood, 2002: 13). All political myths provide a graphic way of linking the past, the present, and the future and are an invaluable tool for decision-makers endeavouring either to justify new policy positions or sustain the status quo. As Edelman (1971: 79) notes, 'myths make the world meaningful' and 'serve constantly to promote conformity and bolster leadership'. But political myths are not easily invented by leaders; they have to be firmly embedded in the political culture in order to represent a resource that can be drawn upon for the purposes of political legitimization.[20]

To generate support for policies that will either bring about a new political order or maintain support for an existing order it is essential to be able to show that these policies make sense in terms of what has happened in the past and what will happen in the future. The problem is that our understanding of the past is as flexible and inchoate as our understanding of the future and so somehow we have to stabilize our image of both the past and the future in order to make sense of the policies being pursued in the present. Narrators in novels often use prolepsis – the anticipation of future events – in order to influence how the reader interprets what is currently happening.[21] Myth-makers employ the same device. It is possible to do this on the basis of myths which take the form of narratives, where the present is viewed as either an episode in an ongoing story or an incident in a dramatic development.

A political myth provides a perspective that dictates what we focus on when we look at the past and the future and from this specific point of reference it then becomes possible to justify the pragmatic steps that are currently being taken to maintain or transform the established political order. These steps make sense in terms of where we have come from and where we want to go. It follows that myths are used by

ideology. The nature of ideology is considered important because it focuses on the relationship between theory and practice. For a general introduction to ideology and ideologies see Heywood (2003).

[20] See Clark (2005) for a discussion of the importance of political legitimization in the context of international politics.

[21] The term prolepsis comes from rhetoric and is a device whereby a speaker anticipates objections and answers them in advance.

policy–makers to establish coherent and meaningful links between the past, present and future and on this basis to build the kind of pragmatic argument that is needed to explain and justify, both to the policy-makers themselves and to their political constituents, how to act at this particular point in time. Political myths, in other words, are drawn upon by theorists and practitioners to render decisions intelligible and meaningful. From this perspective, then, myth-making represents a routine and yet crucial feature of political life.

Metaphors are acknowledged to be very significant myth-making tools because they can help to render complex situations intelligible (Edelman, 1971). This is manifestly the case when the international arena is discussed in terms of a set of weighing scales because the metaphor simultaneously combines a structural conception of power with a graphic image of the international arena. The metaphor encourages us not only to think that the power of states can be weighed but also that we can anticipate that the power of states will change across time. As a consequence, it provides a mechanism that allows us to establish a narrative that links the past, the present and the future. We can look back at the past and see how the structure of power has changed across time, we can assess the structure of power in the present and we can anticipate the distribution of power in the future.

But in the international arena, balance of power metaphors also provide the basis for persuasive myths about how states can maintain their independence. These myths have been propagated most vigorously by political commentators, like Guicciardini, who value the independence of their own state within a system of independent states. The balance of power sits at the heart of these ideological narratives; but here the metaphor is not only providing an image that opens the way for a narrative about how the structure of power has changed across time, it also offers an explanation for how the state can survive. And it is at this juncture that the metaphor takes on the characteristics of a political myth because it not only generates an explanation for what has happened in the past, but it also makes a case for how states should operate in the future.

Explanations for the survival of the European state system hinge on the potential that the metaphors underpinning both adversarial and associational balances of power identify for the emergence of a political equilibrium across the system. The metaphor in the case of an adversarial balance of power reveals that a political equilibrium is equated with scales that are evenly balanced. As Figures 3.5a and 3.5b illustrate, if we assume that an expansion in a state's power or a new alliance between states is considered to create a threat to neighbouring states, then the metaphor indicates very strongly that there will be a response by other states that will restore the system to a political equilibrium. In other words, there is an assumption that self-interested action by independent states will be sufficient to establish an equilibrium. This kind of thinking encouraged the myth that the balance of power reflected the existence of some kind of 'natural law' that ensured the survival of a state within a states system.

The metaphors that define an associational balance of power are much less clear about what a political equilibrium would look like. But the image of the European arch suggests that there is an equilibrium that can be collectively constructed. What the metaphor implies is that the potential exists to establish a political equilibrium on the basis of a consensus whereby the essential security needs of all the major powers are satisfied. An extension of this position is that any aspiring hegemon will be met by an overwhelming collective response.

Critics of the established European political order were never persuaded by these metaphors or the myths that accompanied them. Far from the balance of power providing a sturdy framework that ensured the survival of the European state system, it was linked to pervasive war and instability.[22] Critics made no distinction between equilibriums linked to either adversarial or associational balances of power; indeed, the associational balance was more suspect. Kant argued, for example, that relying on the balance of power to produce a lasting peace was chimerical because 'it is like the house which was built by an architect so perfectly in accordance with all the laws of equilibrium, that when a sparrow alighted upon it, it immediately fell' (cited in Clark, 1989: 55). This mythopoeic assessment of the balance of power ties together the past, present and future in a very distinctive fashion and establishes what Egerton (1983) calls a 'counter-myth'. Ideological critics of the balance of power foster their own firmly accepted myths, such as the democratic peace theory, to promote their own view of world order that reflects a very different set of images of the past, present and future to those promoted by advocates of the balance of power.

---

[22] Claude (1962: 40–93) provides an excellent survey of the critics of the balance of power.

Myth-making and the balance of power

This section examines the complex myth-making role played by the balance of power in Gucciardini's *History of Italy*. It is followed by an assessment of how Winston Churchill and George Bush used the concept in the contemporary era to show how the international arena had been transformed and required new policies for the future.

Myths and the origins of the balance of power

As the medieval era drew to a close, established thinking about power came under challenge.[23] Newly constituted metaphors and myths associated with the balance of power became part of the broader re-conceptualization of power that was taking place at that time. The myths and metaphors that supported the essentially hierarchical view of power that prevailed during the medieval era began to be challenged by very different metaphors and myths that related to an emerging system of states. Ball (1988: 25; x) argues that a dramatic shift of this kind cannot occur simply on the basis of redefining power or adopting a new concept; it requires theorists, practitioners to take on board a new range of 'myths, metaphors, symbols, images, and overarching world pictures'; and such a transformation cannot occur by 'definitional fiat' but requires a 'complex and protracted process of argumentation'. There is substantial evidence to suggest that we may be currently engaged in such a process at the moment, as reflected in major debates about the nature of power and how it is exercised in the contemporary world.

There is no doubt that the Italians engaged in a particularly dramatic shift in the way that they conceived their world during the Renaissance and the re-conception of power was an important dimension of this transformation. The image of Christendom structured on the basis of a hierarchical conception of power was irrevocably challenged. The hierarchical metaphor was certainly not rejected, but it was joined by a new structural conception of power that derived from a counterbalancing

---

[23] There is, however, no point in time when an actual transformation from a hierarchical to an anarchical political system took place. Significant elements of hierarchy persisted through to the nineteenth century. This was most apparent in the Holy Roman Empire. For an illuminating discussion see Haldén (2006).

metaphor. As Mattingly (1962: 60) puts it, by 1400 'Italy was beginning to become a system of mutually balanced parts in an unstable
equilibrium as all Europe was to be three hundred years later, a small
scale model for experiments with the institutions of the new state'.

Guicciardini's *History of Italy* provides perhaps the best known contemporary account of relations among the Italian city states. The book
records the history of the Italian city states from 1490 through to 1534,
the period when France intervened in order to take control of Naples
and thereby starting a process that was to undermine the independence
of the Italian peninsula. Guicciardini (1483–1540) was an active diplomat and appears as a participant in his own history.[24] However, his
reputation has fluctuated wildly across the centuries. In the eighteenth
century, Viscount Bolingbroke, a significant balance of power theorist
in his own right, said that he preferred Guicciardini to Thucydides 'in
every respect' (Hale, 1966: vii); but by the nineteenth century, he was
largely ignored. His reputation recovered in the twentieth century and
Hale (1966: vii) describes him as 'one of the greatest of all writers of
contemporary history'.

Guicciardini is frequently identified as employing some of the first
metaphors that relate to an 'international' balance of power although,
ironically, his history traces the destruction of the Italian balance of
power and its replacement by Spanish hegemony. As a consequence,
from Guicciardini's perspective, the course of events he describes is
tragic because of the value that he ascribes to the independence of the
Italian states and the fact that he presupposes that a balance of power
could have preserved Italian independence. There is, therefore, a significant mythopoeic dimension to the history because of Guicciardini's
ideological commitment to maintaining the independence of the Italian
states and the dramatic and didactic orientation of the narrative that
flows from this commitment.

Although references to the balance of power only appear explicitly
in the opening stage of the history, they perform a very significant function. Guicciardini (1984) begins his account by identifying the end of
the fifteenth century as a stable and peaceful era in Italy's history and
he attributes the peace and stability to factors that can be interpreted
in terms of both an adversarial and an associational balance of power.

---

[24] In the same way, Thucydides appears as a character in *The Peloponnesian
War*.

The key factor was the recognition that Venice 'aspired toward Italian hegemony', the common fear of Venice made it 'easy to maintain an alliance' and the effect of the alliance was to 'create a counterbalance' (Guicciardini, 1984: 7–8). The aim of the alliance was to prevent the Venetians from becoming more powerful and this was a realistic aim because although Venice was 'undoubtedly stronger' than any other city state, it was 'much weaker' than the alliance established to prevent any move towards 'Italian hegemony'. Guicciardini makes it clear that the logic of the situation automatically produced this counterbalance or balance of power, but he goes on to suggest that the alliance did not, as a consequence, reflect 'sincere and faithful friendship'. On the contrary, the allies were full of 'emulation and jealousy among themselves' but as the result of assiduous observation, they maintained the status quo by 'reciprocally aborting all the plans whereby any of the others might become more powerful or renowned'. But in addition to this adversarial balance of power, Guicciardini also hints at an associational balance of power when he focuses specifically on Lorenzo de' Medici, the ruler of Florence who, Guicciardini argues, recognized that the security of Florence depended upon maintaining the existing distribution of power within Italy. As a consequence, Lorenzo acknowledged that war must not break out, because conflict can create the potential for states to acquire additional territory, thereby precipitating a redistribution of power that would destabilize Italy. At this juncture, therefore, Guicciardini (1984: 7–9) moves away from the counterbalancing metaphor and argues that it is essential to ensure that Italy, as an entity, must be 'maintained in a state of balance, not leaning more toward one side than the other'. To prevent this happening, therefore, Lorenzo had to be 'on the watch against every incident'. Guicciardini cites the example of the 'disagreements, hostility' between the princes of Naples and Milan who are of 'almost equal power and ambition' and he suggests that Lorenzo acted as a 'bridle' and could moderate the disagreements and prevent conflict and thus avoid a change in the overall distribution of power.[25]

It is now generally agreed that Guicciardini provides us with an idealized view of this period and, in particular, Lorenzo's diplomacy. Wright (1975: 1) suggests that a close look at Lorenzo's correspondence

---

[25] This metaphor is, effectively, playing the same role as the 'balancer' in more contemporary terminology. For a helpful discussion of the balancer, see Sheehan (1989).

indicates that the period was 'less serene' than Guicciardini depicts, while Gilmore (1952: 142) argues that it is not possible to find at that time a 'conscious application of the principle of the balance of power' and, as a consequence, to interpret this period in terms of the balance of power is 'unhistoric'. But these assessments inevitably encourage us to ask why Guicciardini idealized this initial period and why the metaphors relating to the balance of power essentially disappear with the death of Lorenzo at the start of the book. In the body of the text, replacing the counterbalancing metaphors, Phillips (1977: 136) notes that Guicciardini 'constantly repeats medical metaphors of disease and cure'. For Guicciardini, the disease is identified with the willingness of the Italian city states to ally with outside states that are much more powerful than themselves. He accounts for the start of this development in terms of a shift in the established pattern of alliances, with Milan's ruler, Lodovico Sforza, becoming suspicious in 1492 of what he saw as increasingly close relations between Ferdinand of Naples and Piero de' Medici (who had taken over as ruler of Florence on the death of his father, Lorenzo de' Medici). Lodovico was particularly concerned because he saw that Florence 'on which he used to base his security, was now leaning toward his enemies' (Guicciardini, 1984: 18).

Although Ferdinand, according to Guicciardini, sincerely attempted to remove the source of the dispute, it is then observed that 'the elimination of causes does not always eliminate the effects which have had the origins in those causes' (Guicciardini, 1984: 20). Lodovico's sense of insecurity persisted and in seeking protection from the King of France to alleviate the sense of insecurity, he decided to provoke a French attack on Naples. And it is at this juncture that Guicciadini moves away from balancing metaphors. He does not see Lodovico's move in terms of attempting to establish a counterbalance, but as a 'cure for a disease' that ignores 'how dangerous it is to use medicine which is stronger than the nature of the disease' (Guicciardini, 1984: 20–1). Guicciardini, in other words, associates balancing with moves within Italy whereas, by contrast, the reliance on external states is considered to be an inappropriate medicine for the disease besetting Italy. The 'disease' is linked to 'ill-advised measures of rulers who act solely in terms of what is in front of their eyes: either foolish errors or shortsighted greed' (Guicciardini, 1984: 1). Guicciadini, therefore, is drawing a distinction between appearance and reality, and he associates reality with the impact of moves on the Italian balance. A short-sighted ruler might think that he is making an advantageous move, but if he has ignored its impact on the Italian balance, then he will discover that other states respond in a way that could lead to a long-term deterioration in his position.

From Guicciardini's perspective, the tendency to avoid noting the impact of moves on the Italian balance became a chronic condition after 1492 and led to the French intervention in 1494. In the rest of the book he describes in detail the moves that drew France and then other states into subsequent Italian disputes, eventually leading to Spanish hegemony and the loss of Italian independence. In presenting his history of these terms, Guicciardini adheres to a very clear picture of Italy forming a coherent, civilized unit existing within the much more extensive boundaries of Christendom, but then he also acknowledges states operating beyond the boundary of Christendom. The Turks play a particularly significant role throughout the narrative. But even before the first intervention, Guicciardini (1984: 21) notes that 'the kingdom of France was more populous, had more military power and glory, was wealthier and more influential than any other kingdom perhaps since the time of Charlemagne'. It was clear even at that stage, therefore, that France outweighed every Italian state, even Venice. It is for this reason that Guicciardini does not think it is appropriate to discuss France in terms of a counterbalance, although Guicciardini (1984: 23) is well aware that there are other states in Christendom, such as England, Spain and the Holy Roman Empire, that can pose a threat to the French. But Guicciardini is only concerned about the fate of Italy and once intervention occurred, then Italy's future starts to depend on factors outside of Italy and over which the Italians had no control.

Gilbert (1965: 231) argues, as a consequence, there was a 'crisis in historiography' at that time with the emergence of a new breed of historians who challenged the humanist idea that history is a man-made process. From this new perspective '*Fortuna* was all powerful and man a toy in *Fortuna's* hands' (Gilbert, 1965: 251).[26] Although Guicciardini unquestionably played a part in this reorientation of how history was studied, focusing on factual accuracy and the importance of understanding causal connections, he was also convinced that leaders have the capacity to shape events. His approach is compatible with Porter's

---

[26] *Fortuna* refers to all of those circumstances that human beings cannot control.

analysis of historical explanation. Porter (1981: 11–12) argues that 'the successful actor in history is the person who is most aware of the many possibilities of a situation; and the dramatic quality of historical events does seem to depend on there being alternative outcomes to consider'.

Guicciardini's initial discussion of the balance of power is essentially mythopoeic in function, as a consequence, because it demonstrates that the Italian city states system had the potential to be self-sustaining because security problems could be resolved internally without resort to external forces. This political myth provides the basis for the kind of counterfactual thought experiment that is regularly used by historians to help the reader to understand the consequences of key events in the past. Guicciardini's history starts from the premise that enlightened leaders could have pursued cooperative strategies to maintain an associational balance of power and thereby promote a stable security environment. Instead they made moves that encouraged external involvement and ultimately led to the loss of Italian independence.

The balance of power in the modern world

The mythopoeic role played by the balance of power in the contemporary era is examined, first, in Winston Churchill's 1946 speech entitled 'Sinews of Peace' and then in George W. Bush's 'Introduction' to the 2002 National Security Strategy. Both documents establish narratives that view the present as a turning point, where the future is going to be different from the past. But whereas Churchill draws on the past to show that the balance of power has no relevance in the future, Bush draws on the past to show why the balance of power has to be reconstituted in the future.

The title of Winston's Churchill's speech given at Westminster College in Fulton, Missouri is a metaphor that reveals that the speech is going to discuss ways of strengthening peace, although the speech is primarily remembered for the very graphic image that 'From Stettin in the Baltic to Trieste in the Adriatic an iron curtain has descended across the Continent.'[27] It was a carefully crafted speech designed to convince an American audience that the United States must come to the assistance of Europe in the short term but also build an enduring alliance with

---

[27] The text of the document can be found at www.nationalcenter.org/ ChurchillIronCurtain.html, last downloaded 4 December 2006.

Britain for the long term.[28] Churchill, however, was well aware of the American hostility to the balance of power and so the talk is primarily designed to transcend a world governed by the balance of power.

At the heart of the speech, therefore, is a stark warning to the Americans that there was a threat of global hegemony from the Soviet Union that cannot be met with traditional policies. Churchill did not define the threat in terms of imminent war; he acknowledged that the Soviet Union did not wish to go to war. Instead, he defined the threat in terms of the potential spread of tyranny. What the leaders of the Soviet Union wanted, according to Churchill, was 'the indefinite expansion of their power and doctrines' and to this end they were directing and coordinating the activities of dedicated fifth columns and communist parties in 'a great number of countries, far from the Russian frontiers and throughout the world'.[29] More to the point, as the result of agreements established during the Second World War, Churchill acknowledged that the Soviet Union had been permitted to manoeuvre itself into a position of very substantial strength in Europe by the time that the war came to an end.

Despite the danger, however, Churchill insisted that 'our fortunes are still in our hands and that we hold the power to save the future'. And to this end, he developed a line of argument that embraced a significant mythopoeic dimension. The argument started from the premise that the outbreak of the Second World War was the product of systematic policy failures and that if these policy failures were repeated then the world would have to go back to the 'school of war' for a third time, but at the risk on this occasions of bringing about a 'total destruction' that would return the world to the 'stone age'. Churchill focused on two key policy failures that would in the past have been discussed in balance of power terms: the failure to create a settlement (an associational balance of power) that was acceptable to Germany after the First World War and the failure to respond adequately to the subsequent threat of German hegemony (an adversarial balance of power). In the wake of the Second World War he was concerned about the failure to establish a

---

[28] For an interesting assessment of the rhetorical effectiveness of the speech, see Hostetler (1997). However, he fails to recognize the rhetorical significance played by the balance of power metaphor.

[29] This simply reiterates the argument he develops through his Titanic metaphor in his 1919 House of Commons speech discussed in Chapter 2.

settlement with the Russians but also about the danger of negotiating with the Russians from a position of weakness. He argued that the Russians despised military weakness and, like Hitler, they would take advantage of it. As a consequence, 'the old doctrine of a balance of power is unsound. We cannot afford, if we can help it, to work on narrow margins, offering temptations to a trial of strength.'

What Churchill wanted in the immediate future was a British-American military alliance and a clear commitment to an American military presence in Europe until the European states had recovered economically and militarily and could defend themselves. He talked, however, in terms of a 'fraternal association' and a 'special relationship' before eventually specifying the need for a 'Permanent Defence Agreement' between the United States and Britain. But, of course, this was an agreement that the British needed much more than the United States because the latter, as Churchill admitted, was at the 'pinnacle of world power' although he went on immediately to note that 'primacy in power' went hand in hand with 'an awe-inspiring accountability to the future'.

Having established that Europe was confronting a hegemonic threat from the Soviet Union and that the United States was now the dominant global power, it is important to note that Churchill failed to acknowledge that there had been a fundamental shift in the balance of power since the end of the nineteenth century and that the involvement of the United States in the defence of Europe was now absolutely essential. Not only does he avoid couching his position in balance of power terms, but he also depicts the balance of power as outdated and unsound. Of course, he could have noted in developing his argument about the need for a political settlement with the Soviet Union that Europeans had always recognized the need to establish a 'just equilibrium' in the aftermath of major war. He could also have observed that balance of power thinking had traditionally presupposed that states under threat from a hegemon would establish an overwhelming alliance to confront the hegemon. But he chose instead to adopt a Kantian image of the balance of power. It is likely that this was a self-conscious rhetorical ploy to tap into the longstanding American antipathy to European balance of power thinking. So rather than linking the balance of power to the sinews of peace, he argued that Britain and the United States must cooperate in building a Temple of Peace. He implies that if they had cooperated sooner during the interwar period, then the Second World

War could have been avoided and he says explicitly that cooperation was now essential to avoid a third world war. A formal defence agreement, he insists, would play a part in 'steadying and stabilizing the foundations of peace'. But his vision of the long-term future is even more wide-ranging. Churchill concluded his speech by arguing that if a Defence Agreement between the United States and Britain could be established and maintained, then there need be no 'quivering, precarious balance of power to offer its temptation to ambition or adventure' for the next hundred years.

Churchill's dream of an Anglo-American co-dominion stretching across the globe, replacing the balance of power with a Temple of Peace, was fanciful because it failed to come to grips with the redistribution of international power in the twentieth century, and the fact that the reduction of Britain's status in the world was irrevocable. The United States wished to eliminate not bolster the British Empire. Bluntly, the United States was not going to treat Britain as an equal. Moreover, as the Soviet Union began to appear as a significant threat to US interests, balance of power terminology, far from becoming redundant, was increasingly drawn upon by Americans to define cold war politics. Indeed, when attempts made by Nixon and Kissinger to develop the language of *détente* in the 1970s failed, and public support sagged, the response was to bring balance of power language and thinking to the fore once again (George, 1983: 28).

With the end of the cold war and the subsequent demise of the Soviet Union, however, attention began to focus increasingly on unipolarity and on what, in 1999, Hubert Védrine, the French foreign minister at the time, labelled *hyperpuissance* or the hyperpower possessed by the United States. The rehabilitation of balance of power terminology in the 2002 National Security Strategy (NSS), therefore, is perhaps surprising, although the development can be accounted for in terms of the mythopoeic function that the terminology serves in the document.[30]

In some ways, when the NSS was published, the structural position of the United States in the international system was very similar to the position it held in 1946. Once again, as President Bush admitted, the United States was in 'a position of unparalleled military strength and great economic and political influence'; but just as Churchill pointed to the widespread existence of forces that intended to undermine the

---

[30] Text of the document can be found at www.whitehouse.gov/nsc/nss.html.

influence of democratic governments, so Bush expressed great concern about the dangers posed by terrorists. But in contrast to Churchill, who in deference to the United States, denigrated the balance of power, Bush gives the concept pride of place and argues that the United States intends to 'create a balance of power in favour of freedom'.[31] The document, therefore, represents a riposte to arguments about US unilateralism, unipolarity, and *hyperpuissance*. Bush states explicitly that 'no nation can build a safer, better world alone' and he argues in favour of alliances and multilateral institutions because they can 'multiply the strength of freedom-loving nations'. But more significant is the reference to great powers in the text and the implication that the United States is simply one of a number of great powers. By also referring to the balance of power, the document is alluding to the traditional significance attached to great powers and it opens the way to establishing a link between the past, present and future. It is assumed that the international system has always been dominated by the great powers and that these states continuously prepared for war. Bush is, in other words, defining the balance of power in adversarial terms. But he also argues that there has been a transformation in world politics since the end of the cold war because we are moving into a world where the possibility of the great powers going to war with each other is becoming unthinkable. This does not mean that the great powers are no longer competitive, but it does mean that they are now only interested in engaging in peaceful competition.

But this is not the only change that is noted. It is also argued that the great powers share common interests and increasingly they are coming to share common values. They share common interests, according to Bush, because they are united by common dangers, and, in particular, the problem of terrorism. But they are also united by common values as it is steadily recognized that social and political freedom is the only effective route to 'national greatness'. It follows that in place of the old adversarial balance of power, where there was a chronic danger of war, there is a new kind of balance of power emerging among

---

[31] This was not the first time Bush used this expression. He argued in his 2001 Inaugural Address that 'The enemies of liberty and our country should make no mistake: America remains engaged in the world by history and by choice, shaping a balance of power that favors freedom. We will defend our allies and our interests.' Cited at www.whitehouse.gov/news/inaugural-address.html.

the great powers that is promoting freedom. The great powers are starting to pursue mutually supporting policies and instead of pulling against each other, therefore, they are pulling together and are effectively creating an associational balance of power. The balance of power is being depicted as an arch rather than a tug of war. Three years after this document was published, Condoleezza Rice (2005), the US Secretary of State, replicated the argument that the United States was transforming its relations with the other great powers such as Japan, Russia, the European Union, and 'especially with China and India', and she insisted that collectively they were 'building a more lasting and durable form of global stability: a balance of power that favors freedom'.

Both Churchill and Bush are in essence rejecting the relevance of the historical conception of the balance of power for understanding the role being played by the great powers in the present and the future. There is, therefore, a significant mythopoeic dimension to the argument that they are making. But whereas Churchill is using the metaphor to provide a specific perspective on how power operated in the international system, Bush is using the balance of power as a symbol: for balance of power read great power politics. Although less graphic than Churchill's use of the metaphor, Bush is making the same point that, in the past, great power politics generated war and constant instability. Churchill, then, devises a new metaphor for understanding the future in order to highlight for the United States that there is an opportunity to bring about a fundamental transformation in international politics, provided that they continue to treat Britain as a great power. By contrast, Bush reformulates what he sees as the traditional concept. The balance of power was a source of war whereas it is now a source of freedom. Bush retains the balance of power concept in order to stress that we have not moved into a new unipolar world but remain in a world dominated by a range of great powers that share common values and through cooperation can determine the fundamental characteristics of world politics. In both cases, therefore, the balance of power plays a central mythopoeic role in the construction of an argument that is intended to help us to understand how we move from the past through the present and into a better future. Guicciardini's use of the metaphor is rather different because the preferred future failed to materialize and the balance of power is drawn upon to make the mythopoeic counterfactual argument that Italy did not have to lose its independence.

Conclusion: from metaphors and myths to balance of power models

Models of the balance of power lie at the heart of some of the most important attempts made since the end of the Second World War to develop a theoretical understanding of international relations. From a positivist perspective, these models should be treated as completely independent from the reality that is being investigated. From a post-positivist perspective, however, the idea of a completely neutral social science is an oxymoron, and, as a consequence, there is an inevitable although often veiled mythopoeic dimension to social science research. In other words, the research can, at least potentially, make a contribution to ideological narratives about how to maintain or change social structures. There is a widespread assumption among postpositivists that contemporary realists are continuing to propagate theoretical analysis that sustains an ideological narrative (Guzzini, 1998; Williams, 2006) or myth that has operated as a very successful self-fulfilling prophecy in recent centuries within Europe. The balance of power plays a central role in this theoretical analysis and, as a consequence, in the ideological narratives employed by political communicators, committed to the need to defend a system of independent states, who seek to make events intelligible for their audience.

There is without doubt a good deal of truth to this line of argument. It is certainly the case that the realists have not attempted to establish a more encompassing theory of power. But it is also the case that the postpositivists present a very over-simplified assessment of the realist position. It is simply not the case, as Guzzini suggests, that the realists have been endeavouring to export European diplomatic maxims into American diplomatic culture. Nor is it the case as Williams suggests that the realists adopt a purely materialist and rationalist perspective. The realists are not completely mired in an anachronistic view of the world. Moreover, although the balance of power has a central role to play in the work of the four theorists examined in Part III, it is drawn upon in quite different ways.

Nevertheless, it is unquestionably the case that their attempts to model the balance of power are not inscribed on a blank sheet. Directly or indirectly the realists draw in different ways on the very longstanding metaphorical and mythical status of the concept. Contemporary theorists in International Relations inscribe their models of the balance of

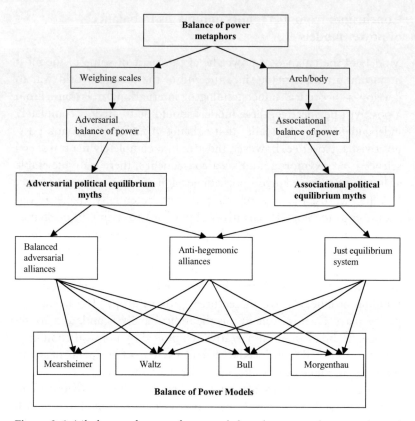

Figure 3.6 A balance of power framework based on metaphors, myths and models

power on a palimpsest on which traces of these metaphors and myths inevitably appear. What I have argued in this chapter is that the myth-makers have drawn upon two different types of metaphorical source. The weighing scales source promotes the idea of an adversarial balance of power, whereas the arch/body source promotes the idea of an associational balance of power. But in both cases, myth-makers have shown the potential for establishing a stable equilibrium. Myth-makers working with the associational balance of power focus on the potential for the European states to establish a political equilibrium based either on the recognition that they can form a coalition that can successfully overwhelm any aspiring hegemon or on their ability to reach agreement on a division of territory that will preserve common security and thereby constitute a 'just equilibrium'. Myth-makers working with the adversarial balance of power, on the other hand, focus on the potential that they always see existing for states to establish an alliance that can match/balance either an adversary with hegemonic ambitions or a group of adversaries seeking to promote their interests at the expense of others.

Figure 3.6 establishes a framework that summarizes the relationship that exists between balance of power metaphors and myths and it anticipates how this relationship impacts on the models of the balance of power developed by the four theorists discussed in Part III. In practice, however, metaphors hardly figure in their discussion of the balance of power and myths make no appearance at all. Of course, this framework concedes quite a lot of ground to Guzzini and Williams, although I would argue that discussions of the balance of power tend to focus on the adversarial balance of power and underplay the importance of the associational balance of power. But in any event, what I hope to show in Part III is that the approach of all four theorists is more interesting and complex than is generally realized, and that a major weakness in the approach to the balance of power is the failure to build on the work of predecessors.

Balance of power models

4 | *Hans J. Morgenthau's* Politics Among Nations[1]

THE BALANCE of power constitutes one of the central concepts in Hans J. Morgenthau's *Politics Among Nations* where it is depicted as 'a necessary outgrowth of power politics' (Morgenthau, 1973: 167). It is over half a century since Morgenthau first wrote *Politics Among Nations* and over thirty years since he produced the fifth and, for Morgenthau, final edition.[2] It is, therefore, a quintessentially cold war text. But it is clear that Morgenthau intended to provide a general theory for students of international politics, and one that would stand the test of time. From the start, however, Morgenthau's attempt to provide a general theory came under fire from many quarters and his concept of the balance of power, in particular, is often severely criticized for being ahistorical, ambiguous and incoherent. Nevertheless, subsequent realists have continued to insist that the balance of power is an intrinsic feature of international politics and that any general theory must take account of the concept. These later realists, however, step back from Morgenthau's very comprehensive approach and refine the concept in an attempt to overcome problems of ambiguity and incoherence. In this process of distillation, however, realism has become increasingly fragmented, with the additional consequence that Morgenthau's approach to the balance of power remains much more expansive than the balance of power theories developed by Waltz (1979) and Mearsheimer (2001) that are discussed in Chapters 6 and 7. As we will see in the next chapter, however, the essential features of

---

[1] An earlier and much shorter version of this chapter is also appearing in Michael J. Williams, ed. *Reconsidering Realism: The Legacy of Hans J. Morgenthau in International Relations*, Oxford University Press (2007).

[2] The first edition was published in 1948 and the fifth edition was published in 1973. This chapter draws on the fifth edition because this effectively represented Morgenthau's final assessment of the thesis, although there have been two more editions published since his death.

Morgenthau's pluralistic and eclectic approach to international politics were picked up by Bull (2002) and other English school theorists.

Although Morgenthau is regularly identified as the father of modern realism, and the precursor of neoclassical realism, there have been relatively few systematic or sympathetic attempts to unpack the theory that is embedded in *Politics Among Nations*. The more prevalent tendency has been to ransack the text, looking for quotations that demonstrate, for example, Morgenthau's credentials as a biological realist (Donnelly, 2000). The problem with this approach is that Morgenthau's assessment of international politics is extraordinarily eclectic and diffuse; as a consequence, it is unhelpful to pigeon-hole him in this way. My pluralistic reading of *Politics Among Nations* presupposes that Morgenthau's theory is underpinned by a model of the balance of power and that a close reading of the text reveals that the model conflates two very different dynamic processes. One associates the balance of power with the unintended outcome of great powers engaged in a mechanistic drive for hegemony. The other dynamic is associated with a complex set of social, ideational and material factors that ameliorate the effects of the first dynamic and assists the great powers in maintaining an equilibrium that promotes their collective security and common interests. These two dynamics correspond to some extent with the distinction between an adversarial and an associational balance of power established in the previous chapter. Morgenthau, however, makes no explicit attempt to distinguish these two dynamics, and so it is important to acknowledge that my reading is imposed on the text. Separating the two dynamics, however, eliminates some of the incoherence and confusion often associated with Morgenthau's approach to international politics.

Once it is acknowledged that the balance of power is associated with two different dynamics, it then becomes much easier to identify and assess the overall thesis that runs through *Politics Among Nations*. What Morgenthau endeavours to show is that the necessary conditions that underlie a stable and self-sustaining balance of power have been significantly eroded over the past two centuries; and, as a consequence, the international system that operated during the cold war was more dangerous and unstable than at any time since the emergence of the modern state system. But, paradoxically, Morgenthau also acknowledged that the bipolar system that emerged after the Second World War possessed the potential to develop the conditions that could lead to the creation of a world state. This ideological commitment to the establishment of a world state gives the text a significant mythopoeic dimension. Unlike Waltz (1979), however, who was also to provide a potentially optimistic scenario for the future, Morgenthau did not link his optimism to the structure of the system, but to the strength of diplomacy and the wisdom of statesmen. Although Morgenthau acknowledges the importance of structural factors, his approach is much more open and flexible than the one adopted by the structural realists who succeeded him. Nevertheless, the idea of structural transformations is central to Morgenthau's argument and his analysis reveals that there have been two major transformations in the modern international system since it emerged in the sixteenth century.

This chapter is divided into six sections. The first looks in more detail at the critiques levelled at Morgenthau's conception of the balance of power and suggests that once the two dynamics associated with the balance of power have been clearly identified, then the collective force of the various criticisms is considerably weakened. It is because key elements of the argument are left underdeveloped or are never clearly articulated that the argument can appear incoherent or contradictory. Clarification is also needed because his overall approach to the balance of power evolves throughout the course of the analysis and is never effectively summarized at any point. The second section explores Morgenthau's conception of power and sketches the two different dynamics that can be associated with his conception of the balance of power. The third section develops in more detail the essential characteristics of the balance of power that emerged, from 1500 to 1789, alongside the formation of the modern international system. The fourth section traces a first major transformation in the international system that was precipitated by the French Revolution, but then was steadily accentuated over the next hundred and fifty years. The fifth section examines the second structural transformation that occurred at the end of the First World War and persisted through the cold war era. In the conclusion I argue that far from Morgenthau subscribing to the idea that international relations can be described in terms of an endless and unchanging cycle of power politics, *Politics Among Nations* can be viewed as a proto-constructivist text that focuses on how international politics has undergone seismic changes as the result of fundamental shifts in the dominant beliefs of the age.

Critiques of Morgenthau

Morgenthau's approach to international politics has been subjected to frequent criticism. Although it is accepted that *Politics Among Nations* was enormously influential in the aftermath of the Second World War, it is now often taken for granted that it is a deeply flawed work.[3] In a recent and comprehensive assessment of realism, Donnelly (2000: 29) agrees with Tucker (1952: 214), who noted soon after the publication of *Politics Among Nations* that Morgenthau's work is riddled with 'open contradictions, ambiguity, and vagueness'. Donnelly (2000: 25) goes on to argue that Morgenthau makes claims that can only be described as 'wildly extravagant'. He depicts Morgenthau as 'an extraordinarily sloppy and inconsistent thinker' (Donnelly, 2000: 35). Finally, he concludes that Morgenthau's sweeping pronouncements 'represent a combination of uninteresting tautology, vague and unhelpful generalities, and patent absurdity' (Donnelly, 2000: 45). But, as the reference to Tucker suggests, Donnelly is coming at the end of a long line of critics who have treated Morgenthau as realism's Aunt Sally, to be set up and then knocked down with a few well-directed critical shots. Like his fairground counterpart, however, Morgenthau invariably seems to pop back up to confront the next generation of critics.

Before assessing Morgenthau's contribution to balance of power thinking, therefore, it is necessary to specify in more detail why his approach to international politics is subjected so regularly to such harsh criticism. One criticism, clearly articulated by Hoffmann, relates to the perceived ahistoricism of his approach. Hoffmann (1960: 30) argues that Morgenthau's general theory of international politics portrays the world as 'a static field in which power relations reproduce themselves in timeless monotony'. Hoffmann (1960: 31–2) goes on to argue that Morgenthau provides a 'mechanistic view of international affairs in which the statesman's role consists of adjusting national power to an almost immutable set of external "givens"'. As a consequence, we are offered an image of 'a frozen universe of separate essences'. The weakness of this approach arises, according to Hoffmann (1960: 33), because the principles of international politics are simply not 'eternal';

---

[3] Vasquez (1983: 17) argues that 'Morgenthau's work was the single most important vehicle for establishing the dominance of the realist paradigm' in the study of international relations.

for example, the Greek city states did not make the 'unsentimental equilibrium calculations' that are seen to be so central to Morgenthau's general theory. Morgenthau, by ignoring the 'forces for change' is seen to reduce the study of international politics to 'a formalized ballet, where the steps fall into the same pattern over and over again, and which has no story to tell' (Hoffmann, 1960: 35). A central aim of this chapter is to show that, contrary to Hoffmann's criticism, the idea of change lies at the centre of Morgenthau's theory of international politics.

A second criticism levelled at Morgenthau's work, in general, but at his concept of the balance of power in particular, relates to a pervasive ambiguity that runs through his analysis. Claude (1962) focuses on this particular weakness, acknowledging that although Morgenthau ascribes four distinct meanings to the balance of power, in practice he frequently fails to highlight which meaning he is drawing upon.[4] Part of the problem is that although Morgenthau (1973: 203) acknowledges that the balance of power is a metaphor, he fails to link the metaphor to the divergent meanings that he attaches to the concept. Morgenthau subscribes to the generic metaphor defined by a set of scales. Drawing on this image, it is possible to conceive of the balance of power as a policy that aims either to keep the scales balanced, or, alternatively, permanently imbalanced in your favour (meaning 1). Alternatively, the balance of power can refer to the position of the scales at a particular point of time (meaning 2). However, Morgenthau presupposes that the most familiar meaning attached to the balance of power is when the weights on both pans of the scales are evenly balanced (meaning 3). Finally, the metaphor draws attention to the fact that whatever the weights are on the two pans, the result is still a balance of power (meaning 4). Claude criticizes Morgenthau for not developing four different labels to convey these different meanings. This criticism, however, fails to recognize that all four meanings are drawing upon a common conception of power that is articulated through the metaphor. Neither Claude nor Morgenthau acknowledge the centrality of metaphors in the way that we understand the world and yet presumably Morgenthau does intend to draw attention to the metaphorical implications of the balance of power and, in particular, the relativity of power and the fact

---

[4] The four meanings are '(1) as a policy aimed at a certain state of affairs, (2) as an actual state of affairs, (3) as an approximately equal distribution of power, (4) as any distribution of power'. Morgenthau (1973: 167).

that a change in the weights in one pan automatically has consequences for the position of the other pan. Claude, is, therefore, undoubtedly correct when he suggests that when Morgenthau refers to the balance of power, the term is being conceptualized as a system. But a more fundamental problem is that while Morgenthau explicitly draws upon the scales metaphor to discuss the adversarial balance of power, he fails to provide any graphic metaphor to capture his conception of an associational balance of power that remains largely buried within the text and requires excavation before it can be exposed.

A third criticism levelled at Morgenthau is that his analysis is incoherent. Donnelly (2000: 29), for example, notes that Morgenthau sees the balance of power as 'a necessary outgrowth' of power politics at one juncture and 'incapable of practical application' at another. It is presupposed that these two statements cannot both be true. By the same token, Donnelly (2000: 29) and Claude (1962: 34) are both impressed by Tucker's (1952) critique of Morgenthau's insistence that his analysis of power politics generates 'iron laws' that can be compared to the law of gravity. It is argued that it is inconsistent, as a consequence, for Morgenthau to suggest at one point that states must necessarily follow these iron laws only to criticize states for failing to observe these laws at another. Morgenthau's counter-argument, that social laws, in contrast to natural laws, can be violated, is given short shrift by Claude (1962: 34). In this event, he argues, the balance of power is essentially 'a redundancy' in Morgenthau's theory of international politics because all it says is that in a power struggle, 'states must and do struggle for power' (Claude, 1962: 37). The overall aim of this chapter, therefore, is to demonstrate that Morgenthau has formulated a much more complex account of the balance of power than is sometimes recognized.

Power and the two competing balance of power dynamics

Morgenthau's (1973: 186) starting point is that if the balance of power is conceptualized as a 'natural and inevitable outgrowth of the struggle for power' then it must be acknowledged to be 'as old as political history itself'. It follows that independent balance of power systems have operated for most of human history in Asia, Africa and America (Morgenthau, 1973: 199). But if, by contrast, the balance of power is associated with 'systematic theoretic reflection' then it must be identified as a European phenomenon that began to emerge in the sixteenth century. Embedded within *Politics Among Nations*, therefore, are two interconnected dynamics that are intimately associated with the balance of power. The first dynamic is depicted in mechanistic terms and is seen to generate an unstable and dangerous balance of power. The second dynamic, conceived essentially as social in orientation, is seen to ameliorate the effects of the first dynamic and helps to produce a much more stable and self-consciously managed balance of power.[5] The essential features of these two dynamics will be outlined in this section of the chapter and in the next three sections there is an examination of how Morgenthau traces the interaction of these two dynamics over the past four hundred years.

When the balance of power is viewed as a universal phenomenon that has operated throughout history and in all corners of the world, the assumption is that statesmen have always been acutely conscious of their own power base and the power possessed by their neighbours. Morgenthau, for example, cites Francis Bacon (1561–1626) who indicated that all princes 'must keep due sentinel, that none of their neighbours do overgrow' (Bacon, 1904: 206). But Morgenthau goes beyond this position and insists that statesmen recognize that power is an extraordinarily difficult phenomenon to measure. This is, in part, because it is so complex, embracing both material factors, such as the number of troops and weapons available to the state, as well as intangible factors, such as troop morale, national character, and the quality of a government and its diplomacy. Morgenthau (1973: 204) argues, therefore, that any attempt to assess the balance of power involves a 'a series of guesses, the correctness of which can be ascertained only in retrospect'. Since the size of any potential miscalculation cannot be known, at the time, Morgenthau insists that statesmen have no alternative, as a consequence, but to attempt to maximize their power position. Morgenthau, therefore, arrives at the same position as the offensive realists such as Mearsheimer (2001), who also argues that great powers seek to maximize their power potential. Morgenthau identifies an automatic law that if one state increases its power capabilities in order to pursue an imperial policy at the expense of a rival, then there will be a 'proportionate increase in the power of the other'. By the

---

[5] But not necessarily a more peaceful international system. Morgenthau accepted that during what he calls the 'golden age' of the balance of power, war was a ubiquitous feature of the system.

same token, if a state is in danger of being overwhelmed by its neigh-
bour, then it will identify other states that are similarly threatened and
form alliances. It follows that states can use their own power, in conjunction with the power of other states, in an effort to counter the
power of enemy states. But Morgenthau (1973: 355) also acknowledges that if this dynamic operated in isolation, then international politics is reduced to the 'primitive spectacle' of 'giants eyeing each other
with watchful suspicion', constantly expanding their military strength
and contemplating preemptive strikes that will eliminate their opponents. Morgenthau (1973: 225) insists, therefore, that a reliance on
power to counter the power of other states in the international system
is 'crude and unreliable'. It effectively reduces the international system to a Hobbesian state of nature. In such an environment, all talk
of a restraining balance of power is ideological, employed by states
that wish to preserve a power advantage possessed at that particular
moment. States, Morgenthau (1973: 211–13) argues, profess an interest in preserving an equilibrium in order to disguise their real interest
in establishing or maintaining a hegemony.[6]

The starting point for the second dynamic, therefore, is the recognition that philosophies that are based on a lust or struggle for power
have proved to be 'impotent and self-destructive'. From Morgenthau's
point of view, the strength of the European tradition is that there have
been self-conscious attempts to 'regulate and restrain' the power drives
that otherwise would tear society apart. Rules and norms supplement
or are superimposed onto the relations among states in a way that
generates limitations on 'the mechanics of power politics' (Morgenthau, 1973: 226). According to Morgenthau, this development was
the product of the mutual recognition that European states were not
monadic units operating in an anomic environment but components
of a European republic. Morgenthau (1973: 216) argues that in the
eighteenth century, princes 'took moral and political unity for granted
and referred as a matter of course to the "Republic of Europe"'. He
readily acknowledges, however, that war persisted as almost a permanent feature of European international politics in the seventeenth and
eighteenth centuries, but he insists, nevertheless, that princes operated

---

[6] Schroeder (1992: 691) makes the same point, indicating that in the eighteenth century, 'Britain and Russia were not alone in saying "balance"
while meaning "hegemony".'

within established rules of the game that were designed to preserve the overall stability of the European republic. Sofka (2001) has challenged this assessment, arguing that the great powers were interested in hegemony rather than parity and that frequently their primary war aim was to dismember their principal rival. It was not the lack of desire but a lack of resources that prevented these hegemonic states from achieving their ambitious objectives. Sofka, in other words, highlights Morgenthau's power politics dynamic but denies the existence of any restraining dynamic.

Morgenthau (1973: 169) is quite clear that a constitutional government illustrates most effectively how the balance of power can restrain political actors. What happens under these circumstances is that the constitution deliberately sets out to ensure that power does not reside in one location, but is distributed in such a way that the power of one sector of government can be checked by another. The closest approximation to the creation of a constitutional government occurs during the establishment of a peace agreement following a major war. In this context, the idea of equilibrium or a balance of power provides the basis for discussion among the participants. According to Morgenthau (1973: 219), the competing states had to 'restrain themselves by accepting the balance of power as the common framework of their endeavours'. Despite the general acknowledgement that power is an extraordinarily difficult concept to measure, there was broad agreement in the eighteenth and nineteenth centuries that the main ingredients of power were territory, population and armaments; and these factors provided a starting point for negotiations (Morgenthau, 1973: 203).[7] Morgenthau (1973: 41–2) notes that 'The particular moment in history which serves as a point of reference for a policy of the status quo is frequently the end of a war when the distribution of power has been codified in a peace treaty'.

A clear illustration of the restraints that were built into the system, according to Morgenthau (1973: 215), is provided by the aftermath of Britain's war with the American colonies in 1783 when, despite the defeat by an overwhelming coalition, there was no attempt to crush Britain by, for example, eliminating their Canadian

---

[7] Gulick (1967: 249–51) documents the detailed statistics that were made available at the Congress of Vienna to facilitate the negotiations. See also Morgenthau (1973: 179).

possessions.[8] Although the dynamics of power politics can show through in times of war, the dynamics of restraint are almost invariably in evidence during the subsequent peace negotiations. At successive peace negotiations, for example, the great powers recognized that European stability depended upon the survival of the individual states that constituted the German Empire, and they endeavoured to consolidate a structure that would ensure this outcome. As Morgenthau (1973: 340) acknowledges, however, this involved a significant reduction in the number of units within the German Empire in 1648 and a further reduction in 1815. But in both cases, the reduction was endorsed by a European consensus. Morgenthau's overall model presupposes, therefore, that there is an interaction between these two dynamics such that, in theory, there should be a progressive erosion of the power politics dynamic with the persistence of the restraining dynamic. The consensus on which the restraining dynamic rests should become stronger across time. Morgenthau argues that during the eighteenth century this moral consensus acted as a feedback mechanism 'strengthening the tendencies towards moderation and equilibrium'. As a consequence, 'under normal circumstances' this development would, according to Morgenthau (1973: 219), make the task of 'overthrowing the system of the balance of power a hopeless undertaking'. But, in practice, circumstances are never normal. Instead, Morgenthau shows how the relative influence of these two dynamics has shifted during the development of the modern state system.

The consolidation of a European balance of power 1500–1789

Although Morgenthau acknowledges that the balance of power associated with power politics can be traced back to the origins of civilization and the emergence of state systems, he is primarily interested in the modern state system, which he traces back to the start of the sixteenth century, when theorists first started self-consciously to conceptualize the balance of power and develop policies based on this conceptualization. It is from this juncture that it becomes possible to observe, in conjunction with the power politics dynamic, a new balance of power dynamic whereby states attempt to manipulate the

---

[8] Morgenthau draws this example from Toynbee (1939: IV: 149).

distribution of international power in order to establish and maintain a stable state system. By privileging this second dynamic, therefore, Morgenthau departs from the familiar periodization of international history that dates the emergence of the modern international system from 1648 when the Treaty of Westphalia brought the Thirty Years' War to an end. He argues that what is significant about the balance of power system that operated over this three-hundred-year period is that it prevented the emergence of a universal monarchy, and that from 1648 through to the first partition of Poland in 1772, it ensured the survival of all the members of the system.

Nevertheless, he acknowledges that the end of the Thirty Years' War did usher in what he calls the 'golden age' of the balance of power (Morgenthau, 1973: 189). He justifies this assessment on two grounds: first, that this was the time when most of the literature on the balance of power was published, and second, that this was the era when princes most explicitly drew on the balance of power to guide their foreign policy.[9] But underpinning these two factors, Morgenthau also argues that this was the era when conditions were most favourable to operating a balance of power. In developing this argument, however, Morgenthau also reveals that this period was very different from the era that emerged in the wake of the French revolutionary wars. In other words, Morgenthau acknowledges that the major transformation in the modern state system occurred much later than is generally presupposed. In developing this argument, he is much more in tune with recent literature that challenges the assumption that the modern state system can be dated from 1648 and his position anticipates a number of the arguments that have been advanced to support this contention.[10]

Morgenthau's starting point is that during the first phase of the modern international state system, international politics had very different characteristics to those that developed in subsequent phases. So in this first phase, foreign policy was dynastic rather than national in character. As Morgenthau (1973: 106) notes, 'identification was with the

---

[9] Members of the English school have similarly argued that what is distinctive about the balance of power is the self-conscious acknowledgement that there is a need to maintain a balance of power (Butterfield, 1966; Bull, 2002).

[10] See, for example, Schroeder (1994a), Osiander (1994; 2001), and Teschke (2003), who all argue that the fundamental change in international politics occurred in the wake of the French revolutionary wars.

power and the policies of the individual monarch rather than with the power and policies of a collectivity, such as the nation'. It follows that during this period international politics can be conceived in terms of inter-dynastic politics based on the very close links that existed among the royal dynasties that ruled Europe at that time. These dynasties formed an international aristocracy that extended across Europe and they constituted what Morgenthau identifies as a cosmopolitan or international society. There was, he argues, 'constant, intimate contact' based on 'family ties, a common language (French), common cultural values, a common style of life, and common moral convictions' (Morgenthau, 1973: 242).

Several important features of international politics during that period are linked by Morgenthau directly to the nature of inter-dynastic politics. In the first place, members of the diplomatic and military services who were drawn from the aristocracy did not regard themselves as state officials, but as 'employees' of a dynastic family. But because they were part of a cosmopolitan society, Morgenthau (1973: 243) also notes that an Austrian ambassador sent to France, for example, 'felt more at home in the court of Versailles than among his own nonaristocratic compatriots'. Under these circumstances it is also unsurprising to find that diplomatic and military personnel 'fluctuated to a not inconsiderable degree from one monarchical employer to another' (Morgenthau, 1973: 243). So during this era, Morgenthau identifies not only a closely knit aristocratic international society that extended across Europe, but also, below this level, a much more fragmented society where loyalties were often much more parochial.[11]

A second feature of inter-dynastic politics noted by Morgenthau (1973: 243) was the 'commercialization of statecraft'. Given that diplomats were part of a cosmopolitan, aristocratic and inter-dynastic society, it is unsurprising that it was considered perfectly acceptable for a government to provide a diplomat from another court with a

---

[11] Morgenthau's position, therefore, is very much at odds with the one adopted by Osiander (2001: 144) who argues that 'in the *ancien régime* rulers, even if called sovereign, were not seen as creating society. Society existed independently of rulers.' Morgenthau's position certainly contrasts with Osiander's (2001: 121) assessment that in most twentieth-century theory in International Relations it is presupposed that there is no international society, that is, no 'pattern of mutual ties of obligation, or at least expectation among individual people'.

pension and also for foreign diplomats to receive payment for their role in helping to conclude a treaty. Morgenthau (1973: 243) argues that these payments provided diplomats with a 'powerful incentive' to expedite negotiations and to 'blunt the edge of international controversies and confine the aspirations for power of individual nations within relatively narrow limits'.

A third feature of inter-dynastic politics that affected the conduct of foreign policy was the existence of a supranational code of morality. Morgenthau (1973: 245) argues that it was 'in the concept and the rules of natural law that this cosmopolitan society found the source of its precepts of morality'. In other words, the members of this cosmopolitan aristocracy were all Christians who accepted that they had no alternative but to observe the laws set down by God. It follows that in pursuing foreign policy, Christian princes were constrained by a common set of moral precepts. Morgenthau insists that these princes did experience a very strong and personal moral obligation to observe these precepts. He argues that 'individual members of this society, therefore, felt themselves to be personally responsible for the compliance with those moral rules of conduct; for it was to them as rational human beings, as individuals, that this moral code was addressed'. This emphasis on personal responsibility then accounts for the importance that was constantly attached to the 'honor' and 'reputation' of the European rulers, which could be endangered if they violated the common moral code in the conduct of foreign policy (Morgenthau, 1973: 245). Morgenthau (1973: 220) argues that the existence of 'a moral consensus' kept the limitless desire for power in check.

For Morgenthau, although traces of these features managed to survive to the onset of the twentieth century, it was after the Thirty Years' War and before the French Revolution that their impact was most felt, and they play a significant role in explaining why this was the 'golden age' of the balance of power. Yet these features were present before and during the Thirty Years' War and so other factors are brought into play by Morgenthau. In the first instance, he depicts the Thirty Years' War in terms of a power struggle between two coalitions of states, both possessing imperialistic or hegemonic ambitions. But such a struggle, he argues, represents the 'most frequent configuration within a balance-of-power system' (Morgenthau, 1973: 189). It is possible, therefore, to portray the war as a particularly complex phase in a power struggle that had been going on since the end of the fifteenth century among the kings of France, the Habsburg rulers of the Holy Roman Empire, and Spain. What was different about the Thirty Years' War was that it displayed a 'ferociousness and intensity not known to other ages' (Morgenthau, 1973: 256). Morgenthau attributes the ferocity of the war to the determination of competing religious groups to universalize their moral code and impose their beliefs on others. He argues that it took nearly a century of 'almost unprecedented bloodshed, devastation, and barbarization' to convince the contestants 'that the two religions could live together in mutual toleration' (Morgenthau, 1973: 542). The religious conflict, therefore, helped to fuel the ongoing power political dynamic that operated among the competing political units.

What was particularly important about the Treaty of Westphalia, therefore, was that it brought an end to the sixteenth-century principle whereby a German prince could determine the religion of his state, and it thereby marks an important stage in the separation of religion and politics in the history of the modern European state system.[12] But, according to Morgenthau, Westphalia also attempted to establish a balance of power that would check the ambitions of the key parties that engaged in the war (Morgenthau, 1973: 189). Osiander (1994: 80–2) disputes the idea that the statesmen at Westphalia were endeavouring to establish a European balance of power. Although he acknowledges that there were references in the diplomatic correspondence surrounding the treaties to equilibrium and the balance of power, he insists that these references relate to the actions of individual states and not to the system as a whole. But because Osiander accepts that this early balance of power thinking was designed to cultivate restraint, his position is not, in fact, incompatible with Morgenthau's position.[13]

Nevertheless, there are tensions and omissions in Morgenthau's line of argument. He argues that because of the difficulty of measuring power, states operate in an extremely uncertain environment and that

---

[12] 'The Peace of Westphalia confirmed this constitutional conception of the modern sovereign state. In other words, the Treaties recognized the inclusion of individual rights in the normative structure of international society' (Almeida, 2006: 67).

[13] Osiander (1994: 80) notes, for example, that Mazarin, the French prime minister, warned that in order not to provoke its neighbours, France should avoid becoming too powerful. But Osiander's central point is that it was not until the Treaty of Utrecht (1713) that there was a self-conscious attempt to think of Europe as a system.

to maintain their security, their optimum strategy is to maximize their power position. But with the removal of religion as a source of contention, after the Treaty of Westphalia, Morgenthau presupposes that the dynamic associated with power politics was very largely suppressed. Foreign policy is now depicted as the 'sport of kings, not to be taken more seriously than games and gambles played for strictly limited stakes' (Morgenthau, 1973: 190). Rulers, it appears, are no longer influenced by the dynamic that pushes them to maximize power. Instead, they are seen to be participating in a 'game' where the goal is to maintain an equilibrium with an even distribution of power between two competing sets of alliances. In fact, Morgenthau effectively reduces the balance of power to a game of alliances.[14] During this era, princes would 'desert old alliances and form new ones whenever it seemed to them that the balance of power had been disturbed and that a realignment of forces was needed to re-establish it'. This is clearly a very different strategy from endeavouring to maximize power.

Morgenthau also seems to undermine the importance that he attaches to international morality when he argues that the movement by princes in and out of alliances to maintain the balance of power was 'impervious to moral considerations, such as good faith and loyalty', although he goes on to say their posture needs to be regarded as 'amoral rather than immoral'. He justifies this position by suggesting that a diplomatic move that 'looks in retrospect like treachery' needs, in the context of the time, to be seen as an 'elegant maneuver' that has been executed 'according to the rules of the game, which all players recognize as binding' (Morgenthau, 1973: 190). It is analysis of this kind that Sofka (2001) wishes to contest. As noted earlier, he argues that it was not the rules of the game that constrained the behaviour of the European states in this era, but rather their inherent weakness. From this perspective, there were no rules of the game. Morgenthau does not make it easy to defend his position at this juncture, because he fails to elaborate on what might be meant by the rules of the game. It is clear, nevertheless, that the basic point he wants to make is that international politics in the eighteenth century operated on the basis of very distinctive principles that need to be distinguished from the ones that operated in the next two centuries.

---

[14] Black (1990: 197) also argues that alliances were the most common way that rulers sought to achieve their political goals.

Despite Morgenthau's failure to elaborate on what he means by inter-dynastic rules of the game, it is possible to draw on more recent literature that has endeavoured to articulate these rules. The significance of dynastic politics is beginning to be acknowledged in the International Relations literature and it is recognized that many states in Europe had still not emerged as depersonalized political units in the seventeenth and eighteenth centuries. States were conceived in terms of dynastic territory. Moreover, as Black (1990: 192–7) notes, even in the eighteenth century there were still very few clearly defined boundaries in Europe. Teschke (2003: 233–7) stresses the importance of viewing international relations at this time from the perspective of inter-dynastic politics. Succession crises, in particular, constituted an integral part of the international fabric. At the end of the seventeenth century, for example, both the Habsburg and Bourbon dynasties had a claim on the Spanish throne and this provoked fears of the French Bourbon family establishing a universal monarchy. To alleviate these fears, the French attempted to get the British and the Dutch to agree to partition Spain. The move failed and the succession crisis sparked a major European-wide war. Teschke also notes that dynastic marriages provided a crucial mechanism for acquiring territory and expanding wealth. His approach presupposes, therefore, that at that time international relations were structured by inter-dynastic family relations. But he also admits that these families were more than willing to carve up each other's territory and then draw on 'often-recondite dynastic genealogical connections' (Teschke, 2003: 234) to rationalize the decision.

The picture that emerges, therefore, is of dynastic families striving to expand their territory on the basis of intersubjectively agreed genealogical rules. This assessment is certainly compatible with Morgenthau's image of international politics in the seventeenth and eighteenth centuries as a 'game'. But there are obvious differences. When Morgenthau draws on the 'game' analogy he is focusing on the use of alliances to maintain an equilibrium, whereas Teschke is focusing on the redistribution of territory. Indeed, Teschke (2003: 233–6) endeavours to establish a sharp distinction between what he calls a 'dynastic predatory equilibrium' and 'the balance of power'. From his perspective, dynasties on mainland Europe used their dynastic connections to expand their territory, but in order to maintain good relations with other major dynasties; they sustained a dynastic equilibrium through a process of mutual absorption of territory.[15] He contrasts this activity with the process of active balancing that Britain began to pursue, in the attempt to prevent territorial expansion on the continent.

Morgenthau certainly agrees that Britain had a distinctive role to play in the European balance of power system which he identifies as the 'holder' of the balance of power, or the 'balancer'. Like Teschke (2003: 260), he accepts that Britain adopted a policy that aimed to 'counter any imperial-hegemonic ambition' on mainland Europe. But he also acknowledges that Britain's aim can be seen to 'keep Europe divided in order to dominate the continent' (Morgenthau, 1973: 194). Morgenthau's position on dynastic expansion, however, is more ambivalent. On the one hand, he acknowledges the importance of mutual compensation and notes how this principle was enunciated at the Treaty of Utrecht in 1713, when most of Spain's European and colonial possessions were divided up between the Habsburgs and the Bourbons.[16] However, whereas Teschke sees the partition of Poland as just another example of dynastic expansion, Morgenthau wants to argue that that it represents a violation of the balance of power rules.[17] As a consequence, he argues that the partition marks the end of the classic balance of power period (Morgenthau, 1973: 179). He adopts this position because he insists that one of the aims of the balance of power is to protect the independence of all states. Teschke (2003: 237) argues, by contrast, that one of the main effects of 'predatory dynastic equilibrium' was for small states to be absorbed by large ones, and he asserts that this accounts for the 'dramatic decline in the number of European sovereign actors between 1648 and the nineteenth century'. By contrast, Morgenthau (1973: 202) insists that the balance of power system succeeded in preserving the existence of all members of the

[15] It is important to note that Teschke is drawing on an essentially Marxist framework and he attributes the expansionist aims of these dynastic states to domestic rather than international factors.

[16] Britain's support of this development poses a problem for Teschke's argument that Britain's power-balancing policy was distinct from the continental policy of dynastic expansion.

[17] Sofka (2001) also sees the Polish partition as characteristic of eighteenth-century power politics. There were three partitions of Poland, in 1772, 1793 and 1795. The kingdom was not restored at the Congress of Vienna. Schroeder (1994a: 524) argues that no one at the Congress thought seriously about this possibility.

modern state system from 1648 to 1772, when the partitioning of Poland started.[18]

Given the importance that Morgenthau attaches to the partition of Poland, it is unfortunate that he does not look at the case in more detail. Schroeder (1994a), by contrast, does examine carefully all three partitions and concludes that the arguments used by Austria, Prussia and Russia to justify the first partition all conform to eighteenth-century balance of power assumptions. In contrast to Morgenthau, moreover, Schroeder (1994a: 67) does set out what he considers to be the rules that governed the balance of power, starting with reciprocal compensation.[19] But he argues that inconsistencies in the balance of power rules made 'cooperative system-conforming conduct indistinguishable from naked aggression'. Schroeder's (1994a: 18) assessment, however, also departs from Teschke's position, because he argues that Poland was partitioned, in the first instance, not so much because it represented a 'tempting prize or a danger to European stability' but because it provided 'a device to avoid a wider conflict and help to settle more important questions'.

The closest that Morgenthau comes to an explanation for the demise of Poland is when he argues that in the eighteenth century, Europe embraced a number of regional balances of power. He argues that as

[18] Presumably Morgenthau arrives at this conclusion by assuming, for example, that when Habsburg Silesia was annexed by Prussia in 1740, it was simply being moved from the control of one great power to another. Teschke and Morgenthau's positions are not necessarily incompatible. Morgenthau notes that the number of states in the German Empire was reduced from 900 to 355 at the Treaty of Westphalia. Napoleon then eliminated 200 of these states and at the Congress of Vienna there were only 36 members of the German Confederation.

[19] Schroeder (1994a: 6) identifies six balance of power rules: 'compensations; indemnities; alliances as instruments for accruing power and capability; raison d'etat; honor and prestige; Europe as a family of states; and finally, the goal of balance of power itself'. He argues that statesmen in the eighteenth century, by and large, abided by these rules. But he insists that the rules, rather than fostering stability helped to precipitate instability. Morgenthau (1973: 179) also notes that the compensation rule was very clearly articulated in 1772 when the first partition of Poland was being discussed. He cites the treaty between Russia and Austria where it was stipulated 'the acquisitions . . . shall be completely equal, the portion of one cannot exceed the portion of the other'.

the result of the growing power of Russia an autonomous balance of power developed in Eastern Europe. The partition of Poland is seen to be the 'first spectacular manifestations of that new system' (Morgenthau, 1973: 198). Morgenthau (1973: 199) goes on to indicate that the partitions were carried out by the directly interested parties 'without any interference of any other nation'. Gulick (1967: 13) notes that during the eighteenth century, both Britain and Prussia had separate ministers for Northern and Southern Europe and he argues that it was not until the nineteenth century that a truly pan-European balance of power system came into existence. There is, perhaps, a presumption that if the European system had been more integrated, then other Great Powers might have come to the aid of Poland. But Morgenthau also accepts that the demise of small states has been a recurrent feature of the balance of power. His explanation for what he sees as a failure of the balance of power is the re-emergence of the dynamic associated with power politics.

First tranformation of the international system 1789–1919

Although Morgenthau treats the first partition of Poland as an early sign that power political balancing was coming to the fore again, for the first time since the Thirty Years' War, the events surrounding the French Revolution and the Napoleonic Wars are considered to provide further evidence of the emergence of untrammelled power politics. In the first instance, Morgenthau associates the French Revolution with the rise of nationalism, which was to become a dominant force throughout the nineteenth century. He recognizes that nationalism represented a fundamental and ultimately fatal challenge to the dynastic world that had prevailed since the sixteenth century. At this juncture, therefore, the state ceases to be regarded as the property of a monarch and his dynastic family and we observe national power and national policies 'replacing identification with dynastic interests' (Morgenthau, 1973: 106). Inevitably, however, this development also marks the onset of a 'gradual decline of the cosmopolitan aristocratic society and of the restraining influence of its morality upon foreign policy' (Morgenthau, 1973: 248). The first fatality of this development, according to Morgenthau, was the balance of power, because neither the French Revolutionary leaders, nor Napoleon, were in any way constrained by the need to maintain an equilibrium that reflected and preserved a European inter-dynastic order. As a consequence, the dynastic rules that governed this order collapsed and they were replaced by a power political drive by states to survive. Fear of Napoleon's expansionist aims eventually produced a winning coalition that ushered in a new attempt to construct a stable equilibrium in Europe.[20]

Although the winning coalition achieved unconditional victory, Morgenthau sets out to show that the attempts to restore order and establish a new balance of power generated contradictions and proved initially to be extremely problematic. The problems arose, he argues, because the new order laid out at the Congress of Vienna was based on two contradictory principles. The first was the inviolability of frontiers, and the second was dynastic legitimacy (Morgenthau, 1973: 216). The two principles pulled in opposite directions. The first heralded a new and very different order from the one that existed before the French Revolution, with the long-established ties between dynasties and territory finally broken. The second, on the other hand, was still looking to the past and attempting to restore the status quo that had been destroyed by the French Revolution. Morgenthau is quite clear that during the course of the nineteenth century it was the new order that slowly but surely overtook the old order, confirming Morgenthau's view that the French Revolution marked the start of a new epoch in history (Morgenthau, 1973: 248). However, Morgenthau is also clear that elements of the aristocratic and dynastic order persisted through to the twentieth century, and that there were determined efforts made after the Napoleonic wars to sustain a dynastic order.

At the heart of these efforts was the importance attached to dynastic legitimacy at the Congress of Vienna, underpinned by the establishment in 1814 of the Holy Alliance by Russia, Austria and Prussia. The ostensible aim of the Holy Alliance was to ensure that the agreements made at the Congress were maintained (Morgenthau, 1973: 42), although the unstated aim was to prevent the occurrence of revolution anywhere

[20] Rosecrance and Lo (1996) challenge this account and argue that European governments persistently chose to bandwagon rather than balance. Whiteneck (2001) disagrees and argues that there was a clear preference among European powers to oppose French hegemonic designs. They only succumbed to French designs after unequivocal military defeats. Schroeder (1994a), by contrast, argues that Britain, Russia and France were all hegemonic powers at that time.

in Europe (Morgenthau, 1973: 216).[21] This unstated aim, however, had the effect of dividing Europe rather than helping to consolidate a consensus around a new balance of power based upon an agreed distribution of territory. Moreover, the problem became intractable when the original signatories of the Holy Alliance formally agreed in a circular, signed in 1820 at the Congress of Troppau, never to recognize the right of any people to circumscribe the power of their king. Such an agreement, Morgenthau argues, was bound to lead to 'intervention into the internal affairs of all nations where the institution of the absolute monarch seemed to be in danger' (Morgenthau, 1973: 440). British statesmen, however, considered that such a move undermined how they conceived of the newly established status quo. They were only interested in defending the territorial settlement agreed at the Congress of Vienna and, in addition, precluding any member of Napoleon's family from coming to the French throne (Morgenthau, 1973: 439). However, the offer by Russia to support collective intervention in the future by sending troops into Central and Western Europe was not seen to be an attractive option by its Holy Alliance partners and so this early attempt at what Morgenthau identifies as international government, based on great power consensus, unravelled almost immediately.

Morgenthau argues, moreover, that the French Revolution and the Napoleonic Wars had initiated so much change in the international system that the survival of the old order would have required 'the continuous use of armed force in order to protect and restore absolute monarchies and their possessions throughout the world' (Morgenthau, 1973: 443). The use of force would have been continuous and essential according to Morgenthau because of the conflict between the principles associated with dynastic legitimacy on the one hand, and the principles of nationalism and liberalism on the other. Morgenthau is also quite clear that there was no way that the dynastic order could survive against the opposition of both Britain and 'the conception of justice

---

[21] Morgenthau argues that the Holy Alliance, as an institution, was based on three treaties, the Treaty of Chaumont, 9 March 1814, the Quadruple Alliance, signed 20 November 1815, and the Treaty of the Holy Alliance, signed 26 September 1815. The Holy Alliance is considered by Morgenthau to have embraced Russia, Austria, Prussia, Great Britain and France.

adhered to by the majority of the people living under the rule of the Holy Alliance'. At the centre of British foreign policy, from the time of Canning, argues Morgenthau, was the desire to promote a new liberal order in Europe. The British, he argues, used the national and liberal movements developing in Europe 'as weights in the scales of the balance of power' (Morgenthau, 1973: 443).

From Morgenthau's (1973: 245) perspective, therefore, what can be observed during the nineteenth century in Europe is a slow transformation away from government by the aristocracy and a movement towards a system of 'democratic selection and responsibility of government officials'. Nevertheless, until almost the end of the nineteenth century, the conduct of foreign policy remained in the hands of aristocratic rulers in most countries. It was only in the twentieth century that officials were 'legally and morally responsible' not to a monarch but to a collectivity (1973: 245–6). Morgenthau, however, is very equivocal about some of the consequences of this development. He believes that nothing has replaced the international aristocratic society that was superimposed on divergent national societies and whose moral code served to restrain the behaviour of dynastic states (Morgenthau, 1973: 249).[22] This moral consensus survived only as a 'feeble echo' in the nineteenth century (Morgenthau, 1973: 444). But he goes on to argue that it was strengthened by 'the humanitarian climate of the times'. In other words, he accepts that the Enlightenment and the political theory of liberalism precipitated an 'increase in the humaneness and civilized character of human relations'. But Morgenthau (1973: 382) also associates this development with 'the rise of the commercial classes first to social and then to political importance' during the nineteenth century.[23] He argues that the commercial classes were strongly opposed to war and international anarchy because they were viewed as 'irrational

[22] In contrast to the English school (Bull, 2002) that accepts that there can be an international society constituted by states, Morgenthau is clear that a society can only consist of individuals.

[23] This position may seem to anticipate the argument developed by Teschke (2003) but whereas Morgenthau sees the rise of the commercial classes as a general European phenomenon, Teschke maintains that the rise of capitalist property relations was distinctive to Britain and reflects a path-dependent history that has to be traced back to the feudal era. But Teschke, like Morgenthau, places Britain at the centre of the transformation of Europe from a dynastic to a liberal capitalist system.

disturbances of the calculable operations of the market' (Morgenthau, 1973: 382).[24]

It is against this background that Morgenthau locates his discussion of the balance of power that emerged after the Napoleonic Wars. Morgenthau argues that this was a very different system from the balance of power system that had existed in previous times. Although he fails to elaborate on how the rules of the game shifted from the eighteenth to the nineteenth century, some of the changes are made reasonably explicit in his text and others can be inferred from his analysis of the period. In the first place, he makes very clear that inter-dynastic politics gave way to international politics.[25] Despite determined attempts, during the nineteenth century, to maintain the position of the absolute monarchies in Europe, the principle of national self-determination 'became one of the cornerstones upon which successive generations . . . tried to enact a stable political structure' (Morgenthau, 1973: 220). This development had two significant consequences for the balance of power. First, it meant that the kind of compensation schemes that were agreed in the eighteenth century could no longer be sanctioned and, as a consequence, national frontiers became relatively fixed. Of course, compensation schemes did still occur. For example, in 1860, France received Savoy and Nice in return for an increase of territory by Sardinia, but the move was sharply criticized by the British as a violation of the balance of power (Morgenthau, 1973: 216). A second consequence was that, later in the nineteenth century, with the unification of Germany and Italy, both justified on the grounds of national self-determination, the political equilibrium established at the Congress of Vienna was very substantially affected. There is no doubt that these unifications precipitated a major change in the European balance of power.

A second fundamental change in the nineteenth century relates to the emergence of international government. Morgenthau cites Friedrich Gentz, who argued after the Congress of Vienna that it was clear that

[24] Whereas Teschke sees an inextricable link between economic and geopolitical relations, Morgenthau draws a sharp distinction and this may account for his failure to examine the significance of mercantilism for the dynastic era. For Teschke, by contrast, mercantilism is seen to underpin inter-dynastic relations.

[25] Schroeder (1994: 578) also notes that dynastic succession disputes ceased to be an international problem after 1815.

the balance of power system had been superseded by 'a principle of general union, uniting the sum total of states in a federation under the direction of the major powers' (Morgenthau, 1973: 438).[26] In other words, as Morgenthau puts it, this was 'government by the great powers', and the principle that was guiding the great powers was 'the maintenance of peace on the basis of the status quo' (Morgenthau, 1973: 439).[27] This distinctive feature of the newly emerged system has led some analysts to question whether it is still appropriate to discuss the system in balance of power terms. Schroeder (1994a: 578) argues that because this new system operated on the basis of distinctively new rules of the game it needs to be distinguished sharply from the balance of power system that operated before the nineteenth century.[28] Morgenthau's position, however, although never clearly articulated, is closer to the position adopted by Teschke (2003: 233) who presupposes that we need 'time-bound meanings of the balance of power'. In other words, from Teschke's perspective, as with Morgenthau's, the nature of the balance of power changed dramatically from the eighteenth to the nineteenth centuries.

Effectively, the great powers agreed at the Congress of Vienna to preserve the balance of power that was defined by the territorial settlement established in 1815. It followed that any changes to that settlement would have to be sanctioned by a great power consensus. This is essentially what happened after the Belgians revolted in 1830 and

---

[26] Gentz was one of the significant balance of power theorists at that time. He was sometimes described as the Secretary of Europe at the time because he acted as the Secretary-General for the Congress of Vienna. See Little (1996).

[27] Morgenthau fails to note explicitly, however, that one of the crucial features of the Congress of Vienna was the recognition and acceptance that the international system was two-tiered, with the top tier being occupied by the great powers. Osiander (1994: 323) stresses that 'this was very much a new phenomenon' and that it is anachronistic and unhelpful to refer to great powers before the nineteenth century. See also Simpson (2004).

[28] Schroeder (1994a) argues that after 1815 it is possible to observe a political equilibrium that has fundamentally different characteristics to a balance of power. By political equilibrium, Schroeder (1992: 695) means 'a condition of international stability, peace, respect for rights and law and the preservation of order, the supervision of international affairs and legitimation of change through the European concert'.

demanded independence from the United Netherlands, which had been established at the Congress of Vienna. Morgenthau (1973: 444) argues that the great powers assumed responsibility for reaching a political settlement between Belgium and Holland, thereby avoiding a major war that could easily otherwise have ensued. Indeed, Schroeder (1994a: 676) goes so far as to argue that 'under no international system other than that of Vienna, could the Belgian crisis have been solved peacefully'.[29] Although Morgenthau does not offer an elaborate justification of his position, it does broadly coincide with Schroeder's detailed discussion of the crisis. Morgenthau notes that the five major European powers, Britain, Russia, France, Austria and Prussia met in London in February 1831 and agreed that they had a duty to ensure that the independence of Belgium did not 'jeopardize the general security and European balance of power'. He goes on to observe that this European concert then attempted to consolidate this position in 1839 when they declared Belgium to be 'an independent and perpetually neutral state' (Morgenthau, 1973: 192).

Although Morgenthau acknowledges that the Concert of Europe was an important mechanism for maintaining the balance of power that was established at the Congress of Vienna, as well as for modifying the agreement in ways that would not destabilize the system, he also recognizes that there were other factors that were, inexorably, bringing about changes in the balance of power system in ways that could not be regulated by the Concert of Europe. The first factor relates to the impact of national self-determination within Europe. The unification of both Germany and Italy during the nineteenth century was justified on the basis of this principle. Although these unifications precipitated a massive change in the balance of power established in Vienna, neither move was either opposed or sanctioned by a great power consensus. In other words, although Morgenthau does not make this point explicitly, the principle of national self-determination effectively trumped the norms associated with the inviolability of international boundaries

---

[29] Schroeder (1994a: 666, 676) argues that the outcome of the Belgian crisis depended on a 'de-emphasis on the balance of power' and 'new rules of the game which all the great powers recognized and were willing to obey and enforce'. This appears to depart from Morgenthau's position, but only because of Schroeder's insistence on viewing the balance of power as an eighteenth-century phenomenon and categorically different from his conception of a nineteenth-century political equilibrium.

and stability. Morgenthau does acknowledge, however, that the unification of Germany created an intractable problem for the European
balance of power that could only be solved by the political recon-
struction of Europe (Morgenthau, 1973: 233). He also recognizes that
traditional balance of power methods failed to manage this problem
and he identifies what has become the European Union as a 'revolutionary departure from the traditional methods by which inferior powers
have tried to counter a superior one' (Morgenthau, 1973: 511). But
in assessing the future success of the European Union he insists it is
necessary to examine the distribution of power among its agencies
as well as the distribution of power that exists between these agencies and the governments of the constituent states (Morgenthau, 1973:
512–13).

A second important factor that lay beyond the control of the Concert
of Europe was the geographical expansion of the system. The Congress
of Vienna effectively treated Europe as a closed system made up of five
equal powers, but this was an unequivocal fiction.[30] During the course
of the nineteenth century, therefore, states outside of Europe began to
play an increasing role in the definition and operation of the European
balance of power. What we observe over the next century according
to Morgenthau (1973: 190) is 'the gradual extension of the European
balance of power into world-wide system'. He views the 1823 Monroe
Doctrine as a particularly crucial development with President Monroe,
arguing that the United States would ensure that the existing balance
of power in the western hemisphere would remain unchanged. In other
words, Monroe indicated that the United States accepted the existing
interests of Europe in the area, but would resist any attempts by the
Europeans to control or repossess those states that had established their
independence (Morgenthau, 1973: 43–4). This position was endorsed
by Britain in a speech by Canning in 1826 when he famously and bom-
bastically declared that he had 'called the New World into existence,

---

[30] Schroeder (1992; 1994a) depicts Britain and Russia as hegemonic and
relatively secure states, thereby possessing radically different security
objectives to Prussia, Austria and France. He argues that what effectively
happened in 1815 was that Russia and Britain were in a position to say to
the other great powers 'Our world spheres of influence are strictly ours;
yours are European and therefore must be shared with us' (Schroeder,
1992: 689).

to redress the balance of the Old' (Morgenthau, 1973: 190–1).[31] The effect of the positions adopted by the United States and Britain was to extend the inviolability of frontiers established at the Congress of Vienna to the western hemisphere.

The expansion of the European system, however, embraced two other dimensions, according to Morgenthau, which were to have significant consequences for the European balance of power. These dimensions relate to a distinction that Morgenthau draws between peripheral areas, on the one hand, that either lay on the boundaries of Europe, in particular the Balkans, or where the interests of the Europeans were marginal, and, on the other hand, what he euphemistically calls 'empty spaces' (Morgenthau, 1973: 444) although he does acknowledge that this 'political no-man's land' was, in fact 'other people's land' (Morgenthau, 1973: 349). In both cases, however, he observes that the European concert and European diplomacy were able to operate with conspicuous success, in the sense that the Europeans were able to resolve their differences peacefully. This 'success' was attributable to the fact that a policy of compensations could so easily be applied. Morgenthau notes, for example, that Africa was 'the object of numerous treaties delimiting spheres of influence for the major colonial powers' (Morgenthau, 1973: 179). As Morgenthau observes, because there was so much 'empty space' there was 'always the possibility of compromise without compromising one's vital interests' (Morgenthau, 1973: 349). Countries as different as Ethiopia and Persia were effectively and 'peacefully' partitioned by the European great powers; and Morgenthau (1973: 180) accepts that this practice was 'organically connected with the balance of power'. Morgenthau (1973: 180) compares these moves to the partition of Poland, but in doing so he fails to note that he saw the partition of Poland as intimating a breakdown in the balance of power, or to recognize that the techniques that the Europeans used in these 'empty spaces' had been effectively eliminated within Europe itself because of the importance attached to the principle of national self-determination. In other words, in Europe it was the consolidation of nations rather than the partition of states that was taking place. This line of argument reinforces Keene's (2002) position that throughout the

[31] Canning was reacting to the decision by France to intervene into Spain in line with Holy Alliance objectives.

nineteenth century it is necessary to distinguish between a European and an extra-European international order.[32]

Morgenthau, however, does recognize that these developments inside and outside of Europe were having structural consequences for the European balance of power. As the 'empty space' outside of Europe was steadily taken over by the Europeans, so the scope for compromise through compensations was being reduced. At the same time, there was no potential for territorial changes at the centre of Europe and, at the same time, the unification of Germany had created insecurities for the other European states. Morgenthau accepts, therefore, that there were structural factors that made it more difficult to maintain the status quo in Europe. But he also insists that there was still room for manoeuvre in peripheral areas, like the Balkans, and that there was scope in 1914 for a settlement of the kind that had been reached at the Congress of Berlin in 1878. But this would have required the European states to acknowledge the peripheral nature of the conflict. From Morgenthau's perspective, therefore, it was 'blundering diplomacy' at least in part, that precipitated the First World War, as 'a conflict at the periphery of the European state system transformed itself into a struggle that threatened to affect the overall distribution of power within that system' (Morgenthau, 1973: 349–50).

Second transformation of the international system 1919–1973

The First World War demonstrated that the European balance of power had become global in extent, but Morgenthau is clear that the war did not bring about a transformation of the international system. It was developments surrounding the war that destroyed the established balance of power and transformed world politics. These developments are seen by Morgenthau (1973: 338–9) to have 'dealt the final fatal blow to that social system of international intercourse within which for almost three centuries nations lived together in constant rivalry, yet under the common roof of shared values and universal standards of action'. This second transformation, therefore, is seen to be more

---

[32] Keene's central point is that the European order was based on the mutual recognition of state sovereignty. Beyond the boundaries of the European order, however, the Europeans attempted to impose a very different kind of order, where sovereignty was divided and the Europeans accorded themselves a right to intervene in order to promote 'civilization'.

dramatic and significant than the one that occurred at the time of the French Revolution. After the Napoleonic Wars, it proved possible to re-establish a balance of power that still had the effect of restraining the international behaviour of states. By contrast, the central feature of Morgenthau's argument is that the changes that occurred in the aftermath of the First World War created 'a new balance of power' that was based on unrestrained power politics. Morgenthau insisted, as a consequence, that it would be 'the most dangerous of illusions' to overlook or belittle the extent of the transformation that took place in the first half of the twentieth century (Morgenthau, 1973: 254).

For Morgenthau, perhaps the most crucial change to take place in this era was the mutation of nationalism. In the nineteenth century, nationalism was closely associated with the development of the nation state. As a consequence, it was still possible for states to oppose each other 'within a framework of shared beliefs and common values which imposes effective limitations upon the ends and means of their struggle for power' (Morgenthau, 1973: 252). But Morgenthau (1973: 253) asserted that during the course of the twentieth century states emerged that confronted each other 'as standard-bearers of ethical systems, each of them national in origin and each of them claiming and aspiring to provide a supranational framework of moral standards which all the other nations ought to accept and within which their foreign policies ought to operate'. Morgenthau (1973: 110) acknowledges that what he calls 'nationalistic universalism' was most evident in fascist Germany but he insists that the United States and the Soviet Union also adhered to a form of nationalistic universalism that was 'only a difference in degree, not in kind'. It follows that in the course of the twentieth century, contests for power 'now took on the ideological aspects of struggles between good and evil. Foreign policies transformed themselves into sacred missions. Wars were fought as crusades, for the purpose of bringing the true political religion to the rest of the world' (Morgenthau, 1973: 108).

Nationalistic universalism can be traced back to the end of the First World War, and it is seen by Morgenthau to have represented the central dynamic that produced a second system transformation. But he also recognizes that there were other crucial developments that provided additional impetus to the transformation. First, he notes that the focal point for the balance of power shifted. Although it is possible to argue that from the end of the nineteenth century a global balance of power had emerged with the result that the First World War had world-wide consequences, Europe still provided the central point of reference.[33] But by the time of the Second World War, this is no longer the case. With the defeat of fascism, Morgenthau (1973: 201) argues that Europe was reduced to being 'a mere function of the world-wide balance'. This global balance of power was also very different from the European balance of power. In the place of nation states competing within a common frame of reference, Morgenthau (1973: 254) argues that what now existed were two 'moral and political systems claiming universal validity' and that they had entered into 'an active competition for the domination of the world'.

Morgenthau is very clear, however, that these two political systems were radically different in scale from the European nation states and he traces the difference back to the nineteenth century. Although all the major nineteenth-century states became interested in expanding into 'empty spaces', Morgenthau nevertheless draws a major distinction between the expansion of the United States and Russia on the one hand, and the European states on the other. The European states entered these 'empty spaces' by establishing overseas empires, and an integral link is established between this move and the European balance of power.[34] By contrast, the United States and Russia, over a longer period, were 'absorbed by the task of pushing their frontiers forward into the politically empty spaces of their continents' (Morgenthau, 1973: 348). And Morgenthau (1973: 348) accepts Toynbee's (1934: 302) argument that the Americans and the Russians were able to expand their territorial base 'unobtrusively', with the result that during this period of expansion they 'did not take a very active part in the balance of power'. The long-term consequence was that in the twentieth century, these two states were continental in scale and, from a territorial perspective, dwarfed the other states in the system.[35]

---

[33] The importance of seeing the First World War from a global perspective is generally acknowledged, although Bourke (2004: 23) argues that Stevenson (2004) is the first international historian to provide a 'truly global history of the conflict'.

[34] As noted earlier, this phase of imperialism was significantly affected by the process of mutual compensation.

[35] Morgenthau fails to note that whereas the United States did effectively move into empty spaces, because so many of the indigenous population were killed by disease, most of the local inhabitants survived the

It was clear to some Europeans from the early nineteenth century that the United States would eventually 'rival or overshadow Europe' (Schroeder, 1994a: 574). For Morgenthau (1973: 331) this point was reached at the time of the Second World War, and since then he argues that it has become 'obvious' that the traditional nation state is now 'obsolescent in view of the technological and military conditions of the contemporary world'.[36] What Morgenthau seems to be saying here is not that traditional nation states will disappear, but that they can no longer hope to operate as great powers with the result that the number of states that can act as great powers in the international system is seen to be greatly reduced. Indeed, in the short run, multipolarity had given way to bipolarity. Morgenthau argues not only that a bipolar system operates very differently to a multipolar system but that the reduction of participants has a 'deteriorating effect' on the operation of the balance of power. Morgenthau argues that in a multipolar system, where the defection of one state can make a considerable difference to the overall distribution of power, then even small states can have a significant role to play. By the same token, states, on the one hand, are very unwilling to operate without the support of allies, but, on the other, they can never be sure that their allies will stay on side. It follows, therefore, that because alliances are so fluid in a multipolar system so too is the distribution of power and this means that multipolarity is associated with a high degree of uncertainty, which then encourages states to be cautious (Morgenthau, 1973: 341–2).

By contrast, in a bipolar system, it is difficult if not impossible for small states to affect the distribution of power by moving from one alliance to another. As a consequence, smaller states are not in a position to restrain one of the dominant states in the system by threatening

process of Russian imperialism. For an illuminating discussion of why the impact of imperialism could be so very different, see Crosby (1986). The implications of the difference, however, were huge, because with a longer time perspective it becomes much more apparent that Russian expansion had a lot more in common with nineteenth-century European imperialism than with American expansion. In particular, it was possible for the Russian empire to collapse because of the opposition of the indigenous populations in conquered territory.

[36] This line of argument was first developed by Herz (1959), although he later retracted and argued that traditional nation states could operate as effective political units in contemporary world politics (Herz, 1969).

to defect from its alliance. But Morgenthau goes on to argue that small states have not only lost any ability they may have had to restrain great powers, they have also lost their own room for manoeuvre. Many states, he argued, now operate within the orbit of one or the other of the two super powers because their 'political, military and economic preponderance can hold them there even against their will' (Morgenthau, 1973: 343). It follows that in a bipolar system, therefore, not only is there very little systemic restraint imposed on the two dominant actors, but smaller states have much less freedom of manoeuvre than in a multipolar system. The bipolar system was further hobbled because of the absence of any actor that could play the kind of balancing role to restrain the two dominant powers. Finally, Morgenthau also argues that in the absence of a colonial frontier, where the great powers expended some of their energies, yet another source of restraint on the two super powers is missing. What Morgenthau (1973: 355) observed, therefore, was the United States and the Soviet Union driven by fear to engage in persistent attempts to increase either their own military potential, or that of their allies. He argues that they 'bend every effort to increase their military potential to the utmost, since this is all they have to count on'.

But it is not only the nature and number of the dominant units that has precipitated such a dramatic transformation in the system. The impact of these two factors was accentuated by the fact that the two dominant states in the international system were also imbued with nationalistic universalism. The presence of nationalistic universalism, in the absence of any of the restraints that had operated in the past, moved the international system onto a completely new and, from Morgenthau's perspective, dangerous and highly undesirable plane. Because both superpowers adhered to a nationalistic universalism, the balance of power also underwent a significant transformation. In the past, the great powers acknowledged the existence of peripheral areas, where they failed to identify any crucial interests and, as a consequence, there were a range of regional and essentially autonomous balances of power. As the consequence of nationalistic universalism, however, not only is the balance of power universal in scope, but the autonomy of regional balances of power has been eroded and they are 'mere functions of the new world-wide balance' (Morgenthau, 1973: 201). Morgenthau (1973: 350) argues that what was the 'periphery of world politics' is now 'one of the main theatres where the struggle between the two superpowers is being fought out in terms of the control of territory and men's minds'.

Nationalistic universalism, therefore, is seen to ratchet up the effects of a bipolarity defined by two super powers, particularly 'the tendency to expand into a two bloc system' (Morgenthau, 1973: 353). Morgenthau (1973: 331) readily acknowledged that traditional nation states were simply too weak on their own to act as 'effective spearheads of the new nationalistic universalism', although he did accept that a state like China could potentially take on the mantle that was currently held by the Soviet Union. But he argued that it would require a fusion of traditional nation states, like France or Germany, to enable them to enter the race to make over the world 'in their own image'. Morgenthau (1973: 331) is very clear, however, that such a move would be catastrophic and that it was vital that supranational unions, such as the European Union, did not travel down this route because he believed that the claim by any political system to have a right to impose 'its own valuations and standards of action upon all other nations' was 'evil'.

It is important to recognize that Morgenthau is not criticizing the values and standards of the United States, or those of the Soviet Union, for that matter. He advocates national self-determination and social justice and believes that 'poverty and misery are not God-given curses that man must passively accept but that they are largely man-made and can be remedied by man' (Morgenthau, 1973: 352). What he found unacceptable in the era after the Second World War was the drive to bring the uncommitted areas of the world into the orbit of either the Soviet Union or the United States at the expense of social justice and national self-determination. But he was clear that there was nothing irrevocable about this drive by the United States and the Soviet Union to impose their views on territory beyond their own national boundaries. He accepted only that the structure of the new balance of power made unrestrained competition possible, but not inevitable. So Morgenthau ends his discussion of the balance of power on a cautiously optimistic note. He cites the work of Fénelon, a French philosopher writing at the end of the seventeenth century, who stressed the potential benefits of a system consisting of two equally powerful states. In such a system, Fénelon argues, the potential exists for at least one of the states to pursue a policy of 'wise moderation' which he associates with the maintenance of a systemic equilibrium and the promotion of common security (cited in Morgenthau, 1973: 355). Morgenthau argued that bipolarity contained the potential for both 'unheard of good as well as for unprecedented evil'. Which of these two possibilities prevailed, he insisted, depended upon whether the prevailing moral and material forces pushed statesmen to promote a hegemony or an equilibrium (Morgenthau, 1973: 355–6).

Conclusion

The analysis of Morgenthau in this chapter challenges the common assumption that because he placed the balance of power at the centre of his theory of international politics he also subscribed to the view that the nature of international politics was fixed and unchanging. His analysis is no doubt open to many criticisms, but it is certainly not the case that he saw international politics in terms of 'a static field in which power relations reproduce themselves in timeless monotony' (Hoffmann, 1960: 30). On the contrary, as I have tried to show in this chapter, from his perspective, the nature of international politics has undergone at least two major transformations over the last three hundred years. Moreover, contrary to conventional wisdom, these transformations have occurred, in part, because the dominant beliefs that underpin the prevailing rules of the game have undergone dramatic shifts.[37] In the case of the first major transformation, the French Revolution is seen to have posed a fundamental challenge to the beliefs of the international aristocracy who had previously dominated the international system. The system of dynastic states and relationships is then slowly but surely seen to have given way to a system of nation states. But even as this system was consolidating, the super powers of the twentieth century were forming on the periphery of the European system.[38] In the aftermath of the First World War, these states not only came to the fore as the dominant states in the system, but also subscribed to very different beliefs to those adhered to by the European nation states, thereby precipitating an even bigger transformation in the system.

---

[37] Checkel (2004: 236) notes, for example, that the realist research programme has undergone a revival, with many arguing for a return to its classical roots. However, this has led observers to question whether such scholarship is not 'smuggling in assumptions on the role of beliefs or domestic politics that are inconsistent with realism's core'. Such an assessment underestimates the pluralist nature of realism's classical roots.

[38] This dynamic was explored in some depth by Dehio (1962; 1967). See also Thompson's (1992) discussion and empirical analysis of Dehio's work.

Construed in this way, *Politics Among Nations* takes on the appearance of an early or at any rate a proto-constructivist text.[39] In the first instance, Morgenthau clearly accepts that there is a structural, mechanistic, or power political dynamic in any anarchic system and because of the problems of measuring power under anarchic conditions, there is a tendency for the structure of the system to push the great powers in a hegemonic direction. But Morgenthau argues that because of what constructivists call intersubjective beliefs, significant restraints can be imposed on the structural dynamics associated with anarchy. The very different beliefs that prevailed before and after the French Revolution both had the effect of reining in the unrestrained dynamics of a power political balance of power. After the First World War, however, Morgenthau observes the emergence of beliefs that had the opposite effect, of accentuating the impact of power politics on the balance of power, driving the superpowers to extend their influence across the globe.

Morgenthau was profoundly critical of this development. But despite the fact that his opposition to the Vietnam War has often been alluded to, there has been a general failure to note that his criticisms of the war flow directly from the analysis of nationalistic universalism that he advances in *Politics Among Nations*.[40] The argument also indicates that the dominance of the United States in the post-cold-war era would have been a source of concern for Morgenthau because, in the absence of external constraints, a unilateralist turn by the United States could give free rein to US nationalistic universalism. Morgenthau was clear, for example, that hegemonic powers tend to ignore international law and he acknowledged that the survival of international law is dependent upon the existence of a balance of power (Morgenthau, 1973: 274). Indeed, given the underlying criticism, it is surprising that

---

[39] The constructivist dimension of Morgenthau's (1971: 352) thinking comes through in his assertion that facts 'have no social meaning in themselves. It is the significance we attribute to certain facts of our sensual experience, in terms of our hopes and fears, our memories, intentions and expectations that create them as social facts. The social world itself, then, is but an artefact of man's mind as the reflection of his thoughts and the creation of his actions. Every social act and even our awareness of empirical data as social facts presuppose a theory of society, however unacknowledged, inchoate and fragmentary'.

[40] See, for example, Griffiths' (1999: 40) assessment of Morgenthau's opposition to the Vietnam War.

Politics Among Nations became and remained for many years the dominant textbook in the United States.[41]

No doubt this was because Morgenthau was so closely identified as a defender of unchanging power politics and this seemed to be a persuasive position to adopt in an era when the United States was seen to be confronting an implacable enemy. But this assessment of Morgenthau is at the very least contestable and also underestimates a significant mythopoeic dimension that underpins *Politics Among Nations*. The text, in other words, contains an ideological narrative that links the past, present and future. From Morgenthau's perspective, international politics has moved across time in a direction that has rendered international politics unsustainable in the longer term. The evolving historical developments that I have discussed in this chapter are all seen 'to support and strengthen each other and move in the same direction – that of a global conflagration' (Morgenthau, 1973: 377). The only long-term solution to this problem for Morgenthau (1973: 519) is the establishment of a world state – a development which he considers 'indispensable' for the survival of the human species. But a viable world state can only be put in place once a world community has been brought into existence and that can only happen over a long period of time. In the interim, because war between the super powers has become unthinkable, there is no alternative but to find diplomatic solutions to conflicts between the super powers.[42] It follows that when Morgenthau (1973:

---

[41] Vasquez (1983) draws on Morgenthau to support his argument that realism represented a hegemonic paradigm in the 1950s and 1960s. His starting point was a poll of International Relations scholars in the American Political Science Association conducted at the beginning of the 1970s (Finnegan, 1972) who were asked to identify the most influential scholars in the field. Morgenthau was named by 47 per cent of the participants, with Deutsch identified by 25 per cent of the participants, as being the next most cited scholar. Vasquez then went on to evaluate the major behavioural research carried out in the 1950s and 1960s and found that the bulk of the variables used related to the realist paradigm. But this is definitely not the paradigm discussed in this chapter.

[42] Craig (2003) provides a fascinating intellectual history of Morgenthau's tortuous thinking about nuclear weapons, flirting in the 1950s with the viability of nuclear war before reaching the conclusion that because of nuclear weapons it is no longer possible to consider war to be a policy of last resort and, as a consequence, realist and idealist approaches to international politics must be merged.

377) considers the prevailing 'simplified balance of power, operating between two inflexible blocs, to be the harbinger of great good or great evil' he is effectively identifying the benign future with an associational balance of power and the malign future with an adversarial balance of power. Diplomacy is identified as the best possible route to sustaining an associational balance of power. This mythopoeic conclusion turns out to be strikingly similar to the one reached by Waltz, although he relies on a structural model rather than the kind of historical model established by Morgenthau.

5 | *Hedley Bull's* The Anarchical Society[1]

THE BALANCE of power plays a privileged role in Bull's (2002: 112) *The Anarchical Society* because it helps to provide 'the conditions in which other institutions on which international order depends are able to operate'. Bull not only identifies the balance of power as one of five key institutions that developed and sustained the European international society of states, but he also argues that it underpins the other four institutions.[2] A closer investigation reveals, however, that the role occupied by the balance of power in *The Anarchical Society* is more complex and less straightforward than Bull formally acknowledges. Although he initially stipulates that the institutional structure of the European international society was underpinned by the balance of power, his analysis demonstrates that, in practice, all five institutions are mutually interdependent. In particular, his analysis demonstrates that the balance of power is to a significant extent sustained by the existence of the other institutions. Because of this mutual interdependence, the balance of power impinges on every aspect of Bull's conception of an international society and so it is intimately associated with much of the complexity in international relations that his approach highlights. But Bull's view of the balance of power is not only more complex than is apparent at first sight, it is also less straightforward. What complicates his approach to the balance of power is the distinction that he draws between an international society and an international system. The distinction provides one of the important threads that runs through *The Anarchical Society* but it also impinges on Bull's assessment of the balance of power in ways that are never adequately

---

[1] This chapter is an extended and substantially reworked version of 'The Balance of Power and Great Power Management' in Richard Little and John Williams, eds., *The Anarchical Society in a Globalized World*, Houndmills: Palgrave, 2006.

[2] The other institutions are international law, war, diplomacy and the great powers.

clarified. Despite the centrality of the balance of power in Bull's thinking, as with Morgenthau, the implications of the concept are never fully
worked out. One of the central aims of this chapter is to explore how
the balance of power relates to Bull's distinction between an international system and an international society. It then becomes possible to
see that Bull's approach provides a bridge between the classical realism
of Morgenthau and the neorealism of Waltz.

If Morgenthau's *Politics Among Nations* is viewed as the founding
text of realism, then Bull's *The Anarchical Society* provides the classic English school account of international relations. Hurrell (2002:
vii) argues, for example, that Bull still offers 'the most elaborate and
powerful exposition' of the argument that states constitute an international society.[3] Hoffmann (2002: xxiv), however, asserts that scholars
in the United States were initially slow to recognize the significance
of Bull's text because of the dominance of Morgenthau's realism and
then later because of the overwhelming influence of Waltz's neorealism.
For scholars steeped in realist thinking, Hoffmann argues, references
to an international 'society' seem 'strange'. But as the previous chapter
demonstrates, this assessment rests on an over-simplified view of Morgenthau and, as Chapter 6 reveals, Hoffmann's view of Waltz is also
problematic. What this chapter shows, however, is that when attention
is focused on the balance of power, then a surprising amount of overlap
between Bull and Morgenthau emerges. Both share a similarly complex
approach to the concept, and the source of the complexity relates, at
least in part, to the conceptual distinction that Bull establishes between
international systems and international societies. Both, however, provide a clearer understanding of international societies than they do of
international systems. It was left to Waltz to clarify how the balance of
power can be conceptualized in the context of an international system.

Although Morgenthau does not distinguish as explicitly as Bull
between an international system and an international society, the distinction can nevertheless be discerned in *Politics Among Nations*. By
the same token, the two balance of power dynamics identified in the

---

[3] *The Anarchical Society* was originally published in 1977. Bull died in 1985
but the book was reissued as a second unaltered edition in 1995 with a
foreword by Stanley Hoffmann. It then came out as a third edition in
2002 with an additional foreword by Andrew Hurrell. Although the text is
identical in these editions, there are slight differences in page numbering.

previous chapter map very closely to the distinction that Bull draws between a fortuitous and a contrived balance of power. But Bull does not, in fact, tie the fortuitous balance of power very neatly to the international system or the contrived balance of power to the international society. Nevertheless, his overall position does seem to presuppose that within an anarchic international system, a balance of power can only emerge accidentally or fortuitously among the component states as a transient phenomenon that cannot provide the basis for a stable international order. By contrast, an institutional balance of power is viewed as a contrivance of the great powers that provides a vital source of order in the European international society.

The assumption that realism and the English school adhere to a similar model of the balance of power is highlighted, in part, by Hurrell (2002: ix) when he insists that both schools recognize that the balance of power 'is a conscious and continuing shared practice in which the actors constantly debate and contest the meaning of the balance of power'. However, Hurrell also assumes that both classical realists and English school theorists eschew the neorealist idea that the balance of power can also be a 'mechanical arrangement' and the product of a 'constellation of forces that pushes and shoves states to act in particular ways from outside'. The problem with this latter assessment is that both Morgenthau and Bull do, in fact, make provision for this 'mechanical arrangement'. It is possible, as a consequence, to discern in both Bull and Morgenthau an awareness of the distinction identified in Chapter 3 between adversarial and associational approaches to the balance of power.

Although Bull articulates the differences between accidental and contrived balances of power on the one hand, and system and society on the other, much more explicitly than Morgenthau, he fails nevertheless to establish a clear relationship between the two sets of concepts. Yet on the face of it, the distinction between a system and a society does seem to have important consequences for Bull's divergent conceptions of the balance of power. But despite frequent references in the literature to the system/society distinction, there have been few attempts to explore how the two concepts are related to each other. Outside interest in the English school is centred almost exclusively on Bull's conception of the international society and his conception of an international system is almost completely ignored. It has been left to analysts working within the English school to dissect the distinction and the emerging consensus, as we will see, is that it serves no useful purpose. But this assessment is challenged here. I argue in this chapter that the distinction plays a crucial role in Bull's analysis although it is never fully spelled out. The issue is complicated by the fact that Bull articulates the relationship between system and society in three radically different ways. As a consequence, it is necessary to distinguish his different approaches to the system/society divide and then sort out how they relate to his divergent conceptions of the balance of power.

In the first place, Bull views the system/society divide as a heuristic tool in a role analogous to the one associated with the state of nature in Hobbesian analysis. In other words, it is intended to help us to understand why states want to constitute an international society and establish institutions that help to sustain the society. But Bull takes the argument further and he gives the distinction an ontological twist in order to help him to analyse world politics. On the one hand he argues that there are international systems that operate in the absence of an international society, while on the other he argues that international societies are necessarily underpinned by international systems. By giving the distinction an ontological as well as a heuristic status, however, Bull renders it both problematic and confusing. The problems and confusion become particularly acute when Bull focuses on the geographical expansion of the European international society. He argues that the European international society operated in the context of a global international system. So as the society expanded, it encroached on and absorbed the system. If this approach to world politics is accepted without reservation, then it suggests that whereas the great powers were able to contrive a balance of power within Europe, any balance of power in the global international system could only have been an accidental result of power politics. In fact, Bull fails to adhere to this position himself; instead, his analysis suggests that long before the establishment of a global international society, the Europeans extended a contrived balance of power well beyond the boundaries of Europe. This inconsistency seems to give weight to the argument that the system/society distinction should be dissolved.

In this chapter, however, I follow a very different route and argue that it is possible to extrapolate from Bull a much more elaborate model of the balance of power to the one that he formally presents. Although the extrapolated model remains largely implicit within the text of *The Anarchical Society*, it can be identified in the context of two crucial moves made during the course of Bull's overall exposition of international politics. One move relates to the establishment of the system/society distinction and the other relates to the emergence and geographical expansion of the European international society. What needs to be exposed is that these two moves are much more closely intertwined than is apparent at first sight. In the first instance, however, it is necessary to separate the elaborate model, which draws on Bull's conception of a contrived balance of power, and distinguish it from a much more basic model, which links the idea of a fortuitous balance of power to an international system that operates in the absence of an international society (see Figure 5.1). The more elaborate model focuses on international settings where the international society is underpinned by an international system. The model reveals that the contrived balance of power embraces two different dynamics: an associational dynamic that is related to the international society and an adversarial dynamic that is linked to the international system. Both system and society are global in extent, but whereas the adversarial dynamic operates in the same way across the system, the associational dynamic operates on the basis of different rules inside and outside of Europe (see Figure 5.2).

The aim of this chapter is simply to sketch the basic outlines of the model of the balance of power that is embedded within *The Anarchical Society*. However, perhaps unsurprisingly, the international society dimension of the model emerges more clearly than the international system dimension. Moreover, the relationship between the two dimensions remains unclear. However, the distinction between system and society is raised again in the discussion of Waltz's *Theory of International Politics* in Chapter 6 where it is argued that the international system is discussed at the expense of international society. I return to the question of whether it is worthwhile linking the balance of power to the system/society distinction in the final chapter.

Although Bull argues that academic interest in the balance of power was waning by the 1970s, when he was writing *The Anarchical Society*, because of the welter of conceptual and normative criticisms levelled at the concept over the previous thirty years, he insisted that it is not possible to make sense of contemporary international relations without taking account of the balance of power. But, in fact, Bull's view of the balance of power has had remarkably little impact on the study of international relations and, indeed, neither has Morgenthau's, because

Figure 5.1 The balance of power when an international system operates in the absence of an international society

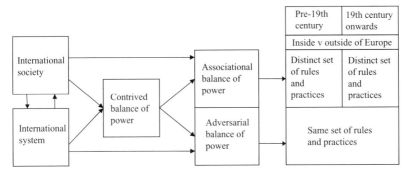

Figure 5.2 The balance of power when an international system operates in conjunction with an international society

their emphasis on the associational, institutional or societal approach to the balance of power was quickly overwhelmed by Waltz's systemic and adversarial approach. As a consequence, the potential space that Bull created for a more pluralistic approach to the balance of power that embraced a societal as well as a systemic dimension was very quickly swept to one side.

This chapter is divided into four main sections. The first focuses on how Bull formally conceptualizes the balance of power. The subsequent sections then expand on the system/society division and the emergence and expansion of the European international society in an attempt to flesh out the more elaborate model of the balance of power that is implicit within *The Anarchical Society*. The second section concentrates on Bull's idea of an international system. After exploring the growing consensus within the English school that favours abandoning the system/society distinction, the section examines the three different ways that Bull conceives of the international system and explores their implications for his model of the balance of power. The third section then identifies the complex role played by the balance of power in international society by examining the mutually interdependent relationship that the balance of power has with the other four institutions identified by Bull. The fourth section examines the history and geographical expansion of the European international society and shows how Bull's approach to the evolution of the European international society impacts on his implicit model of the balance of power. The implications of this assessment of Bull's approach to the balance of power are then explored briefly in a concluding section.

Bull's conception of the balance of power

The overall aim of this chapter is to present a comprehensive account of Bull's model of the balance of power. This is not a straightforward task because the chapter in *The Anarchical Society* devoted to the balance of power is primarily concerned with a taxonomic exercise of identifying the different variables that have been used to characterize the balance of power (simple vs. complex balances, general vs. local balances, subjective vs. objective balances, and fortuitous vs. contrived balances), examining the various functions that the balance of power performs in the international society, and examining the impact of nuclear weapons on the balance of power. So to provide a comprehensive understanding of the balance of power from Bull's perspective it is necessary to locate the concept within his overall account of international politics. In practice, the concept provides a theme that runs through the text, like a leitmotiv, and has the effect of pulling the various strands of Bull's thesis together. As a consequence, it is necessary to examine *The Anarchical Society* through a lens defined by the balance of power. It then becomes possible to highlight the crucial and integrating function that the balance of power plays in Bull's approach to international politics. Once this tactic is adopted, however, it then becomes apparent that there are gaps in the thesis and loose ends that are not tied together. This is not so surprising because as Vigezzi (2005: 79) argues, *The Anarchical Society* is 'a largely experimental book' and was part of a larger project that is still in progress. However, it is not intended in this chapter to plug the gaps or to knot the loose ends although it will be necessary to return to these lacunae at the end of the book.

Before examining the various moves made by Bull where the features associated with the more complex albeit implicit model of the balance of power are elaborated, it is necessary to start by looking at how he more explicitly deals with the concept. Bull relies, in the first instance, on a definition formulated in a publication from 1758 by Emmerich de Vattel (1714–1767), a Swiss jurist and diplomat. Vattel defined the balance of power as 'a state of affairs such that no one power is in a position where it is preponderant and can lay down the law to the others'.[4] For Vattel, therefore, the balance of power is contrasted with hegemony and it applies to a political arena where there is no overarching authority. It is a term that tells us much more about the nature of the political arena than about the units operating within that arena. Bull, however, quickly extends the concept beyond a description of how power is distributed and argues that the balance of power constitutes an institution.[5] When Bull refers to institutions, he is not talking about formal organizations, but rather 'a set of habits and practices shaped towards the realisation of common goals'. What then is the common goal that the balance of power is designed to realize? The most obvious answer to this question is to prevent the emergence of a hegemonic power. But it is clear that Bull wants to go beyond this point. He argues that the balance of power implies 'self-restraint as well as the restraint of others' (Bull, 2002: 102). The goal is to preserve an arena where the units are independent. An institutional balance of power not only presupposes that all states wish to preserve their own autonomy, but also that they acknowledge a common interest in maintaining the essential characteristics of the society within which they operate. So not only must the states prevent the emergence of a hegemonic state that will eliminate the autonomy of the units that make up the international society, but they must also refrain from pandering to their own hegemonic ambitions. The institutional balance of power, therefore, lies at the very heart of Bull's conception of an international society and it reflects the existence of a collective commitment to the survival of such a society.

Bull recognizes, however, that there are at least six factors that complicate his formulation. First, he acknowledges that polarity has an important impact on institutional practices. When there are only two great powers in the system, there has to be a rough parity of power

---

[4] Cited in Bull (2002: 97).
[5] Buzan (2006; 2004a) provides useful discussion of the role played by institutions in English school thinking in general, and Bull in particular.

between them; but parity only entails an institutional balance of power when at least one of the two great powers adheres to the goal of preserving an even distribution of power. When there are a number of great powers, however, even 'gross inequalities' of power do not necessarily put the strongest state in a position of preponderance (Bull, 2002: 98).[6] This position suggests that it might be easier to preserve a stable balance of power in a multipolar system, than in the kind of bipolar system that Waltz (1979) depicts as more stable. Bull, however, does not address this issue. As will become more apparent in the next chapter when we look more closely at the role of polarity in Waltz's conception of the international system, part of the problem with Bull's approach to international politics arises because he is unable to clarify the basis on which he distinguishes between an international system and an international society.

The second complicating factor relates to the fungibility of power, although this is not a term that Bull uses. In contrast to Waltz (1979), who assumes that power is fungible, Bull accepts that it is necessary to acknowledge the significance of different types of power.[7] Military power must be distinguished from economic power, for example, because the latter can be highly influential within its own domain. As a consequence, Bull (2002: 108) argues that 'international politics moves are made on "many chessboards"'. It follows that during the cold war, for example, the United States and the Soviet Union may have constituted the major players on the nuclear deterrence 'chessboard', but in the areas of trade and investment, Japan replaced the Soviet Union as a major player. Distinctive balances of power can be identified on

---

[6] Buzan has developed the most sophisticated discussion of polarity in recent literature. He endorses Bull's line of argument in the context of the contemporary world, indicating that in the aftermath of the cold war 'the United States was nowhere near powerful enough to have eliminated the possibility of great power balancing, let alone being able to transform the international system from anarchy to hierarchy' Buzan (2004b: 55).

[7] International relations theorists who believe that power is fungible see different types of power as reinforcing each other. For example, if power is fungible, then a state can translate its economic power into military power, and vice versa. Waltz (1979) is often seen to be the leading advocate of this view. Keohane and Nye (1977) are leading advocates of the argument that there are different types of power and that they are not fungible. There is also a major debate about the degree of fungibility between hard power and soft power.

the different 'chessboards'. But Bull draws back from the more radical implications of this position by arguing that the different 'chessboards' are, in practice, interrelated, so that a strong position on one board may be brought to the table where a different game is being played. Because the different boards are interrelated, it is essential to accept that there is an indispensable concept of 'overall power' that relates to a general balance of power (Bull, 2002: 109). As we will see in the next chapter, this line of argument takes Bull in the same direction as Waltz and it has the effect of inhibiting Bull from exploring the full implications of his differentiated approach to the balance of power.

The third complicating factor focuses on the geographical distribution of power. Bull accepts that power is not evenly distributed across the international arena and so it is necessary to distinguish a general balance of power that embraces all the great powers from local balances of power that form in specific regions. Bull acknowledges that the institutional rules governing the general balance of power have much less leverage at the local level where great powers can sometimes move into a preponderant position.[8] The implications of this discrepancy are significant for Bull's model because it suggests that the great powers occupy a very privileged position in the international society. We will come back to this issue when we explore more explicitly the institutional relationship that exists between great powers and the balance of power.

The fourth complicating factor relates to perceptions of how power is distributed. Bull is well aware of the problems of assessing power and he recognizes that there is often a mismatch between the subjective and the objective balance of power.[9] Although he does not explore the issue in depth, he acknowledges that for the balance of power to operate as an institution there has to be a self-conscious recognition of how power is distributed among all the great powers. But this is considered to be a necessary and not a sufficient condition for the formation of a stable

---

[8] Bull fails to discuss the specific dynamics that can operate between these two levels. By contrast, as we will see in Chapter 7, Mearsheimer (2001) does look closely at the relationship between local and general balances and incorporates this dimension into his overall model. But he is not sympathetic to the institutional view of the balance of power developed by Bull. See also Buzan and Waever (2003) on the importance of a regional approach to security.

[9] For a good discussion of this point, see Wohlforth (1993).

balance of power. Stability is seen to require an accurate perception of power. Any significant mismatch between the objective and subjective balance of power is seen to result in a balance of power that is 'fragile and impermanent' (Bull, 2002: 100). Bull, therefore, does not open up the issue raised by Morgenthau that power is, ultimately, impossible to measure. This insight pushes Morgenthau down a more constructivist route that recognizes the need for an intersubjective agreement about the nature of the balance of power. Although Bull does not travel down this particular route he also draws on cases where the balance of power is established on an intersubjective basis.

The fifth complicating factor relates to the development of nuclear weapons. Bull argues that their impact has been so great that it has generated an institution of nuclear deterrence that needs to be distinguished from the balance of power.[10] Bull establishes the distinction on four counts. First, because nuclear deterrence focuses on one element of 'overall power', it only involves an aspect of the balance of power. Second, whereas the balance of power in a bipolar world presupposes power parity, this is not the case with nuclear weapons where the emphasis is on mutual assured destruction, which can exist even when there is a huge discrepancy in the volume of weapons possessed by the two sides. Third, the balance of power rests primarily on the objective power possessed by the great powers, whereas nuclear deterrence rests on the subjective belief that both sides have the will to retaliate. Finally, the objective of the balance of power is to preserve international society, and this may well involve war, whereas nuclear deterrence is purely intended to preserve peace.

In the aftermath of the cold war and the demise of the Soviet Union, however, the institutional dimension of deterrence identified by Bull may appear to be increasingly suspect. Indeed, even before the end of the cold war, nuclear weapons appeared to be losing some of their privileged status as a deterrent. Certainly the United States displayed much more interest in developing missile defence than maintaining what can be seen as the outmoded institution of nuclear deterrence. There are, however, good reasons to think that some of the fundamental practices associated with nuclear deterrence remain intact. In particular, there is a presumption that the great powers can no longer contemplate

---

[10] Bull sees nuclear deterrence as both a manifestation of the balance of power and as a distinct sixth institution.

war as a rational strategy. This assumption is certainly embedded in the US 2002 National Security Strategy discussed in Chapter 3. As a consequence, although the United States possesses much more military power than any other state in today's world, the presumption by other great powers seems to be that it will not be used against them. The assumption that war among the great powers is effectively obsolete has led Buzan (2004a) to question whether the balance of power will persist as an institution in the future. As his discussion of the balance of power operating on different 'chessboards' makes clear, this is not a conclusion that Bull would endorse.

The final complicating factor relates to the distinction that Bull draws between fortuitous and contrived balances of power. This distinction, however, needs to be related to the system/society divide and has important implications for the implicit and more elaborate model that is embedded in *The Anarchical Society*. As a consequence, discussion of this is held over for the next section.

Having clarified what Bull means by the balance of power and examined the factors that complicate the overt model of the balance of power that he develops in *The Anarchical Society*, we can now turn to his two crucial moves that open the way to a more expansive model of the balance of power. The first move relates to the distinction that he draws between an international system and an international society. An international system exists, he argues, whenever 'states are in regular contact with one another and where in addition there is interaction between them, sufficient to make the behaviour of each a necessary element in the calculation of the other' (Bull, 2002: 4). By contrast, an international society exists when states, on the one hand, are 'conscious of certain common interests and common values' and, on the other, 'conceive of themselves to be bound by a common set of rules in their relations with one another, and share in the working of common institutions' (Bull, 2002: 13). This distinction is frequently referred to whenever Bull's work is discussed. But having noted the distinction, attention is then almost invariably focused on his conception of international society. There is, in other words, very little attempt to examine the significance of the distinction. Yet, as Vigezzi (2005) makes clear, the distinction is one that had long exercised Bull in his discussions with the other members of the British Committee on the Theory of International Politics – the precursor of the English School.

International systems and the balance of power

Before trying to clarify what Bull meant by an international system in *The Anarchical Society* and how it relates to the balance of power, it is worth noting that there is an emerging consensus among contemporary theorists working from an English school perspective that the distinction between system and society is unhelpful and should be dispensed with. The consensus is significant because it extends across the very diverse analytical perspectives that are now embraced by the school. James (1993), who initiated the attack on the distinction, insisted that it is simply not possible to conceive of an international system that does not embrace the features that Bull associates with the existence of an international society. By the same token, any meaningful conception of an international society must make the systemic assumption that its members will take each other's behaviour into account. It follows, according to James, that Bull has set up a false dichotomy and the most practical step is to discard the idea of an international system because it is the societal dimension that needs attention.

Jackson (2000: 113–16), on the other hand, accepts that the two terms highlight a useful distinction, but he argues that it is better captured by distinguishing between instrumental and non-instrumental behaviour. Instrumental behaviour is based on strategic conceptions of self-interest that necessarily take the actions of other actors into consideration. Failure to take account of others will all too easily give rise to self-defeating strategies. By contrast, non-instrumental behaviour is based on legal and moral obligations that necessarily embrace the legitimate interests of others who will be affected by this behaviour. Jackson accepts that both forms of behaviour need to be accommodated in any analysis of international society. He objects to the use of international systems terminology, however, because it too easily gives rise to a mechanistic view of behaviour that encourages what Jackson considers to be the utterly mistaken notion that human beings can be pushed around by social structures. However, he insists that when Bull refers to the international system he is not suggesting that human behaviour can be structurally determined.

Buzan (2004a: 98–108) provides a third significant discussion of the distinction. He acknowledges Jackson's view that Bull is endeavouring to capture two distinct types of social behaviour, but he insists, nevertheless, that Jackson fails to get at the essence of Bull's position on the international system which does represent a 'physical mode of interaction typical of the mechanistic, realist-style analyses of the balance of power as an automatic process rooted in the relative material capabilities of states' (Buzan, 2004a: 99). In other words, according to Buzan, Bull's view of the international system generates a very distinctive approach to the balance of power, one which assumes that the behaviour of states can be accounted for by the changing distribution of power in the international system. As we will see in the next chapter, this approach to the balance of power corresponds almost exactly with the one adopted by Waltz (1979). It is certainly intriguing that Bull's definition so closely matches how Waltz conceived of an international system. But if this is how Bull thought about an international system then it is ironic that he anticipated Waltz's approach but has been credited with promoting an approach that eschews and undermines Waltzian thinking. In any event, Buzan then argues, in line with Jackson, that Bull's view of an international system can be captured perfectly well within the context of an international society, thereby rendering the need for a system/society divide redundant.

The difficulty with all three of these assessments, however, is that they fail to accommodate the complexity of the divide in Bull's thinking. But, as a consequence, clarifying the nature of the divide is not easy because Bull seems to use it in three rather different ways. In the first instance, the distinction is used for heuristic purposes that correspond to the distinction that Hobbes draws between the state and a state of nature.[11] In other words, an international system that lacks all norms and institutions can be compared to a state of nature. Indeed, Bull says quite explicitly that the existence of an international system in the absence of an international society would 'exemplify the Hobbesian state of nature' (Bull, 2002: 241). But there are problems with this move. Indeed, Bull himself draws attention to the obvious flaws in establishing a 'domestic analogy' between a Hobbesian state of nature and the anarchic international system (Bull, 2002: 46–9). So, for example, it is self-evidently the case that states in an international system are not nearly as vulnerable as individuals in a state of nature. As a consequence, in contrast to the level of existential or absolute insecurity

---

[11] Bull makes similar use of the system/society distinction when he explores future alternative world orders. One future scenario depicts an international system that has lost all traces of society.

experienced by the individual in the state of nature, states experience relative security. It follows that alliance formation becomes a realistic option for states, whereas such a strategy could not be countenanced by individuals in the state of nature.[12]

This line of argument, however, rests on the assumption that all that Hobbes was concerned with was the persistence of chronic insecurity in the state of nature. Williams (2005) has persuasively demonstrated for an international relations audience that this account of Hobbes is underdeveloped and that it needs to be acknowledged that the implications of the state of nature are much more profound for Hobbes and, as a consequence, for any analyst with serious pretensions to work within the realist tradition of thought. Williams' starting point is the recognition that Hobbes was a philosophical sceptic who accepted that our understanding and knowledge of the world is radically and necessarily insecure. There are, for Hobbes, no unequivocal epistemological or ontological foundations on which we can proceed to build firm and secure knowledge about the world. This is not such a surprising position for Hobbes to have adopted given that he was living at a time when there had been ferocious wars fought within and between states about the most fundamental beliefs that human beings adhere to. The state of nature, therefore, identifies a situation or condition of radical ontological and epistemological uncertainty. It is a world where there is no common language or shared beliefs. But the desire for a common language and shared beliefs stems from a fundamental human need that, from Hobbes' perspective, can only emerge with the establishment of a centralized state.

It follows that the existence of the state, on this reading of Hobbes, entails far more than the provision of physical security. And, by the same token, when attention is focused on relations between states, there is also much more at stake than threats to physical security and this explains why sovereigns are 'in the state and posture of Gladiators; having their weapons pointing and their eyes fixed on one another . . . which is a posture of warre' (Hobbes, 1953: 65, cited in Bull, 2002: 45). The sovereign is protecting the state, but in doing so it is preserving the existence of a common language and shared beliefs that are absolutely essential ingredients of the human condition. The

---

[12] Waltz (1979) fails to take this position into consideration when he argues that a common logic prevails in any kind of anarchic system and that the logic is unaffected by the nature of the units that make up the system.

ontological and epistemological uncertainty that characterizes the state of nature has now been pushed up to the level of the international system, which can be seen to lack any common language or shared beliefs. The absolute insecurity of the state of nature may have been eliminated, but the even more fundamental uncertainties associated with the state of nature have now been projected onto the international system.

What are the implications of this assessment for the balance of power? From Bull's perspective, the concept has no meaning in the context of an international system because it is an institution that requires the existence of a common language and shared beliefs. In the absence of these features, there can be no provision for an international balance of power. Bull does not deny that an even distribution of power may emerge, but this will be completely contingent on strategies that have absolutely no relation to Bull's conception of an institutionalized balance of power. A systemic balance will emerge 'quite fortuitously, in the absence of any belief that it serves common interests, or any attempt to regulate or institutionalize it' (Bull, 2002: 63). Bull assumes that such a fortuitous balance of power is the most likely outcome in a situation where two dominant states are both striving to achieve hegemony within an international system. He argues that in a bipolar, anomic world with the two dominant powers aiming at absolute aggrandizement, we can only imagine the balance of power to be 'a moment of deadlock in a struggle to death between two contending powers' (Bull, 2002: 100–1).

Such a development will be a fleeting moment in the history of the international system and Bull insists that there is simply no 'inevitable tendency' for this kind of unintended balance of power to arise in an anarchic system (Bull, 2002: 107). From Bull's perspective, the power political argument that an unintended balance of power will be a permanent feature of any international system presupposes that 'all states seek to maximize their relative power position' (Bull, 2002: 107). But, following Hobbes, Bull accepts that to survive, any sovereign has to satisfy domestic interests, and it follows that there are often persuasive reasons for states to disregard the power political requirement to maximize their international power.[13] This position reinforces Bull's general argument that the emergence of a balance of power will necessarily be

---

[13] Williams (2006) provides an excellent discussion of why the formation of the state necessarily imposes severe limitations on the options available to any sovereign.

a fortuitous and transitory feature of any international system.[14] As a consequence, the resilience of the European balance of power is an extremely unusual feature of world history and is best accounted for by the emergence of an institutional balance of power.

Already, however, the analysis has moved beyond the idea of the international system as a heuristic or tool for thinking about what world politics would look like in the absence of an international society through to his second use of the system/society distinction. Here, there is a clear presumption by Bull that there have been historical periods when international systems can be identified in the absence of any international society.[15] Indeed, Bull (2002: 241) argues that there is 'ample historical precedent' for international systems operating in the absence of international societies and he refers, for instance, to the contacts made by the Spanish with the Inca and Aztec Empires, the interactions between the British and the Maori in New Zealand, and the threat to Europe posed by Genghis Kahn. But these examples are all problematic because it is far from clear that any of them can really be said to provide instances of sustained international systems. They are all essentially examples of episodic 'first encounters'.[16] Nevertheless,

---

[14] In contrast to Bull's approach, Wendt (1999: 266–7) accepts that a balance of power may form in an anarchic system. On the other hand, like Bull, he accepts that 'a balance of power in this context is not really a balance of power. Mechanical equilibrium there may be, but actors are unaware of it as such.' There is powerful evidence that suggests, moreover, that in the absence of an institutional balance of power there is a significant tendency for world politics to move from operating within an anarchy through to operating in a hierarchy. See Kaufman *et al.* (2007) and Hui (2004; 2005).

[15] Bull (2002: 11) argues, however, that to develop a world history of international relations requires moving into 'unchartered territory'. Since Bull was writing in 1977, Adam Watson (1992) has provided an account of how international relations has evolved across world history. See also Reus-Smit (1999), who compares the international society in ancient Greece with various phases in the evolution of the European international society, and Buzan and Little (2000).

[16] Wendt (1999) provides an important discussion of the implications of first encounters. See Jones (2007) for a sophisticated discussion of the complex international relations that developed in the Americas after the Spanish invasion, that examines both the local balancing failures of the immediate pre-conquest period and the failure of indigenous states to balance the Spanish following the initial conquests.

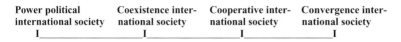

Figure 5.3 Buzan's spectrum of international societies

these encounters did last in some cases for long periods of time and the issue needs to be reassessed in the later section on the geographical expansion of Europe.

There is, however, a third use that Bull makes of the system/society distinction that is particularly problematic for his societal approach to world politics and for his conception of the balance of power in particular. Bull presupposes that although an international system can exist in the absence of an international society, every international society is necessarily underpinned by an international system. It is difficult, however, to link the fortuitous balance of power and the raw and brutal first encounters that exemplify an international system operating in the absence of an international society, with the complex social relations that Bull associates with the institutional balance of power that he identifies with an international society. Buzan (2004a: 190–5) circumvents this problem by dispensing with the system/society distinction. He equates Bull's international system with a power political international society, which lies at one end of a spectrum. Next along the spectrum lies a coexistence international society (the kind of international society that Bull focuses on) followed by a cooperative international society. At the far end of the spectrum there is a convergence international society, where all states share the same values (see Figure 5.3).

There is, of course, considerable merit in establishing ideal types of this kind and Bull certainly favours this as an approach. But in *The Anarchical Society* he is also wanting to establish a framework that helps to make sense of the last few centuries in international politics and at the heart of his position is the belief that the essentially power political orientation associated with the international system, and institutional orientation associated with international society, co-exist and that both exert a significant influence on decision-makers responsible for managing international relations. It is very apparent, moreover, that Bull is not just conceiving of the international system as a 'virtual' reality, akin to the state of nature, that co-exists with the actual reality provided by the theory and practices associated with international society. Bull is not viewing the international system as a distopian idea that encourages statespersons to operate within the norms and practices of international society. He insists that international politics is constituted by a mix of divergent and sometimes competing practices that contribute to a complex and multidimensional reality. He argues, moreover, that there are theorists who have captured the essential elements of the practices that he associates with an international system and the practices that he associates with an international society. So 'the element of war and struggle for power among states' that he associates with an international system needs to be distinguished from 'the element of co-operation and regulated intercourse among states' that he associates with an international society (Bull, 2002: 39). The thinking of theorists associated with both of these traditions of thought is seen to have evolved over the past five hundred years and helps to capture the essence of the changing reality of world politics that has gone on during this period. Bull (2002: 49) insists, therefore, that it is important not to reify either of these elements, so, for example, 'it is always erroneous to interpret events as if international society were the sole or the dominant element'.[17]

From this perspective then, the international system and the international society are defined by different sets of practices. In the formal model that Bull establishes, there is no doubt that the practices associated with the balance of power are firmly linked to international society. But if Bull's assessment is taken at face value, then he is short-changing what power politicians have had to say about the role of the balance of power in an international system. According to power politicians, European great powers recognized that they were engaged in an adversarial relationship with each other and, as a consequence, they monitored changes in the overall distribution of power very carefully and responded in such a way as to ensure that their own position within this distribution of power was not adversely affected. The responses could take a number of forms although most attention has been focused on military expansion, arms races, alliance formation and war. The persistent attempts by states to improve or at least maintain their power position can be associated with a competitive or adversarial balance of power. Bull (2002: 100) also acknowledges that theorists who adopt a

---

[17] Bull further complicates the argument by pointing to the existence of transnational practices that can be observed in world society and that co-exist with the practices that can be observed in the international system and the international society.

power political perspective frequently identify an automatic tendency for the system to balance, so that 'whenever a threat to the balance arises, some countervailing tendency will be brought into being to check it'. He also accepts that this is an example of a contrived balance and, therefore, very different from a fortuitous balance. In other words, he is acknowledging that systemic behaviour in an international society differs from systemic behaviour that has not been mediated through an international society. Indeed, Bull (2002: 40) argues that during a major conflict, when the two sides fiercely deny that they are members of a common international society, the concept 'does not disappear so much as go underground, where it continues to influence the practice of states'.

Bull's view of the relationship between the international system and the international society remains profoundly underdeveloped, although his overall thesis becomes easier to understand and more plausible if the relationship is elaborated. The balance of power becomes particularly significant in this context because although never clearly distinguished, two very different balance of power dynamics can be discerned within Bull, one linked to the international system and the other linked to the international society. Once this move is accepted then it also becomes possible to show that the institutional framework associated with international society has a profound impact on how the balance of power operates within the international system. In his formal model of the balance of power, Bull does hint at the existence of two dynamics. One dynamic involves restraining others and the other dynamic involves restraining self. As Bull puts it, the contrived balance of power implies that 'each state should not only act to frustrate the threatened preponderance of others, but should recognize the responsibility not to upset the balance itself'. Restraining others inevitably involves an adversarial relationship whereas mutual self-restraint presupposes an associational relationship. In his formal model, Bull's emphasis is on the adversarial dynamic. He argues, for example, that the 'most elementary form of contrived balance of power is a two-power balance in which one of the parties pursues a policy of preventing the other attaining military preponderance' and the dynamic is then extended to multipolar situations and the emergence of 'grand alliances' against 'potentially dominant powers' (Bull, 2002: 101–2). Bull, however, fails to anticipate the full structural logic that Waltz (1979) articulated soon after *The Anarchical Society* was published. Nevertheless, this is the logic that Bull is striving towards in his discussion of the adversarial dynamic, although the nature of the logic becomes much clearer in the wake of Waltz's *Theory of International Politics*.

Ironically, in Bull's formal model there is scarcely any discussion of an associational balance of power that 'implies self-restraint' and a recognition that the preservation of the balance of power should be 'the common goal of all states' (Bull, 2002: 102). Nevertheless, the associational dynamic comes much more clearly into focus when Bull discusses the other institutions, great power management in particular, and examines the implications of the geographical expansion of the European international society. Once the geographical dimension is brought into the picture it also starts to become apparent that the norms and practices associated with the associational balance of power outside of Europe diverged from those within Europe (see Figure 5.2). Bull's assessment of the other institutions also helps to clarify how the adversarial balance of power is mediated by the international society and why it is so different from the fortuitous balance of power that operates within an unmediated international system (see Figure 5.1).

International society and the balance of power

Bull (2002: 102) not only identifies the balance of power as one of five institutions that generates order in the contemporary international society but he also argues that it represents a foundational institution because it helps to provide 'the conditions in which other institutions on which international order depends (diplomacy, war, international law, great power management) have been able to operate' (see Figure 5.4). In practice, however, Bull depicts these institutions as interdependent and it is more accurate to describe the balance of power in Bull's thinking as a central institution, sustained, at least in part, by the existence of the other four institutions. The relationship between the balance of power and the other four institutions is examined in this section, although most attention is focused on the link with great power management because it is the self-conscious desire to preserve the international society by the great powers that is seen to distinguish the European balance of power from the balances of power that have formed in other contexts. Although the idea of a European balance of power is central to English school thinking, there is an unresolved tension in Bull's position. On the one hand he accepts Butterfield's (1966: 133)

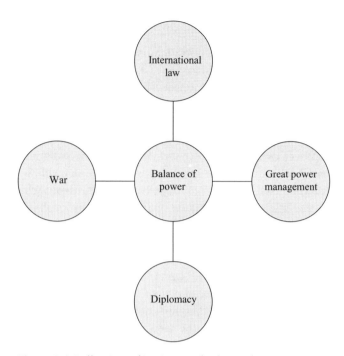

Figure 5.4 Bull's view of institutional relationships in international society[18]

position that the idea of a general balance of power 'seems to come from the modern world's reflection on its own experience'.[19] On the other hand, Bull (2002: 111) also argues that the European balance of power was 'only one manifestation of a phenomenon that has occurred in many periods and continents'. Bull fails to address this tension. But it is clear that it can be resolved if it is accepted that an adversarial balance of power can form in an international system independently from the associational balance of power that evolved in the European international society.

[18] The figure represents how Bull formally depicts the institutional relationships, with the balance of power playing the central role. But the discussion developed in this section not only suggests that there is mutual interaction among all the institutions but also that this figure masks the difference between an associational and an adversarial balance of power and the way in which these institutions mediate the adversarial balance of power.

[19] According to Bull (2002: 312), Butterfield 'argues persuasively' that there was no conception of the balance of power in the ancient world.

International law and the balance of power[20]

Bull establishes a complex but also contradictory relationship between the balance of power and international law. In doing so, he is working within a tradition of thought established by jurists and publicists writing prior to the twentieth century. Within that tradition there was a fundamental debate between those who saw the balance of power as providing essential support for international law and those who saw the balance of power as eroding international law. By the twentieth century, however, both sides of this argument were set to one side by international law theorists.[21] Nevertheless, there are good reasons why Bull focuses on the link between international law and the existence of a balance of power. In particular, the absence of a 'common power' in international society has been the source of a long-running debate about whether the rules that operate in international politics can be given the designation of law. Bull's (2002: 130) view is that because these rules are 'believed' to have the status of law, a whole range of activity that plays a crucial role in the working of international society becomes possible. He is also of the view that 'most states obey most agreed rules of law most of the time' (Bull, 2002: 131). The regular and unproblematic movement of money, goods and visitors across state boundaries every single day is a reflection, Bull argues, of this ubiquitous obedience to rules associated with international law.

Although conformity to international law reflects a 'social reality', Bull insists, however, that law is not an independent or 'motive force in world politics' (Bull, 2002: 133). He argues that states obey international law primarily because they 'judge it in their interests to conform to it' (2002: 134). At first sight, it would seem that Bull is anticipating here the argument developed so forcefully by Krasner (1999), that international law is not a highly institutionalized feature of international politics and although states may justify their actions in terms of international law, the real reasons are much more self-interested. Bull

[20] For a discussion of Bull's view of international law, see Armstrong (2006).
[21] Vagts and Vagts (1979: 555) note 'The existence of a significant relationship between the concept of the balance of power and international law would be regarded as improbable by most modern international lawyers'. See also Kingsbury (2002). There has, however, been a growing interest in recent years in re-establishing the link between international law and international politics. See Byers (1999; 2000) and Simpson (2004).

(2002: 134) insists, however, that although states only obey international law for 'ulterior motives', this does not mean that international law should not be taken seriously. It is a crucial institution that helps to maintain order by performing a range of vital functions. The first and most critical function is to identify the existence of a society of sovereign states. The second function has been to identify the rules of co-existence that govern relations among these units. The third function is to help mobilize compliance with both the rules of co-existence and the rules of cooperation.

It follows that international law and the balance of power are performing mutually interdependent roles because both help to underpin a society of sovereign states. All states have an interest in the survival of this society and over the centuries a complex body of rules has developed that gives specificity to this common interest and helps to ensure that it is fulfilled. Bull notes that the most basic rules promoting this common interest, for example, the rules governing sovereignty, non-intervention and diplomatic immunity, depend for their effectiveness on the principle of reciprocity. But this principle presupposes a balance of power, because if there is a preponderant state, then it can disregard the rights of other states.

Bull acknowledges, however, that international law and the balance of power will not always prove to be mutually reinforcing because, paradoxically, to maintain the balance of power – viewed as a necessary condition for the survival of international law – it will sometimes be necessary to violate international law. For example, a pre-emptive strike against a state with the potential to undermine the balance of power violates international law. Although Bull discusses this illustration of the paradox, he fails to provide any examples of it. Nevertheless, Bull is clear that the need to maintain a balance of power takes precedence over international legal considerations. On the other hand, international law is designed to promote conditions that make such moves unnecessary. Most of the time, therefore, international law and the balance of power represent mutually compatible and reinforcing institutions. This whole line of argument, however, becomes much more persuasive when it is acknowledged that Bull is making reference to the adversarial balance of power. A rising hegemonic power is clearly posing a direct challenge to the rules of co-existence and cooperation and so cannot expect to take advantage of these rules in order to satisfy its ambitions.

Diplomacy and the balance of power[22]

Bull argues that the consolidation of the European balance of power and the emergence of diplomacy as a central institution in the European international society were closely inter-related. Indeed, he argues that it is difficult to see how a balance of power could be identified in the absence of the complex and sophisticated diplomatic network that developed in Europe. By the start of the eighteenth century, it was widely acknowledged that all the states of Europe were linked together in a common society with the result that any major change within a state had knock-on consequences for all the other states in the society. This feature was seen to account for the emergence of permanent diplomatic missions across Europe that constantly monitored what was going on within each state and would then report back to the home government. Because all states were interlocked, moreover, it was argued that moves made by the very smallest states could still have ramifications that could affect the most powerful states. By the same token, it was argued that no state was so small that it would not be considered as a potential friend or ally by the strongest states in the European arena.[23] It was also argued that diplomats were more likely than princes to see what was in the interests of the state and identify the common interests that were shared by all the members of the European republic.

The assumption that Europe formed a 'single field of forces' was central to the idea of a balance of power, and it simultaneously implied that it was also necessary for all states to have knowledge and understanding of what was happening in all the other states. So a key function of diplomats was to gather intelligence and information about the countries where they resided. In particular, there was a need to know about the distribution of military resources across Europe. However, Bull (2002: 164) only identifies the existence of 'reciprocal interests of states in permitting information on a selective basis'. In other words, states were anxious to impress potential enemies with their military strength in order to promote deterrence, while on the other hand they also wished to deny access to information that would help these potential enemies to develop countervailing strategies. Without the constant

---

[22] For an assessment of Bull's view of diplomacy, see Hall (2006).
[23] Bull draws on François de Callières who developed this line of argument in *On the Manner of Negotiating with Princes*, which he wrote in 1716.

flow of information that formed the lifeblood of the diplomatic network, however, it is difficult to see how states could have made balance of power calculations, even in principle. So the systematic development of diplomacy as a European institution represented an essential structure underpinning the formation of a balance of power. Here again, however, it is clear that Bull is discussing an adversarial rather than an associational balance of power.

War and the balance of power[24]

Bull's approach to war is also intimately related to his conception of the balance of power. He recognized that war can threaten the very existence of an international society. But at the same time, because war has always been used by states as a crucial instrument of policy to pursue legitimate as well as illegitimate interests, it was essential to find ways to institutionalize and constrain war. One important source of constraint was international law that recognized the legitimacy of war, provided that it was fought within limits set by agreed rules. But although international law has always sanctioned war, the rules determining legitimacy have changed dramatically across time. Bull notes, for example, that it was only with the consolidation of international society that private wars were outlawed. This development was seen to provide an important curb on the ubiquitous violence that went on during the medieval era. But since rendering private wars illegal, there have been persistent attempts from within international society to limit how wars are fought, and the circumstances when states can legitimately go to war. Although there has always been the desire to outlaw war completely, this position has been considered impractical by states, and international lawyers have accepted that there are always going to be some circumstances when states can legitimately go to war. In an anarchic arena, where there is no common power to enforce the law, there have been occasions when states have resorted to war in order to uphold international law. By the same token, if a rising power has threatened the independence of other states, war has been needed to defend the balance of power. Bull argues, however, that in the aftermath of the Second World War and the development of nuclear weapons, there was a fundamental reassessment of the role of

---

[24] For an assessment of Bull's conception of war, see Jones (2006).

war in world politics and the perception that war poses a threat to the survival of international society now prevails. As a consequence, the possibility of war being used to enforce international law, preserve the balance of power, or effect just change 'is now qualified by a sense of the overriding need to contain war within tolerable bounds' (Bull, 2002: 191).

Nevertheless, Bull insists that war can still be viewed in institutional terms as an instrument for promoting the common interests of international society. He depicts war as an essential institution in international society, a fundamental building block that has a crucial impact on how other features in world politics are defined. He argues that war is 'so basic that even the terms that we use to describe the system – great powers and small powers, alliances and spheres of influence, balances of power and hegemony – are scarcely intelligible except in relation to war and the threat of war' (Bull, 2002: 181).[25] But he goes further than this and suggests that when viewed from the perspective of the international system, war represents the 'basic determinant of the shape the system assumes at any one time'. In the final analysis, according to Bull, it is war, or perhaps more accurately, war and the threat of war, that has determined the number of states that are operating in the system, the shape of the boundaries that define these states, how disputes between states are settled, and whether a balance of power prevails or the system is dominated by one state. It follows that it has been war and the threat of war that has determined whether a balance of power has been preserved. But it is also clear from Bull's reference to the international system rather than to international society that he is thinking in terms of an adversarial balance of power. With the evolution of nuclear deterrence, this assessment extended into the cold war era. However, it can be argued that because of the fear of war, the Soviet Union permitted a largely peaceful transformation of the political landscape at the end of the cold war, suggesting that war has become a much less significant institution in international society. Bull recognized, however, that war is unlikely to disappear from the international agenda. On the contrary, he argued that non-state actors were now proving to be the architects of 'new wars' that operate outside the societal rules that were designed to constrain inter-state war. He insists

---

[25] Bull constantly slips between references to the international system and international society.

that international society has to find ways of bringing these new forms of war within 'the compass of its rules' (Bull, 2002: 193).[26] This has yet to happen, although so far these new wars have not impacted on the balance of power.

Great power management and the balance of power

From Bull's perspective, great powers presuppose the existence of both a balance of power and an international society. He insists that great powers represent a kind of club, with rules of membership. It follows that there must be more than one member to form a club and so neither Rome nor imperial China constituted great powers. By the same token, Bull (2002: 195) suggests that if the United States became 'the single dominant power, it could no longer rightly be called a great power or a super power'. Bull, of course, was writing before the end of the cold war and since then it has frequently been argued that the world has been restructured, with the United States emerging as a 'hyper power' that operates in a unipolar world. Bull was certain, however, that even at the end of the Second World War, when the distribution of power most favoured the United States, it was far from ready to 'assume the mantle of Rome'. As the cold war progressed, Bull identified the movement of former great powers, such as China and Japan, back into the great power club. It is improbable, therefore, that Bull would have changed his position in the light of more recent events; instead, it is more likely that he would continue to argue that the idea that we are operating within a unipolar world fails to identify the real distribution of global power that still reflects the existence of a contrived balance of power.[27] Far from being able to 'lay down the law' for international society, the United States, time and again, is finding it necessary to opt out of evolving international law, while continuing to insist that it is operating in good faith as a member of the international community.

---

[26] Jones (2006: 185), however, makes the point that these 'new wars' are not new and that the period when inter-state wars prevailed was brief, starting from the beginning of the nineteenth century, so that Bull is peddling a kind of 'continuity realism' that is 'modernist and statist from head to toe'.

[27] This view is now beginning to be rearticulated. For a sophisticated discussion of the issue, see Buzan (2004b).

Great powers, therefore, are simultaneously linked by the balance of power and the existence of an international society. Bull insists that there would be no great powers in a hypothetical international system because the rights and duties associated with being a great power presuppose the existence of such a society. It follows that states like Napoleonic France or Nazi Germany that reject these rights and duties and aim to overthrow the international society 'are not properly speaking great powers' (Bull, 2002: 196).[28] Great powers are restrained by the existence of an international society and simultaneously help to reproduce the society. Bull establishes six inter-related roles that are linked to the rights and duties of states. First, they have a duty to preserve the central or overarching balance of power; second, they must try to ensure that their actions do not create crises for other states; third, they must eschew war whenever possible and limit its extent if they do become involved in war; fourth, they must be willing to exercise control in areas where their power is preponderant; fifth, they must be willing to establish spheres of influence when the opportunity arises for international society to expand; and sixth, they must be willing to cooperate in order to promote common policies across international society.

These roles are all related to the management of the international society, and because the great powers are seen to have a duty to manage the international society, they are accorded a number of rights, such as the right under certain circumstances to go to war or to establish spheres of influence. Bull traces some of these rights a long way back into European history. So, for example, spheres of influence are seen to originate in the fifteenth century. Bull's position has been challenged, however, by Simpson (2004) who argues that the idea of great powers having rights and duties only emerged after 1815. But on closer inspection it is clear that Simpson is talking about formal rights and duties that were written into the treaties that were established after the Napoleonic Wars, whereas Bull is interested in both formal and informal rights and duties, and there is a presupposition that these rights and duties operated on an informal basis in earlier centuries.[29]

---

[28] Halliday (1999) provides an excellent discussion of how revolutionary states can get re-socialized back into international society.

[29] However, Bull (2002: 36) also acknowledges that the 1815 Vienna settlement formally endowed the great powers with special rights and duties, reflecting 'a new doctrine of the hierarchy or grading of states, in place of the old hierarchy of inherited status and precedent, based on the facts of relative power and the consent of international society'.

Great power management presupposes collective or concerted action (Simpson, 2004: 73) and action of this kind is most apparent in the aftermath of war. It is the peace negotiations, not war, as Bull suggests, that prove to be the 'basic determinant of the shape the system assumes at any one time' (Bull, 2002: 181). The most significant changes that occurred in Europe took place as the result of the great powers acting in concert in the aftermath of systemic war. Every great power had an outcome that it favoured on these occasions but it was recognized that the eventual outcome had to be acceptable to the other great powers and at least tolerated by the small and medium powers. From the Treaty of Utrecht in 1713 onwards, such agreements were formally discussed in terms of establishing a balance of power or a just equilibrium. As Osiander (1994) and Bobbitt (2002) demonstrate, however, it was not only the future of the balance of power that was at stake at these peace conferences. Essentially the future constitutional structure of the international society came under discussion. By comparing the agreements that were established at these major conferences, therefore, it is possible to observe how the structure of international society changes across time. Osiander (1994) insists, however, that the balance of power only came into play in 1713; but earlier agreements also had to be based on a consensus about how power was going to be distributed. While the discussions may not have made formal reference to the balance of power, the final outcome reflected, effectively, an informal agreement on the balance of power.

Peace negotiations necessarily take place in the wake of war, and so Bull is undoubtedly correct to point to the institutional consequences of war, but there is also an independent associational dynamic generated by the large-scale peace negotiations that follow systemic war. Although the parties start from competing positions, there are powerful pressures to produce a great power consensus that have often involved substantial shifts in the established distribution of power. The major reduction in the number of European states, for example, occurred at the Treaty of Westphalia and the Congress of Vienna, thereby illustrating a point made repeatedly by Bull that the great powers have always been more interested in the future stability of the international society than the preservation of all its members.

What this section has demonstrated is that there is a strong sense of mutual dependence among the five institutions that Bull identifies, but that the nature of the mutual dependence becomes much clearer if there is a distinction drawn between an associational and adversarial balance of power where the former is linked to international society and the latter is linked to the international system. What then becomes apparent is that the adversarial balance of power is significantly mediated by the other four institutions with the consequence that it takes a radically different form to the fortuitous balance of power that Bull identifies in an unmediated international system. But this section has also identified the significance of an associational balance of power which is also tied very closely to the other four institutions but, unlike the adversarial balance of power, it takes an institutional form itself, playing a crucial role in the way that international society is structured. Although Bull fails to elaborate on this role in his formal model, it becomes more prominent when he looks at the historical development and geographical expansion of the international society.

The emergence and geographical expansion of the balance of power

There is relatively little explicit discussion of how the international society changed over time in *The Anarchical Society* because Bull is interested in the statics rather than the dynamics of world politics. In other words, he wants to establish what the idea of international order involves rather than demonstrating how the historical institutions that embody international order are subject to change (Bull, 2002: 19). His approach is very different to the one adopted by Morgenthau in *Politics Among Nations* where the interest is focused on how international society has changed across time. Nevertheless, Bull (2002: 26) acknowledges that the ideas underpinning international society have undergone a significant 'metamorphosis' over the last three or four centuries. At the time of Grotius (1583–1645), in the era immediately preceding the Treaty of Westphalia, for example, Bull argues that there was no conception of an international society and the fundamental institutions associated with such a society were either absent or still at a very underdeveloped stage of development. International law, for instance, had yet to emerge and natural law regulating individuals rather than states prevailed (Bull, 2002: 26–31). Treaties were still viewed as private contracts that were established between individuals and were not binding on successors. Grotius assumed that individuals existed within a universal society and so he operated on the basis of solidarist rather than pluralist assumptions.[30] It follows that significant changes had to take place before the contemporary conception of an international society of states emerged.

Bull acknowledges, therefore, that the character of international society underwent significant and persistent change over the next four or five hundred years. Jones' (2006: 185) argument that Bull is guilty of 'continuity realism' and that he is 'modernist and statist from head to toe' (see footnote 26) is not entirely fair. Nevertheless, it is true that he fails to explore the implications of change in international society for his understanding of the balance of power. Moreover, the problem is compounded by the conflation of the adversarial and associational balance of power. But there are some references to change in the text that help to establish his basic position. His starting point, however, is that there was no conception of the balance of power when Grotius was writing because there was no conception of sovereignty. Instead, the Roman-law notion of *dominium* or private property prevailed. As a consequence, territory and the people occupying that territory were regarded as the patrimony of the ruler. It follows that in the same way that individuals can buy and sell property, so a ruler could barter and exchange territory and population in a way that became increasingly difficult as the idea of sovereignty was consolidated and, more espe-cially, after nationalism became a potent force in world politics.

Bull acknowledges, however, that this practice had a crucial impact on the associational balance of power because prior to the nineteenth century the emerging great powers were mainly associated with hered-itary monarchies and the principle of international legitimacy was dynastic. Indeed, this dimension of the associational balance of power persisted into the nineteenth century and even at the Congress of Vienna it was assumed that territory could be divided or joined together in the interests of establishing a just equilibrium. But as we move through the nineteenth century, there is much less freedom of manoeuvre on that front.

---

[30] This distinction is now embedded in English school literature. In essence, pluralists privilege state rights over individual rights whereas solidarists insist that individual rights must be privileged. However, Buzan (2004a) has challenged this assessment and argues that it is more useful to locate the distinction on a continuum of interstate relations that extend from one end where power politics prevails through to convergence at the other end where all states subscribe to the same values.

At the time Bull was writing, as noted earlier, he also acknowledged that nuclear weapons had brought about another fundamental transformation to the balance of power, with established rules becoming outmoded by the evolution of nuclear weapons. In the pre-nuclear era, war was seen to be a crucial institution needed to help preserve a balance of power under threat. Nuclear weapons were considered to have radically changed this calculation because of the emergence of an overwhelming common interest in preventing the outbreak of war. Provided they were willing to play by the deterrent rules, it follows that the two main nuclear weapons states could cooperate in order to produce an increasingly stable deterrent/balance of power; so nuclear deterrence was an associational feature of international society for a brief period.[31] However, because of the persistent capacity for technological innovation nuclear deterrence was never as stable as its early advocates hoped. Nevertheless, the strategic use of nuclear weapons remains highly unlikely and so too does the possibility of war between any of the major powers in the international arena. Thinking along these lines has led to the conclusion that if war is becoming a redundant institution, then it follows that the balance of power could also be downgraded as an institution in the near future (Buzan, 2004a: 193). However, Buzan does not acknowledge the system/society divide that has been employed in this chapter, so it is necessary to return to this issue in the final chapter.

Although Bull is not primarily interested in the historical evolution of the European international society, this element is necessarily present in his discussion of the putative geographical expansion of the European international society across the globe. Of course, Bull is better known for his discussion of this expansion through his work with Watson (Bull and Watson, 1984), but, unsurprisingly, some of the basic ideas are foreshadowed in *The Anarchical Society*. The links with the balance of power, however, are largely submerged in this text and a certain amount of excavation has to take place before they can be exposed. But once this is done, it quickly becomes apparent that the impact of European expansion on the balance of power is more complex than might at first sight be anticipated. In the first instance, Bull uses the system/society distinction to get some leverage on Europe's relationship

---

[31] Adler (1992; 2005) provides a fascinating account of how the United States persuaded the Soviet Union to accept the value of a deterrence rather than a defence posture.

with the outside world. For most of Europe's history, he argues, the European society of states operated within the context of a very much more extensive international system.

From the sixteenth century to the late nineteenth century, European states participated in an emerging global international system. Despite communication, exchange of envoys, and agreements with states beyond the frontiers of Europe, not only about trade but also about war, peace and alliances, Bull insists that these contacts took place 'outside the framework of any shared conception of international society'. He accepts that there were occasions when a sense of common interests, albeit 'tentative and inchoate' began to emerge. But he acknowledges that he is not in a position to provide a detailed account of when and how the European international society expanded across the established international system. Any attempt to provide such an account, he argues, would quickly confront the 'difficult problems of the tracing of boundaries' (Bull, 2002: 15).

The difficulty of establishing these boundaries, however, should not obscure a more deep-seated problem with Bull's formulation. For an international system to exist, interaction among the members has to be sufficient 'to make the behaviour of each a necessary element in the calculation of the other' (Bull, 2002: 10). But this kind of calculation was simply not being made on a world-wide basis prior to the end of the nineteenth century. Indeed, when the Europeans began to explore beyond the boundaries of Europe, it was some time before these probes began to impact on European diplomatic relations or the balance of power, although the existence of two spheres was acknowledged from a very early stage. Wight notes, for example, that the Peace of Cateau-Cambrésis, 1559, recognized that Europe formed one sphere, with the creation of colonies operating within an outer sphere. The treaty established 'amity lines' that separated Europe from areas where colonization was taking place. The amity lines distinguished a zone of peace in Europe from a zone of war elsewhere, and Wight (1977: 125) observes that this division 'became almost a rule of law, giving freedom to plunder and attack and settle without upsetting the peace of Europe'. Although Wight argues that this rule of law persisted for some time, by the eighteenth and nineteenth centuries, states had become very concerned about the colonial possessions of their neighbours and they certainly figured in the peace settlements that followed major wars.

But this development was essentially a Eurocentric phenomenon, with European states assessing how the acquisitions across the globe by

other European states affected the European balance of power. This is
not an example of the European international society expanding into an
established international system, but rather the European international
system/society penetrating separate systems/societies in other parts of
the world. There is a growing recognition that there are fundamental
problems with the way that Bull thought about the expansion of the
European international society and that the whole issue needs to be
re-conceptualized.[32]

There is a second related problem with Bull's image of the European
international society extending across an established international system. It fails to take sufficient account of the distinctive way that European states related to the outside world during the nineteenth century.
Keene (2002) argues that there were two distinct international orders
operating during this period, with one set of rules operating among
the European states, and a second international order that built upon
a very different set of rules that defined relations between European
states and the outside world. This second international order is also a
Eurocentric phenomenon that fails to take account of the longstanding
order that had prevailed in many parts of the world before the impo-
sition of European rule (Onuma, 2000). To some extent, Bull is aware
of these developments. He notes, for example, that as the conception
of Christendom dwindled, the specifically European character of the
society of states was strengthened and in the process 'so also did the
sense of its cultural differentiation from what lay outside' (Bull, 2002:
32). Hobson and Sharman (2005: 87) go further than this, however,
and argue that the Europeans defined great powers in essentially racial
terms as states that 'can govern over large areas of land in the "inferior non-European" world'. International lawyers are shown to have
played a crucial role in propagating the idea of a racial hierarchy.[33]

---

[32] The first generation of English school writers focused on the idea of a
'standard of civilization' that states like Japan had to achieve before they
could join the European society of states (Gong, 1984). But this approach
sidesteps the whole colonial process (Buzan, 2004a; Callahan, 2004).
More recent thinking is focusing on the power political implications of
the expansion of European international society (Suzuki, 2005).

[33] Hobson and Sharman draw attention, in particular, to John Westlake,
M. F. Lindley and James Lorrimer. It was extraordinarily easy for the
Japanese to buy into this racial view of the world and to legitimize their
own imperial expansion in these terms.

Given this perspective, moreover, it was easy for the Europeans to justify their occupation of Africa. But they also managed to divide Africa by acting in concert. Fourteen European states met at the Berlin conference, 1884–1885, to start a process that was to reduce almost all of Africa to colonial status. By 1914, through a complex process of give and take, Africa had been divided arbitrarily among the Europeans states into fifty distinct territories. The process of colonialism, therefore, was intimately linked to the dynamic that defined an associative balance of power. The process of establishing European spheres of influence, moreover, was not restricted to Africa. Bull (2002: 213) notes, for example, the spheres of influence deals over Persia and Siam that helped to dampen rivalry among the great powers as European influence extended across the globe.

Conclusion

What I have endeavoured to do in this chapter is to show that Bull created a considerable amount of space for thinking about the balance of power and that he provided some of the tools needed to promote a comprehensive remapping of the concept. In some ways, Bull was following in Morgenthau's footsteps because he also provided the basis for an expansive concept of the balance of power at the heart of his approach to international politics. At the same time, his focus on the international system also anticipates Waltz. But what is most obviously distinctive about Bull's approach is the emphasis that he places upon the idea of the balance of power as an institution and the complex links that he identifies with the other institutions associated with the contemporary international society. Less obvious, but equally striking, are the implications for the balance of power that follow from the distinction that Bull draws between the international system and the international society. Although there have been powerful arguments advanced that the distinction should be eliminated in favour of a more comprehensive conception of the international society, I have argued in this chapter that there is a utility to retaining the distinction when the focus is on the balance of power. If the distinction is maintained, then it becomes apparent that embedded within Bull there is a much more complex view of the balance of power than is apparent at first sight.

The distinction allows Bull to develop the argument that the nature of the balance of power is radically different in the international system depending on whether or not it is mediated by an international society. Bull's distinction between a fortuitous and a contrived balance of power explicitly makes this move. However, he does not then make a clear distinction either in terms of terminology or analysis between the operation of the contrived balance of power in the international society and the international system, although the distinction is clearly implicit in his formal model. In an effort to fill out the concept, attention is drawn to the two dynamics, one linked to an adversarial balance of power and the other to an associational balance of power that can also be discerned in Morgenthau. The former clearly anticipates the Waltzian neorealist approach to the balance of power. The latter has been much less clearly referenced within the literature, and although it represents Bull's distinctive contribution, it is left underdeveloped. Nevertheless, it can be inferred from Bull that the institutional practices linked to the associational balance of power changed across time. So, for example, the European practice of reallocating territory to maintain a balance became more difficult to implement in nineteenth-century Europe. Bull is also aware that very different associational practices operated inside and outside of Europe. So, for example, as the dynastic practices of cutting and paring territory in Europe to preserve the associational balance of power died out, they were taken up with a vengeance in Africa and elsewhere in the nineteenth century. By contrast, there is a presumption, never clearly spelled out, that the practices associated with the adversarial balance of power have remained unchanged across time. This assumption proves absolutely central to the Waltzian approach to the balance of power.

Ever since the end of the cold war, assessments of international order have tended to be couched in terms of hegemony, unipolarity, hyperpower and empire. All these terms tend to suggest that the long-established international order associated with the balance of power has given way to a new form of international order that represents the negation of the balance of power, with one state setting the rules and then ruling the roost. It is unlikely, however, that Bull would have accepted this characterization of the current international order. It is much more likely that he would be sympathetic to Buzan's (2004b) argument that the United States represents a super power operating within a clutch of great powers that unquestionably have the potential to balance the United States. Bull insisted that during the cold war there was a balance of power that embraced the United States, the Soviet Union and other 'near or potential great powers'. On the other hand, he makes it clear that he is talking in terms of an adversarial balance of power when he insists that 'this balance differs from the European great power balance of the last [i.e. nineteenth] century in important respects'. During that era he identifies an associational balance of power defined as 'a concert or system of general collaboration among the great powers for the maintenance of the balance' (Bull, 2002: 287). He acknowledges that in the cold war there were elements of an associational balance of power, but that it required 'strengthening Soviet-American collaboration' and extending to include the other great powers.

It may be the case, as Buzan suggests, that as the likelihood of war among the great powers wanes, so too does the relevance of the adversarial balance of power. But if this happens, then more space is opened up for an associative balance of power to come into play, with the great powers bargaining to reach a consensual outcome that optimizes their various interests. Defensive and offensive realists have been so preoccupied with the insecurity associated with anarchy that they have failed to explore this dimension of international politics. Yet, the great powers have, over several centuries, demonstrated a capacity to reach agreements that have had the effect of consolidating their position in international society. In the years since the end of the Second World War, this feature of international politics has been institutionalized in international forums. During the cold war, however, many of these forums were restricted to western states, although the World Trade Organization, a post-cold war institution, has extended its membership to include China, but not yet Russia. International institutions and the regimes that have been developed within these institutions have primarily been explored by liberal institutionalists. As a consequence, there has been a failure to take on board that these institutions are dominated by the great powers and that the regimes emanating from the institutions are based on a bargained consensus that promotes the interests of the great powers, very often at the expense of the weaker members of the international society. If it is the case that the adversarial balance of power is becoming redundant, then the need for a better understanding of the associative balance of power increases.[34] Ironically, as we will see in the next chapter, Waltz's structural analysis pushes him in the same direction.

[34] Gruber (2000) provides an important guide, associating the great powers in supranational institutions with 'go-it-alone' power.

Bull (2002: 307) is extremely sensitive to the mythopoeic dimensions of his text and he acknowledges that 'the argument has taken a definite direction' which dictates how the future should be shaped. As he sees it, the argument indicates that although the international society is 'in decline', every opportunity should be taken to defend and promote it. From his perspective, following in Morgenthau's steps, the international society was endangered by the fundamental ideological clash between East and West and the dominance of an adversarial balance of power. At the same time, however, and indeed as a consequence of these features, he rejects the idea that the international system is 'in decline' (Bull, 2002: 266). But despite the implicit defence of international society, Bull (2002: 308) insists that the study of world politics 'is an intellectual and not a practical one' and he resists the suggestion that his work can make a contribution to an ideological narrative that carries us forward into the future. Nevertheless, there is a powerful ideological dimension to the text although Bull seems reluctant to spell it out, in part, because he argues that his text has focused on order at the expense of justice.[35] But, in practice, his position on justice is reasonably clear. His starting position is that 'human society at present is characterized by massive economic and social injustice' and that 'it is surely the duty of all intelligent and sensitive persons, however conscious they may be of the obstacles standing in the way' to recognize and work for a world society that has eliminated such injustice (Bull, 2002: 278). While sensitive to the arguments that both the international system and society are a source of this injustice, he insists that the existence of injustice has deeper causes than the existence of states and that it is not inconceivable that the international society will become 'infused with a stronger consensus about goals of economic and social justice' (Bull, 2002: 282). But such a hope takes us back to the operation of the associational balance of power.

---

[35] It has often been pointed out that the distinction between order and justice rests on a false dichotomy. For a sophisticated discussion from a post-structural perspective of the issue see Edkins and Zehfuss (2005).

6 | *Kenneth N. Waltz's* Theory of International Politics

WALTZ (1979: 117) insists that if there is any 'distinctively political theory of international politics, balance of power is it' and in *Theory of International Politics* he attempts to formulate and clarify the basis for such a theory. He recognizes, of course, that there is no agreed statement of the theory, and that even the meaning of the balance of power is the source of endless disagreement. As a consequence, he ponders whether it is not 'quixotic' to attempt to cut through the confusion that surrounds the idea. Nevertheless, this is the aim that he sets himself and in attempting to establish a model of the balance of power he produced one of the most widely cited and controversial books in the field. Although, on the face of it, much of the book is not directly concerned with the balance of power, its entire contents are designed, in practice, to establish what constitute the necessary conditions for a successful theory of international politics and to explain why the balance of power provides the most effective candidate for developing such a theory.

The main aim of this chapter is to explicate the essential features of Waltz's model of the balance of power, but in the process, two incidental but significant insights that run directly counter to conventional assessments of *Theory of International Politics* also and somewhat unexpectedly emerge. First, although it is generally accepted that Waltz provides the best-known model of a competitive or adversarial balance of power, the logic of his argument also reveals the potential for an associational balance of power to emerge. It is intriguing, given the intensive scrutiny of *Theory of International Politics*, that this feature of his work has been almost completely ignored.

A second and equally surprising product of this assessment of Waltz's model is that it points the way to the emergence of a unipolar system and the absence of any sustained discussion of unipolarity represents, as a consequence, a significant weakness of *Theory of International Politics*. This weakness is exposed in Waltz's (2000a: 55–6) subsequent assessment of world politics in the post-cold war era where he has consistently argued along the lines that 'both friends and foes will react as countries always have to threatened or real predominance of one among them: they will work to right the balance. The present condition of international politics is unnatural.' This argument runs directly counter to the position that he develops in *Theory of International Politics*, which does not suggest that there is anything 'unnatural' about unipolarity and shows, very clearly, moreover, why balancing strategies will do nothing to change the unipolar structure of the system.

There are two diametrically opposed reasons why *Theory of International Politics* has proved to be so influential and enduring. On the one hand, Waltz was the first theorist in the field of international politics to argue so unequivocally why only a structural approach can provide the foundations for a successful theory of international politics. The major exemplar for successful structural theory is seen to be economics, and Waltz returns time and again to show why he thinks economists have been so successful in developing theory and, perhaps even more important, why he thinks he can draw directly on economic theory to develop a model of the balance of power. In essence, the reason derives from his conviction that the structural constraints experienced by economic actors take a similar form to those confronted by actors in the international political system. The structure of an oligopolistic market and the anarchic international system are seen by Waltz to be identical or at least isomorphic in structure. As a consequence, Waltz is convinced that the parsimonious theory found in economics can be replicated in international politics. Given the prestige so often attached to economic theory, this has been considered, at least in some quarters, to be both a laudable and an attractive goal.

On the other hand, *Theory of International Politics* has also endured, paradoxically, because it continues to provide such a perfect example for constructivist critics of how not to develop a theory of international politics. From their perspective, in striving for parsimony, Waltz drains his theory of any meaning at all. While constructivists accept the need for a structural approach to international politics, they argue that Waltz provides an erroneous assessment of the nature and role of structures in international politics. Anarchy, they insist, is not a structure but an empty concept that must be given social meaning before it can play a structural role in international theory. Whereas Waltz turned to economics to assist him in his task of developing international theory, the constructivists have turned to social theory. It is no accident that Wendt (1999), who has provided perhaps the most sophisticated and detailed constructivist response to Waltz, entitles his text *Social Theory of International Politics*. By following this route, Wendt wishes to demonstrate that the putative attempt by Waltz to define structure in purely material terms is, from a philosophical perspective, incoherent. Drawing on social theory, Wendt demonstrates that there must be intersubjective agreement about social structures for them to have an impact on the behaviour of social actors. When this logic is applied to anarchy, then it follows that the concept can take a variety of forms, depending upon the prevailing international culture: hence Wendt's familiar aphorism that 'anarchy is what states make of it'. This constructivist move has now become so firmly embedded in the study of International Relations that it is too significant to ignore. As a consequence, when discussing Waltz's approach to the balance of power it is necessary to take the constructivist critique into account at each stage of the argument.

Since the end of the 1970s when *Theory of International Politics* was published, there has been a second line of attack from theorists and analysts who accept (what constructivists see as) Waltz's materialist bias but who insist, nevertheless, that the theory simply fails to stand up under either empirical investigation or logical scrutiny. According to these critics, however, rather than accept criticism of this kind and abandon a balance of power theory, advocates of the theory have endeavoured to save it by adding on ad hoc features that are designed to circumvent the problems thrown up by its opponents (Schroeder, 1994b).[1] So, for example, Walt (1987) has drawn a distinction between balance of power theory and balance of threat theory and he argues that the latter incorporates the idea of power but subsumes it, in conjunction with geography, offensive capabilities and intentions, within the more general concept of threat. He then goes on to argue that whereas the balance of power theory predicts that states will ally

---

[1] Schroeder is one of the few diplomatic historians who has engaged seriously with international relations theorists. His attack on Waltz gave rise to an important exchange of views. See Schroeder (1994b) and Elman, Elman and Schroeder (1995). This was, in fact, the second debate about the balance of power initiated by Schroeder. On an earlier occasion there was another robust exchange of views about behavioural attempts to operationalize the concept. See Schroeder (1977a); Alexandroff, Rosecrance and Stein (1977); Small (1977); and Schroeder (1977b).

against the strongest state, the balance of threat theory predicts that states will ally against the most threatening state. An even more significant move, initiated by Schweller (1996), develops the argument that because Waltz's theory presupposes that states are security-maximizing units, it follows, logically, that they will favour the status quo. But such a presumption, according to Schweller (1994), overlooks the existence and importance of revisionist states in the international system. Once these states are taken into account, contrary to Waltz's theory, bandwagoning rather than balancing will prove to be the prevailing strategy in any anarchic international system.[2] After surveying evidence of this kind, and applying the metatheoretical approach developed by Lakatos (1978), Vasquez (1997) concludes that there is now enough evidence, gathered by realists themselves, to demonstrate that Waltz's theory has turned into a degenerative rather than a progressive research programme.[3]

The aim of this chapter, however, is not to provide a comprehensive survey of the complex debates and issues that have been spawned by *Theory of International Politics*. Such an endeavour would generate a substantial book and so what is attempted here instead is the recovery and, in the process, reassessment of the balance of power theory as it was originally presented by Waltz. This chapter, therefore, charts a similar route to the one established by Goddard and Nexon (2005) who are also interested in recovering what they depict as Waltz's 'paradigm lost'. They argue that it needs to be recognized that Waltz's approach has been profoundly influenced by the social theory associated with structural functional thinking.[4] Once this approach is factored into Waltz's view of theory, then it becomes apparent that his approach is more sophisticated and sociological than is often acknowledged and, as a consequence, many of the constructivist critiques of *Theory of International Politics* are misdirected. This leads Goddard and Nexon to the conclusion that although structural functionalism represents a flawed social theory, because of its status quo bias, by taking account of Waltz's

---

[2] This line of argument has become so successfully established that it has created a schism among structural realists, with Waltz's approach being designated as defensive realism to distinguish it from the offensive realist approach, most closely associated with the work of Mearsheimer (2001).

[3] Vasquez's 1997 article sparked a considerable debate which is reproduced and extended in Vasquez and Elman (2003).

[4] As a consequence, they are critical of Wendt's assumption that Waltz's approach lacks any foundation that builds on social theory.

insights about structural continuity and the dynamics of anarchy the way is then opened for a potential synthesis of structural realism and constructivism. Such a synthesis, they argue, could lead on to a more progressive systems theory. In particular, they suggest that by taking account of Waltzian ideas about the distribution of power, constructivists can thereby overcome a tendency towards cultural reductionism. It also becomes apparent that there is a much closer link between Bull and Waltz than is generally recognized.

Although this chapter does not pursue the argument followed by Goddard and Nexon, it draws upon some of their conclusions, for example, their claim that Waltz deploys the essentially constructivist argument that structure and units are mutually constituted.[5] But their most crucial claim that is co-opted into the argument developed here is the assertion that Waltz, drawing on structural functionalism, insists on the need, for analytical purposes, to separate out different elements of the international system. So it follows that there is a need, for instance, to distinguish an economic system from a social system. However, the system that Waltz wants to focus upon is the international political system, although he is well aware that there is a complex body of social norms, rules and values that operate within the overall international system, and that the content of these norms, rules and values are profoundly affected by the structure of the international political system. Nevertheless, following the social theory associated with structural functionalism, his concern in *Theory of International Politics* is exclusively with the operation of the international political system.[6] From Waltz's perspective, therefore, the weakness of the constructivist position is the failure to acknowledge the need to accommodate the impact of the political system on the social system. Indeed, by arguing that anarchy can take different forms, Wendt effectively collapses the distinction that Waltz wants to establish between political and social systems.[7] Once the distinction is collapsed, then it is no longer possible

---

[5] This line of argument is explored in more detail in Buzan, Jones and Little (1993).

[6] There is no doubt that the theoretical exposition in Buzan, Jones and Little (1993), and Buzan and Little (2000), could have been reinforced by exposing the implicit structural functional assumptions that underpinned some of the analysis.

[7] The synthesis proposed by Goddard and Nexon (2005), therefore, is also at odds with Waltz's approach because they wish to establish a single international structure that embraces culture as well as politics.

to explore the relationship that Bull (1977) posits between the international system and international society.[8]

The constructivists have unquestionably mounted a powerful case against Waltz's assertion that it is both possible and necessary to identify an independent political structure within the international system. The first section of this chapter, therefore, will reassess Waltz's position that we can, from an analytical perspective, identify an international political structure, defined by anarchy and power distribution, in the light of constructivist arguments that anarchy is an empty concept and that power is a socially constructed concept. The second section of the chapter reassesses Waltz's argument that the balance of power theory accounts for the persistence and reproduction of the international political system. It looks specifically at the two processes that Waltz associates with the maintenance of the balance of power: competition and socialization.

The two processes are then applied to multipolar and bipolar systems and are seen to operate in radically different ways. Whereas the instability and uncertainty generated by multipolarity can lead to the danger of 'underbalancing', bipolarity by contrast can generate a third process, which Waltz identifies as 'management' and this can lead to 'reverse balancing'.[9] Waltz, however, fails to explore the implications of this third process for his assessment of the balance of power.

The international political structure

Waltz's starting point assumes the existence of a fundamental divide between the natural and social sciences.[10] He attributes the difference, among other things, to the fact that social units are influenced by the

[8] Of course, the issue is complicated by the fact that many realists (including Waltz) privilege international politics at the expense of international society, thereby mirroring the move made by the constructivists. See, for example, Krasner (1999).

[9] Underbalancing is Schweller's (2004; 2006) term, although he explains the phenomenon – in line with his neoclassical credentials – at the unit level. 'Reverse balancing' is my term and identifies collaborative policies that are designed to promote stability by reducing the level of arms or implementing measures that are designed to inhibit the use of weapons. Note that Waltz fails to identify management as a distinct process.

[10] Waltz (1979: 68) argues that 'The subject matter of the social and natural sciences are profoundly different.'

structure of the systems of which they form a part. So, in the case of international politics, states do not have a completely free rein to do whatever they want because they are constrained, to some degree or other, by the structure of the international political system. If the structure has no significant causal impact, then the reason for identifying an international system is negated. Waltz is not denying, of course, that states are, in a sense, free agents, and can try to do whatever they want, but he insists that if they move beyond the constraints set by the structure of the system, then there will be a systemic response. Waltz (1979: 40) aims to show 'how the structure of the system affects the interacting units and how they in turn affect the structure'. In other words, the structure of the system pushes the states to take actions that have the effect of reproducing the structure of the system. But Waltz also wants to find a way of escaping from the idea that the international system can be compared to a mechanistic self-regulating system like a boiler with a thermostat.[11] In that case, the system has been established to achieve a goal – to maintain the water at a constant temperature. In the case of the international system, there is no overarching goal. The reproduction of the system is the unintended consequence of the actions of the component units that set themselves the common goal of survival.

Waltz insists, however, that if this approach is going to be effective, then it is essential to establish a clear analytical distinction between the component units and the structure of the system. From his perspective, a major problem with the use of systems theory in International Relations is that there is a persistent tendency to incorporate internal characteristics of the units, such as the ideology of the state, into the structure of the system.[12] For example, although the cold war ideological schism between the Soviet Union and the United States is often treated as a structural feature of the international system it is, in fact, a feature of the units and not the political structure of the system. Treating ideology as a systemic feature erodes the sharp distinction

---

[11] This is the metaphor that Hopkins and Mansbach (1973: 17–19) employ, although with some reservations.

[12] Aron (1966), for example, distinguishes between homogeneous and heterogeneous international systems. In a homogeneous system, states share a common ideology, whereas in a heterogeneous system, states subscribe to competing ideologies.

that Waltz wants to draw between units and structure. By maintaining the distinction there is a major pay-off from Waltz's perspective, because whereas the defining features of states have changed dramatically across time, the defining features of the international political structure, at least according to Waltz, are a constant feature of international politics. As a consequence, he is able to draw on this unchanging political structure to account for what he sees as the extraordinary degree of continuity that can be observed in international politics. As he sees it, the 'texture of international politics remains highly constant, patterns recur and events repeat themselves endlessly' (Waltz, 1979: 66). This is true whether we are talking about the political interactions within the Greek city states in the fifth century BCE, the dynastic states in seventeenth-century Europe, or the nation states in late nineteenth-century Europe.[13] There are radical differences between these types of states, but what Waltz wants to demonstrate is that the international political structure within which they interact takes exactly the same form. As a consequence, these very different units operate under identical structural constraints.

To understand how these structural constraints work, however, Waltz assumes that politics is about power and, more specifically, about how power is organized, because it is only possible to talk about a political system if power is organized in a meaningful and discernible way that produces order. He goes on to argue that there are two and only two types of political order: one related to a domestic political structure based on the organizing principle of hierarchy and another related to the international political structure based on the organizing principle of anarchy. Although he readily acknowledges that these two types of order represent the ends of a spectrum and that there are innumerable types of order in between, he insists that the only way to make theoretical progress is by working with simplifying assumptions.[14] So he

---

[13] It is this kind of assertion that constructivists find so objectionable about the structural realist approach. They insist that there are fundamental differences between these periods. If we accept the assessment of Waltz advanced by Goddard and Nexon (2005), however, it is possible to argue that Waltz can accept that there are fundamental differences in the international social system and insist that it is only in the political system that the commonalities can be observed.

[14] Although all social scientists accept this methodological procedure, in principle, it has been argued that Waltz takes the argument too far in

insists that there are two mutually incompatible ways of positioning units from a power perspective. Either the units are positioned on a hierarchical basis, so that one unit is in a superior position to another or the units are positioned on a horizontal plane, with no unit willing to acknowledge the superiority of another unit. These two ways of positioning units is not a property of the units, but 'a property of the system' (Waltz, 1979: 80).

Although Waltz identifies and discusses the essential features of a political structure defined by hierarchy, he is primarily concerned with the less complex structure of anarchy. Hierarchy is a more complex structure than anarchy because the units are functionally differentiated, and the power associated with each functional unit is distributed to produce anything from a very steep hierarchy to a very shallow hierarchy. Waltz accepts, moreover, that the political order associated with hierarchy is potentially very fragile. He observes that it is all too easy to lose sight of the fact that it is a reasonably common occurrence for a hierarchical political order to break down and give way to a Hobbesian state of nature (Waltz, 1979: 103). By contrast, anarchy is a less complex and, Waltz implies, more robust political structure. For this structure to collapse, all the units would have to disintegrate simultaneously, and this is a very improbable outcome. On the other hand, anarchy could transform into a hierarchy. But for this to happen, either one unit would have to have to take control of the system against the wishes of the others, or the units would all have to agree to transfer their power to a higher authority. Both of these outcomes are possible, although structural constraints make them highly unlikely. For Waltz (1990: 37), therefore, there is a powerful 'logic of anarchy' that derives from its structure and generates patterns of behaviour that reproduce the system and this logic operates 'whether the system is composed of tribes, nations, ologopolistic firms or street gangs'.

To understand how this logic operates, however, we need to say more about the structure of an anarchic system both in terms of anarchy as an organizing principle and the distribution of power as a structural

---

this case. Ruggie (1986) is the best known exponent of this view. He insists that it is simply not possible to characterize the medieval period as either a domestic or an international political system. It represents a third type of political order. Wendt (1999) takes issue with Waltz on the grounds that his international category masks fundamental structural differences.

attribute. Waltz (1979: 89) acknowledges that neither of these elements is easy to conceptualize, and he turns to economic theory to provide an analogy that can help to illuminate what is meant by an anarchic political structure. However, he goes even further than this to suggest that an economic market is structurally similar to the international political system. Economists, however, recognize that the market can be structured in a number of different ways. They draw clear distinctions between the market as a monopoly, a duopoly, an oligopoly and perfect competition. These markets have different structural characteristics and so Waltz's argument about structural similarities operating in different domains needs to be treated with some care. In the first instance, however, Waltz (1979: 173) draws on the broad distinction that economists make between perfect competition and oligopoly. The former tells us 'about the market and not about the competitors' whereas oligopolistic theories 'tell us quite a bit about both'.

In the context of perfect competition, because there are so many buyers and sellers operating in the market, none is able to affect the price at which goods are bought and sold. Under these conditions, certainly for producers and sellers of goods, the structure of the market is a 'tyrannical force' (Waltz, 1979: 133). When the price of the goods being produced falls, producers have to make a strategic decision about whether to expand production in order to maintain their levels of income. But if all decide to expand production, then the structure of the market will simply force the selling price down even further. This is a bad outcome, but any alternative strategy will produce even worse consequences. This is the 'tyranny of small decisions' and it can only be overcome by intervention from the political system, with the government introducing measures designed to mitigate the effects of the market. It follows, Waltz (1979: 133) argues, that under conditions of perfect competition 'the individual producer is free of tactical constraints and subject only to strategic ones'. The significance of this distinction is easier to understand when we compare perfect competition with an oligopolistic market where both tactical and strategic constraints come into play.

The key point that Waltz wants to make when comparing the structures of these two types of market is that it is the number of units involved, not their attributes or functions that make the difference. Under conditions of perfect competition there are so many producers/units, that if a unit is added or deleted, it makes no difference to the operation of the system. It follows that knowing the precise number of producers/units operating within the market does not increase our understanding of the system and it is assumed that units are constantly moving in and out of the market. Moreover, because outcomes are determined by the impersonal structure of the market, the power of individual buyers and sellers never enters the equation and so there is no sense of conflict between them. Producers/units acknowledge the power of the market and recognize, as a consequence, that they can effectively ignore what their individual competitors are doing. The producers, therefore, can be viewed as autonomous agents, positioned on a horizontal plane, that have no tactical interest in endeavouring to outwit their competitors or to exert authority over them. They simply have to respond strategically to the changing conditions set by the market. The situation is very different, however, in the context of an oligopolistic market that is dominated by a limited number of large firms. Here, the producers are still autonomous and are positioned, effectively, on the basis of the organizing principle of anarchy, but now distribution of power among the units enters into the structural equation. If power is defined by the share of the market, then it makes a big difference whether a producer has control of 20 or 50 per cent of the market.[15] It follows that the producers/units are acting under both strategic and tactical constraints. As Waltz (1979: 133) argues, in an oligopolistic market the decisions of large firms are not dictated by 'impersonal market forces unalterable by their own actions' and, as a consequence, they are 'impelled both to watch their competitors and to try to manipulate the market'.

What this line of argument indicates is that the structure of the market associated with perfect competition provides only a very limited amount of insight for a theorist interested in international politics. Waltz uses this kind of market to demonstrate that there are human systems where the behaviour of units is constrained primarily by the structure of the system. But this is not seen to provide a useful exemplar for international politics because in such a setting, the units make

---

[15] Kaplan (1962: 16–17) also recognized the importance of this distinction between perfect competition and oligopoly and discussed the former in terms of system dominance and the latter in terms of subsystem dominance. For Waltz, however, subsystem dominance is an oxymoron – eliminating the utility of the systems framework.

no attempt to influence each other's behaviour. On the other hand, Waltz does think that the theory of oligopolistic markets has relevance for international politics, provided that theorists are willing to accept a move that economists often make. Economists agree that in a system where there are a large number of firms, their interactions can be understood, although not fully predicted, 'if the number of consequential firms reduces to a small number by virtue of the pre-eminence of a few of them' (Waltz, 1979: 131). Waltz makes this crucial move when he argues that international politics can be studied in terms of the 'logic of small number systems'. His theory of international politics is, in fact, a theory that focuses almost exclusively on the great powers. When he talks about the political structure of the international system, therefore, he is restricting the definition of this structure to the composition of the great powers.[16] There may be large numbers of other states in the international system, but they have no impact on the way that Waltz conceptualizes the international political structure. From this perspective, as a consequence, there is no distinction to be drawn between an international system that consists solely of two empires and the international system that prevailed, for example, during the cold war with two super powers operating in an international system that contained many more states. Of course, Waltz is not suggesting that there is no difference between these two types of international system. But he is suggesting that the same model can help to explain how these two very different systems are maintained and reproduced.[17] By the same token, Waltz knows that by focusing exclusively on the international political system, he is necessarily ignoring many significant features of the international system. But he justifies this move by using the same methodological procedure that economic theorists have used, with some success, when, equally unrealistically, they 'conceive of an economy operating in isolation from its society and polity'

[16] Waltz (1979: 72) argues that 'the theory, like the story, of international politics is written in terms of the great powers of an era. This is the fashion among political scientists as among historians, but fashion does not reveal the reason lying behind the habit.' He goes on to argue that 'units of greatest capability set the scene of action for others as well as for themselves.'

[17] It follows that Waltz's model bypasses discussions about whether there is hierarchy in the international system. It simply fails to take account of whether or not the Warsaw Pact should be depicted in terms of a hierarchy.

(Waltz, 1979: 89). So in the same way, Waltz eschews international economics and international society when looking at the international political system. As Goddard and Nexon (2005) argue, this methodological procedure is endorsed by structural functional theorists.

For the logic of small systems to come into effect, Waltz's model of the international political system assumes that either there are only a small number of actors in the system or there are a small number of actors that can be set apart from the other actors by the level of impact that they have on the system. These actors are multi-functional and effectively this is a state-centric model.[18] Waltz acknowledges that there are other powerful non-state actors operating within the international system but he argues that these actors operate within a framework that is established by the dominant states in the system. It is also the case that Waltz (1979: 97) assumes that the identification of these dominant states is essentially unproblematic and he argues categorically that the 'great powers of an era have always been marked off from others by practitioners and theorists alike'. Despite this confident claim, Waltz is well aware that although it may have been relatively easy to identify great powers in the past, by the 1970s there was considerable debate about whether the international system should be characterized as bipolar or multipolar. He identifies two familiar ways of unravelling his own claim that the international system was unequivocally bipolar at that time. To illustrate the first way, he cites Kissinger, by then a practitioner as well as a theorist (and so according to Waltz equipped twice over to make the assessment), who insisted that power is no longer 'homogenous' so that although, militarily, there were only two super powers, economically there were at least five major actors. To illustrate the second way of contesting bipolarity, Waltz (1979: 130) cites President Nixon who 'slipped easily from talking of China's becoming a superpower to conferring superpower status on her'. But Waltz insists that both of these moves are mistakes and he argues that the 'economic, military and other capabilities of nations cannot be sectored and separately weighted'. Instead, a state's rank depends on how it scores on '*all* of the following items: size of population and territory, resource

---

[18] It is probably more accurate to say that they are state-like actors. Waltz is clear that the model can apply to tribes or street gangs or indeed in any situation where a small number of actors are interacting under anarchic conditions.

endowment, economic capability, military strength, political stability and competence' (Waltz, 1979: 131). The potential problem with this formulation, from Waltz's (1979: 97) perspective, is that it seems to violate his injunction 'to keep unit attributes out of structural definitions'.

We need to come back to this point, but before doing so, it is necessary to examine a problem that is potentially more significant that has been raised by Waltz's constructivist critics who argue that Waltz's position is inherently incoherent, with the knock-on consequence that his whole enterprise is misconceived. The constructivist position, moreover, is increasingly being taken on board, even by some self-styled realists, such as Buzan, who are broadly sympathetic to Waltz's aim of examining world politics from a power perspective.

The starting point for constructivists is that realists, like Waltz, simply cannot lay exclusive claim to such central concepts as power or assert by fiat that power can be defined without difficulty in material terms. Constructivists, therefore, aim to identify a way of approaching power so that it can no longer be hijacked by realists or assumed to take a material form. Such a move is essential, they assert, because by drawing on arguments that have already been long-established in the field, the realist or materialist approach to power proves, on closer examination, to be unsustainable. This is because power is, ultimately, constituted by ideas and not material forces. Constructivists accept that although there could be useful theories that provide explanations by reference to what are sometimes called 'brute' material forces, they do not include theories that are based on power. Wendt (1999: 94) argues that although International Relations theorists have largely ignored the extent to which the 'material base' of international politics is constituted by ideas, the issue is an important one 'that bears on the transformative potentials of the international system'. In making their case, constructivists argue either that realist theories rest on an incoherent material conception of power that needs to be replaced by an idealist conception or that realist theories rest on 'suppressed constructivist assumptions about the content and distribution of ideas' (Wendt, 1999: 96).

The claim that a material conception of power is incoherent draws on well-established literature showing that a composite conception of power is not susceptible to measurement. Constructivists argue that this poses realists with an insuperable problem because for their position to be sustained, it has to be possible to measure power and have it play an 'analogous role to money in utilitarian theory'; this is because realists are seen to associate power with capabilities and this then translates into the 'capacity to control outcomes' which in turn provides an 'indicator for ranking international actors' (Guzzini, 2004: 537).[19] Problems arise for realists because they have always acknowledged that there is no single measure of power – as Waltz's list given above demonstrates. But if there are different components of power, then it can be questioned whether the various components of power operate across different domains. Does military power have any purchase in the economic arena? Or does economic power have any purchase in the military arena? If a positive answer can be given to these questions, then it indicates that power, like money, is fungible.[20] But it is widely accepted that power is not fungible and so, as Kissinger notes above, it then becomes necessary to specify the domain within which a state exercises power. If power is not fungible, then it becomes impossible to establish a composite measure of power, for example, by adding military capabilities to economic capabilities. By the same token it is also argued that it is a mistake to privilege one domain over all the others: to assume, for example, that what really counts in international politics is military power. Baldwin (1989: 167) concludes, therefore, that 'it is time to recognize that the notion of a single overall international power structure unrelated to any particular issue area is based on a concept of power that is virtually meaningless'. And Guzzini (2004: 541) agrees that 'there is no case for a "lump" concept of power, as balance of power theories would require'.

These lines of argument, however, run completely against the grain of Waltz's analysis because they are endeavouring to undercut his attempt to develop a structural conception of power. We need to return, therefore, to the question of how Waltz establishes a structural conception of power. It takes three distinct moves to establish his position. First, he disputes the assumption that power capabilities must be translated into the 'capacity to control outcomes'. He is adamant that although there

---

[19] Guzzini (1993; 1998; 2004) has produced some of the most sustained and comprehensive attacks on realist thinking about power, in general, and Waltz's notion of structural power, in particular.

[20] There is now a substantial literature on power fungibility. As Guzzini (2004: 539) notes, although Aron (1966) argued against using this economic analogy many years ago the debate persists. See Art (1999) and Baldwin (1999).

have often been attempts to define power in behavioural or relational terms as the ability of A to get B to do something they would not otherwise have done, he considers this an unhelpful way of trying to conceptualize power.[21] As Waltz (1979: 191–2) sees it, the equation of power with control reflects a 'pragmatically formed and technologically influenced American definition of power', and one that 'takes much of the politics out of politics'. Power is only one factor, and not necessarily the most important, that determines an outcome. So Waltz (1979: 192) prefers 'the old and simple notion that an agent is powerful to the extent that he affects others more than they affect him' and this leads him to the conclusion that to be 'politically pertinent, power has to be defined in terms of the distribution of capabilities'. Crudely expressed, Waltz assumes that a state with very extensive power resources can have a very large effect – often unintentionally – on states with very limited power resources, whereas the small states will have an insignificant impact on the large state. Power flows one way when there is a large power differential between two states and two ways when there is no power differential (see Figure 6.1)

The advantage of moving away from a behavioural concept of power is that it does away with the question of whether, for example, the Vietnamese exercised power over the United States during the Vietnam War. From Waltz's perspective, the defeat by the United States was the result of a large number of complex factors. But, at the end of the day, the United States had a very large impact on Vietnam, whereas the impact of Vietnam on the United States was much less significant. The flow of power is effectively one way. This is the necessary first step in Waltz's attempt to formulate a conception of power as a property of the international system rather than a property of a specific state. It means that when attempting to establish the political structure of the system, it is only necessary to identify the major powers in the system. Waltz's second move is to argue that there is only ever a small number of states in international politics with sufficient power to affect all other states in the system.[22] To move into this select band of great powers, these states,

---

[21] Guzzini does accept this formulation of power, which he derives from Dahl (1968). Waltz also associates the relational view of power with Dahl (1957).

[22] If there are a large number of states, then the structure of the system would take a radically different form akin to the structure of the market under conditions of perfect competition.

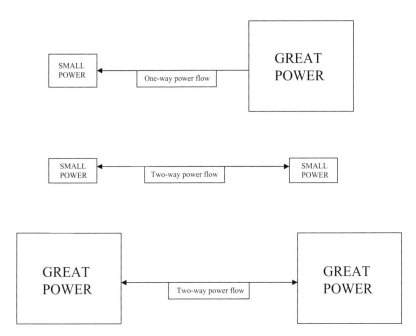

Figure 6.1 The impact of power differentials

as already noted, have to possess substantial capabilities across all key dimensions. To be a great power at the end of the twentieth century Waltz argued that immense resources were required so that the state could maintain every type of capability and exercise these capabilities at strategic and tactical levels. He concluded that the 'barriers to entering the superpower club have never been higher or more numerous' (Waltz, 1979: 183). Even with very rough and ready measures, Waltz argues, it quickly becomes apparent that throughout European history, there have been relatively few states that cross the great power threshold. The numbers then drop even further when we move into the era of a global international system. But for Waltz, the key factor that follows from the very restricted number of states that fall into the great power category is that the logic of small numbers can be applied to international politics.

Waltz's third move is absolutely crucial for his structural conception of power and is essentially an extension of the previous two moves. Not only does he assume that the amount of power a state possesses can be calculated, but he also assumes that the calculation necessarily depends upon the amount of power possessed by the other states in the system. It follows that as the number of states in a system increases, so the level of power possessed by each state is necessarily reduced (see Figures 6.2 to 6.4). Of course, there is no reason to suppose that the great powers in a system will all possess the same amount of power, but the point Waltz makes is that the power possessed by a state is structurally determined by the power possessed by the other states in the system. As a consequence, the amount of power possessed by a state can only be expressed as a percentage of the total amount of power that exists within the system. So, if the power possessed by one state increases, then the power possessed by the other states must decrease by a proportionate amount. Waltz's move from a behavioural conception of power to a structural conception of power is, in fact, identical to the change in the meaning that occurs when power is metaphorically linked to a balance of power as discussed in Chapter 2. The fact that theorists and practitioners habitually discuss developments in international politics in terms of the balance of power indicates, moreover, that whatever constructivists argue, it is widely assumed that power can be measured but that the measurement is only meaningful when it is cast in structural terms.

Constructivists, however, are unconvinced by this argument. They insist that although it may be true that practitioners often seem to agree on the components of power that come into play, and the thresholds that have to be crossed before a state qualifies as a great power this is not because there is an external and 'objectivized measure' of what constitutes a great power. On the contrary, a measure exists because diplomats have come to an agreement about what has to be counted. So, far from power being a 'materialist necessity', it can only be seen as 'a social (and often politically bargained) construct' (Guzzini, 2004: 542). But, tucked away in a footnote, Guzzini (2004: 561) then admits that there must, as a consequence, be some similarity between money and power because they both represent what Searle (1995) calls 'social facts', although Guzzini insists that money is much more institutionalized than power.

The constructivist view of power has been gaining ground. Buzan (2004b: 31), for example, who provides one of the most searching and systematic analyses of polarity and who takes it for granted that 'understanding the global power structure is an essential starting point for thinking about international relations', accepts the need to take

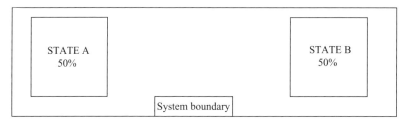

Figure 6.2 Power distribution in a bipolar system

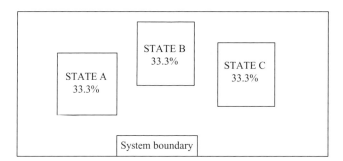

Figure 6.3 Power distribution in a tripolar system

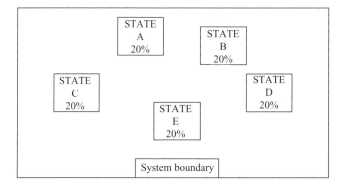

Figure 6.4 Power distribution in a five pole system

constructivism on board in conjunction with Waltz's materialist approach to power. He argues that Waltz's approach promotes an undifferentiated conception of great powers that derives from a Euro-centric view of the world. Buzan associates this position with 'simple polarity' and his aim is to develop a conception of 'complex polarity' that not only makes more sense of the contemporary world, but also makes it possible to rethink how Europe developed from a global historical perspective. Europe engaged in a process of global expansion that persisted for more than 400 years and over time opened up a fundamental difference between the European great powers that engaged in expansion and those that did not. Buzan (2004b: 48) argues that although this distinction failed to register during the era of European expansion, a much richer conception of polarity can be established if it is now taken on board. We can then see Europe as a region in a global system rather than simply the cockpit of world politics. This perspective then permits Buzan to distinguish those major European powers that only had regional interests and concerns from those that also had extraregional interests. This move allows him to reclassify some major European states as regional rather than great powers.

In an even more radical move, Buzan argues that the contemporary distinction that is sometimes drawn between super powers and great powers needs to be clarified and applied to both global and contemporary history. The resulting threefold distinction that he establishes between super powers, great powers, and regional powers, provides the basic structure for his analysis of complex polarity.[23] He recognizes, of course, that distinguishing states on this basis is not at all straightforward and that relying exclusively on a material approach to power becomes inadequate. He agrees with the constructivists that realists have not managed to establish an effective composite measure of power, and that disaggregating power is not an effective solution on its own. However, he accepts that attempts to use formal recognition of great power status are also unsatisfactory, as the widespread criticism of the current membership of the Security Council in the United Nations illustrates. Instead, in line with constructivist thinking, he relies on a reputational approach, arguing that 'the main criterion for a state to be a system-level power is that it is treated as such by the other powers' (Buzan, 2004b: 67).[24] He goes on to suggest that a system-level power assumes 'not only that its security depends on the

---

[23] Huntington (1999) develops a similar classification but fails to offer allocation criteria.

[24] Although Buzan does not cite the reference, this line of argument was developed in an important and now undercited piece of research by Singer and Small (1966), that uses the establishment of diplomatic missions to establish the reputational status of states in the international system.

global power structure but also that it is able to influence that structure'. It follows that other states will view it as a potential hegemon or crucial member of the global balance of power.

On this basis Buzan then stipulates that super powers require 'broad-spectrum capabilities exercised across the whole of the international system'. In the nineteenth century Britain, France and arguably Russia occupied this rank. In the interwar period it was held by the United States, Britain and the Soviet Union. In the cold war Britain dropped out of the equation, and after the cold war, the Soviet Union followed suit, leaving the United States as the lone super power. Great powers, unlike super powers, do not require system-wide capabilities in all sectors. For Buzan what then distinguishes great powers from regional powers is that 'they are responded to by others on the basis of system-level calculations, as well as regional ones'. Drawing on this formulation, he identifies Germany, the United States and Japan as great powers at the end of the nineteenth century. After 1919, France drops down to this level and the United States moves up to super power status. Then, in the cold war, China, Germany, Japan (and possibly Britain and France) all possess great power status. After the cold war, Buzan associates Britain, France and Germany with the European Union representing a composite great power in conjunction with Japan, China and Russia.[25] The super powers and great powers identified by Buzan are, of course, disputable.[26] But, nevertheless, Buzan's formulation of a three-tiered system allows him to break free of the Eurocentric framework that continues to bedevil the study of international relations. So during the nineteenth century, countries like Italy and the Austro-Hungarian Empire drop out of the systemic framework and into the European regional framework. The fact that Waltz retains these states in his list of great powers is the product of his purely materialist and Eurocentric methodology. Their elimination from Buzan's list reflects one of the strengths of his approach, although it perhaps underestimates the extent to which Europe at that time still constituted the hub

---

[25] Buzan (2004b) focuses primarily on the systemic level of analysis, whereas Buzan and Waever (2003) develop the regional level of analysis.

[26] Buzan, for example, acknowledges that Schweller (1993) establishes a different set of super powers for the interwar period – the United States, Russia and Germany. But this is based on a purely materialist basis, rather than the more nuanced and constructivist formulation that Buzan employs.

of the international system, or, at any rate, the extent to which members of the international system operated on this basis; and that is a
key to Buzan's designation of super/great/regional powers.

On the face of it, an important advantage of Buzan's approach is that
there are also no structural consequences to distinguishing between
super powers and great powers because there is nothing categorical
about the distinction; it is primarily a question of lowering the entry
threshold. Great powers are just like super powers, but with fewer
material capabilities and a lower commitment to influencing or maintaining the existing power structure. Both of these criteria are considered compatible with Waltz's approach. Waltz is very clear that as
well as bringing more autonomy and a greater level of safety, increased
power 'permits wider ranges of action', on the one hand, and 'a bigger
stake in the system and the ability to act for its sake', on the other
(Waltz, 1979: 194–5). In the cold war era when he was writing, Waltz
did not think that, with the possible exception of Europe, there were
any states that had any possibility of developing a global role in the
near future – by which he meant before the start of the new millennium.
And for Europe to enter the picture, what was to become the European
Union would have to develop both military power and political competence.[27] Although Waltz (1979: 179–80) accepted that these developments were possible, he saw no country coming close to challenging
the leading position occupied by the United States and he concluded
that the question to ask is not 'whether a third or fourth country will
enter the circle of great powers in the foreseeable future but rather
whether the Soviet Union can keep up'.

If the answer to this question had been that the Soviet Union could
not keep up, then the implication that followed from Waltz's analysis was crystal clear: bipolarity would give way to unipolarity. Given
this assessment, it was remiss of Waltz not to open up the question
of unipolarity. If he had done so, then it is possible that he would
have been compelled to anticipate Buzan's move and to lower the
great power threshold and distinguish between great powers and super

---

[27] Only in the twenty-first century did this capacity start to develop. As *The
Economist* (2006: 29–30) argued, 'If the ability to project force is now
the hallmark of an independent foreign policy, the EU could be said, at
last, to be getting a bit more bloody, bold and resolute.' It adds, however,
that 'Europe's foreign policy is too young to be judged by its record.'

powers. On the other hand, he also might have been more willing to entertain the possibility of an enduring unipolar world. In practice what he seems to have done in the wake of the Soviet Union's demise is to lower the great power threshold. But apart from the fact that he fails to address this issue explicitly, the very logic of his approach should have encouraged him when writing *Theory of International Politics* to explore the implications of unipolarity. No economist would refuse to take monopoly seriously on the grounds that it is 'unnatural' – Waltz's description of unipolarity – and yet that essentially is the position that Waltz (2000b) has adopted in the post-cold war era. Given the significance that Waltz attaches to the economics analogy and the importance that economists attach to monopoly, the failure to open up the issue of unipolarity in *Theory of International Politics* is surprising, while the focus on multipolarity in the post-cold war era becomes distinctly odd.

Because the Soviet Union not only failed to keep up with the United States but actually fell apart, Waltz was left with a theoretical lacuna which he made no attempt to fill. Confronted by the lacuna, instead of following in the steps of Wohlforth (1999) who does endeavour to identify the theoretical consequences of unipolarity, Buzan chooses to jump ship and join the constructivist bandwagon arguing that 'there does not seem to be much theoretical mileage in hanging on to general hypotheses based on simple numbers' (Buzan, 2004b: 74); and he is confident that his notion of complex polarity will give him more theoretical purchase than Waltz's notion of simple polarity.[28] Buzan argues, for example, that if constructivists are right and 'anarchy is what states make of it' then it should be the case that polarity is also what states make of it. Drawing on Wendt's notion of culture, Buzan hypothesizes that the impact of polarity will be different depending on whether the system is made up of friends, rivals, or enemies.[29] But as we will see in the next section, Buzan's line of argument considerably underplays

---

[28] It is revealing that Buzan makes no attempt to critique Wohlforth's attempt to use structural theorizing to open up the idea of unipolarity.

[29] Wendt (1999) opens the way for this move when he examines the role of the balance of power in the context of Hobbesian, Lockean and Kantian anarchies. But Buzan is building in more complexity by arguing that, at least in theory, the impact of culture will vary depending upon the degree of polarity.

the 'theoretical mileage' that can be obtained from polarity.[30] Waltz should, in fact, have made more of the argument that 'anarchy is what polarity makes of it', although he could have developed this argument more effectively if he had extended his theory to embrace unipolarity. What Buzan is endeavouring to do, by contrast, is to establish a synthesis between Waltzian neorealism and Wendtian constructivism. If Goddard and Nexon's account of Waltz is accepted, then this move is unproblematic, from Waltz's perspective, provided that it is accepted that Buzan is looking at the impact of the cultural system on the political system.

Having looked at the role that anarchy and the distribution of power play in establishing the political structure of the international system, it is necessary to look briefly at the character of the units that constitute the international system. This represents a third factor that defines the international political structure. It is much more important in the context of hierarchical political systems because there the units are functionally differentiated. By contrast, the logic of anarchy dictates that the units are 'alike in the tasks that they face, though not in their abilities to perform them' (Waltz, 1979: 96). In the next section we will see how this feature of the units is reproduced and, indeed, reinforced. But before looking at how the political structure of the international system affects the behaviour of states we need to examine one more criticism levelled at Waltz by the constructivists that relates to the character of the units. Wendt argues that despite Waltz's insistence that his concept of the international political structure eschews all unit level factors, it does, in practice, embrace an implicit motivational factor. Following Schweller (1993; 1994; 1996), Wendt argues that, for Waltz, states are 'security-seeking' agents that want to preserve what they already have. It follows that Waltzian states are 'satisfied' or 'status quo' states as opposed to 'revisionist' states that want to make fundamental changes to the international system. Wendt (1999: 105) insists that he is not criticizing Waltz for making this move, because from a constructivist perspective, even the most structural of theories have no alternative but to make motivational assumptions. But he insists that an anarchy of status quo states will have very different characteristics to an anarchy of revisionist states because the meanings that anarchy and the

---

[30] It would have been more difficult to do this if he had taken Wohlforth (1999) into account.

distribution of power have for these two sets of states will be quite different. He agrees with Schweller that while status quo states may aim to maintain a balance of power, revisionist states will bandwagon in aggressive coalitions that aim to maximize their chances of changing the system. As a consequence, Wendt argues that the effects of anarchy and the distribution of power will depend on what states want and will, as a consequence, reflect the underlying distribution of interests that exists among the states.

This line of argument has proved to be extraordinarily persuasive and it is now widely accepted that Waltz needs to be classified as a defensive realist, to distinguish him from offensive realists, like Mearsheimer (2001), who assume that states are necessarily expansionist or revisionist in orientation. There is no doubt that Mearsheimer's theory does embrace a motivational dimension, but it is equally clear that Waltz's aim is to eschew motivations.[31] Waltz (1979: 91) accepts that survival 'is a prerequisite to achieving any goals that states may have'; but he is also clear that beyond the survival motive 'the aims of states may be endlessly varied; they may range from the ambition to conquer the world to the desire merely to be left alone'.[32] The central point that Waltz wants to make, however, is that anarchy persists whatever the motivations happen to be and it is this phenomenon that he wishes to explain.[33] Whereas Wendt argues that the ideas underpinning the prevailing culture will determine the nature of the balance of power, Waltz insists that it is the distribution of power. The aim of the next section is to examine why and how Waltz privileges the power distribution in his account of the balance of power.

The balance of power

Waltz's balance of power theory is animated by the logic of small numbers and it presupposes that the structure of the international system is defined by a limited number of great powers. It is, of course, possible

---

[31] Waltz (1979: 122) acknowledges that his theory 'makes assumptions about the interests and motives of states without explaining them'.

[32] Wendt (1999: 104) argues that it is 'trivially true' that states aim to survive.

[33] From Mearsheimer's (2001) perspective, Schweller fails to take account of the radical uncertainty generated by anarchy, making it impossible to distinguish between status quo and revisionist states. But as we will see in the next section, this is not a route that Waltz wishes to pursue.

to envisage an international system that is made up of a very large number of states that are approximately equal in power, but the logic of anarchy associated with such a system would take a very distinctive form that would contrast sharply to an international system that is regulated by the logic of small numbers. Although Waltz's theory does not attempt to embrace an international system characterized by large numbers, it can be inferred from his overall position that interaction within such a system would take on some of the characteristics associated with an economic system or market defined by perfect competition.[34] It might seem, therefore, that a system of this kind would look like a state of nature because, for example, there is no incentive to engage in alliance formation. But economists would certainly treat this analogy as inappropriate because they assume that the market is embedded in a social and political system. As a consequence, they take it for granted that a shopkeeper, for example, will hand over an expensive item in return for a cheque, which is, in fact, a piece of paper with no intrinsic value. Economic theory cannot explain this behaviour, but economists do not see the need to, because they buy into Goddard and Nexon's structural functional argument that we can separate out political, social and economic systems for analytical purposes. One of the factors underpinning this chapter is the extent to which Waltz also draws on this argument.

Central to Waltz's argument is the assumption that because the political structure of the international system is defined by a small number of great powers, as the number of great powers changes, so there are critical points where step level shifts occur and the prevailing logic of anarchy takes on fundamentally different characteristics. Although Waltz accepts that marginal changes will occur whenever a great power is added to or subtracted from the existing number, he is only interested in what he considers to be the most dramatic shift that occurs with a movement from a multipolar to a bipolar system.[35] The logic of anarchy takes a very different form when the number of great powers increases from two to three or more. From Waltz's perspective, it is not that 'anarchy is what states make of it', in Wendt's memorable phrase, but rather 'anarchy is what polarity makes of it'. Change the structure,

---

[34] Kaplan (1962) argues that systems of this kind display system dominance.
[35] Waltz accepts that a tripolar system is also distinctive, but it is subsumed within the multipolar system. But see Schweller (1993; 1998).

here defined in terms of the number of great powers in the system, and the nature of anarchy can undergo a very substantial transformation. What Waltz should also have observed, therefore, is that a diminution from two great powers to one, represents just as big a shift in the logic of anarchy as multipolarity to bipolarity. Extending the line of argument developed in *Theory of International Politics*, Waltz should have argued in the wake of the Soviet Union's demise that unipolarity was going to be a very enduring feature of the international system. Instead, there was a significant lobby that argued that there would be a rapid return to a multipolar system. This prediction runs completely counter to the core logic of Waltz's theory and it reflects a failure by neorealists to take the full implications of structural thinking on board. To some extent, neorealists cannot have processed the full implications of how the logic of anarchy changes with the shift from multipolarity to bipolarity. Once the two logics are exposed, it then becomes easier to see how unipolarity generates a third structural logic which makes a shift back to either bipolarity or multipolarity extremely difficult to achieve.

In this section, however, we look in more detail at how the structural logic derived from anarchy plays out in the context of multipolarity and bipolarity. Waltz's starting point is that the anarchic structure constrains the behaviour of states in such a way that both systems will be reproduced by structures and processes that produce a balance of power. From Waltz's perspective, therefore, it really does not matter if the system is made up of revisionist states or status quo states, because whatever aims individual states may have, the international structure pushes them to pursue policies that result in a balance of power and the reproduction of the system. Waltz is very clear, however, that the system has not been designed or programmed in some way to achieve this common outcome. The structure of the international system does not operate like a boiler with a thermostat that maintains a constant temperature. Indeed, it is not possible to observe how the international structure operates, because there is only a set of interacting states: two in the case of bipolarity and more than two in the case of multipolarity. But the system gets reproduced because the interactions are profoundly affected by two 'pervasive processes' – competition and socialization – that are generated, according to Waltz (1979: 74), by the anarchic structure. It follows that states are only indirectly constrained by the structure of the international system. Although socialization and

Structures		Processes	Outcomes
Ordering principle	*Distribution of power*		
Anarchy	Bipolarity	Socialization *internal balancing* Competition/Management	Bipolar balance of power
	Multipolarity	Socialization *internal and external balancing* Competition	Multipolar balance of power

Figure 6.5 Waltz's structural conception of the balance of power

competition are very different processes, Waltz argues that both are a product of anarchy and each of them then significantly constrains the behaviour of states. So Waltz's position is that anarchy precipitates two processes that constrain states to act in a way that ensures that the anarchic system is constantly reproduced (see Figure 6.5). However, because bipolarity and multipolarity are distinct systems, Waltz recognizes that the two processes reproduce their structures in rather different ways.

Waltz, however, does not make it easy to understand either competition or socialization in international politics because he explains both primarily in the context of large number systems and, as already noted, the logic of these systems does not translate neatly through to small number systems. This is particularly true in the context of competition and socialization, because Waltz argues that both of these processes work on the consequentialist argument that those units failing either to compete effectively or to conform to the rules of the system (thereby remaining unsocialized) are eliminated from the system. The logic associated with perfect competition is used to illustrate the competitive process. Waltz (1979: 137) argues that firms that are 'proficient survive, while others, less skilfully managed, go bankrupt' and he goes on to acknowledge that the elimination of inefficiency 'is a condition for the good performance of the economy'. But as Waltz recognizes, this is not a very useful model for thinking about international politics, because economists are interested in the efficient production of goods and services, whereas in international politics, by contrast, interest is primarily focused on the fate of the great powers. More to the point, while economists accept that bankruptcy is a common phenomenon under conditions of perfect competition, great powers rarely go out of existence.

To account for the survival of units, a more sociological approach is required. But having assessed Waltz's use of competition and socialization, Wendt (1999: 101) concludes that there is 'little that is "social" about his theory'. But this assessment relies too heavily on the use that Waltz makes of perfect competition. As noted in the previous section, Waltz stresses that the logic associated with small number systems is quite different from the logic associated with large number systems. In small number systems, units are required to take account of each other as well as the structure of the system and so they are inherently more social in orientation than the firms operating in a market defined by perfect competition. Socialization and competition, therefore, take on a different form when applied to great powers in the international political system. The most effective way to clarify the nature of competition and socialization in the context of small number systems, therefore, is to see how Waltz actually applies these processes to bipolar and multipolar systems.

Although bipolarity and multipolarity are both maintained in Waltz's theory by a balance of power, Waltz offers very different assessments of how the balance of power operates in these two systems because this is essentially what his theory is designed to do. Waltz (1979: 71) insists that a systems theory 'explains changes across systems, not within them'. On the contrary, systems theory can only 'explain and predict continuity within a system' (Waltz, 1979: 69). In comparing and contrasting these two systems, however, Waltz locates them within specific historical contexts. Multipolarity is identified with the European great power system and bipolarity is discussed in terms of relations between the United States and the Soviet Union during the cold war. Waltz's main aim is to show that a bipolar system is much more likely to promote stability than a multipolar system because the structural constraints associated with bipolarity generate a more stable balance of power than those associated with multipolarity.

Multipolarity and the balance of power

Focusing first on multipolarity, Waltz (1979: 162–3) acknowledges that it makes a 'consequential' difference if a multipolar system is constituted by three or four great powers rather than six or seven.

However, he demonstrates that if we focus on the period from 1700 to 1935, there was never a time when there were fewer than five great powers interacting. His analysis of multipolarity, therefore, works on the premise that there are at least five great powers in existence and that it makes no consequential difference if numbers rise beyond this point because the main structural constraints are not fundamentally affected by the entry of additional great powers into the arena.

Waltz's (1979: 70) general assessment is that politics among the European great powers 'tended toward the model of a zero-sum game'. In other words, the European states operated under conditions where a material gain for any one of the great powers came at the expense of the others. So, for example, when Germany acquired Alsace and Lorraine from France in 1871, Germany's gain was exactly equivalent to France's loss.[36] Waltz is very clear that his theory could not have predicted this move by Germany, although his theory does presuppose that moves of this kind will take place. Indeed, a consequence of all great powers wishing to survive as independent actors is that, on the one hand, they can never be sure what other states are going to do in the future, while on the other, and just as importantly, they can be quite certain that their relative power capabilities will change over time in ways that cannot be foreseen. Because all the great powers are committed to their own survival, both of these factors have to be taken into account. And by pursuing strategies that enable them to survive, the great powers simultaneously and, from Waltz's perspective, unintentionally, ensure that the anarchic structure of the international system is reproduced. By reproducing a multipolar anarchy, however, the great powers are also perpetuating the conditions of uncertainty about the future that require them to rely on a self-help posture and competitive strategies to ensure their own survival. It follows that great powers are perpetually insecure and are unwilling to make any move that results in any deterioration of their existing position.

Although the emergence of additional great powers does, according to Waltz, increase the existing level of uncertainty, it does not alter the basic structural constraints that he associates with multipolar anarchy. This structural feature of the international system presupposes that self-help is 'necessarily the principle of action' for the great powers

---

[36] This example, however, ignores the growth of nationalism. Acquiring a hostile population could prove to be a liability.

(Waltz, 1979: 111). Two important factors follow from this insight. First, each great power has no alternative but to spend 'a portion of its efforts, not in forwarding its own good, but in providing the means of protecting itself against others' (1979: 105). Second, the great powers are predisposed to eschew cooperation and to adopt a persistently competitive attitude towards each other. Waltz advances a number of reasons why great powers prefer to go it alone rather than establish enduring cooperative links. On the one hand, they fear that cooperation can lead to dependency and so they prefer to push in the direction of autarky and self-sufficiency and/or to engage in 'imperial thrusts to widen the scope of their control' (Waltz, 1979: 106).[37] On the other hand, great powers also fear that the fruits of cooperation will be divided in a way that leaves them at a disadvantage. Drawing on the theory of oligopolistic firms, Waltz (1979: 106) argues that great powers 'must be more concerned with relative strength than with absolute advantage'.[38] This phenomenon makes cooperation extremely difficult to achieve because in a situation where a set of great powers can all benefit by cooperating, the parties will still not agree to cooperate despite the potential for absolute gains all round, if one of the partners is due to receive a larger gain than the others and thereby improve its relative position. Waltz is certainly not saying that cooperation is impossible under conditions of anarchy. But he is suggesting that anarchy generates a competitive environment that militates against cooperation.

The constraints associated with anarchy, however, only provide half of the story that lies behind Waltz's structural account of the multipolar balance of power. The other half is linked to the distribution of power. In any anarchic system, Waltz argues, the units are acutely conscious of their relative power positions. So, any move made by a great power to increase its internal strength will be observed and monitored by the other great powers. Waltz goes onto argue, moreover, that because of the fear of falling behind, there is also a powerful tendency to emulate such moves by the other great powers. The result is that the great

---

[37] Waltz does not develop this theme at length. But it is not only economists who have been interested in this phenomenon of exchange leading to power differentiation. See Blau (1964).

[38] The distinction between relative and absolute gains has given rise to a substantial body of literature and debate. See Baldwin (1993) for an assessment of this debate. For a more recent discussion, see Mosher (2003).

powers develop an increasing number of common features over time, leading Waltz to characterize them as 'like units'.[39] This internal process, therefore, is intimately connected with the distribution of power and represents a crucial dimension of the balance of power. Waltz refers to this process as internal balancing, which he views as a systemic response. In other words, the great powers are not simply reacting to each other, they are also aware of reacting to each other in the context of the system of which they form a part. 'Each is playing a game *and* they are playing the game together' as Waltz (1979: 75) puts it.

But emulation is only one aspect of the socialization process. Waltz is also aware that the international political system operates in the context of a body of norms and rules that help to regulate the behaviour of the great powers. Waltz's theory is not intended to account for the emergence or the maintenance of this international social system except insofar as it impinges on the international political system. To survive in a competitive multipolar system, the great powers know that there are times when they need each other's assistance and, as a consequence, Waltz (1979: 128) identifies the existence of 'successful practices' that facilitate these links. He cites the conventions of diplomacy as an example of such practices. It is clear, however, that for Waltz these conventions are not maintained because the great powers have internalized the values that underpin them. They are maintained on utilitarian grounds. But what then happens when a nonconformist great power emerges and decides to ignore such conventions? Waltz argues that it will be socialized by the system as the nonconformist state discovers that other great powers are unwilling to form alliances with it.[40] As a consequence, the more competitive the environment, and the closer

---

[39] Although this tendency has been observed by other theorists (Tilly, 1990), it has been argued that very different kinds of political actors persisted in the aftermath of the medieval era and that the emergence of the nation state as the dominant form of actor took some considerable time; this argues against the emulation thesis and requires a different kind of explanation (Spruyt, 1994). Nevertheless, emulation does seem to have been an element in the way that great powers have evolved. Waltz (1979: 124) insists, however, that the theory does not lead to the expectation that 'emulation among states will proceed to the point where competitors become identical'.

[40] Armstrong (1993) and Halliday (1999) provide important discussions of how nonconformist states get drawn into international society.

the nonconformist great power is to the centre of the system, the faster it will be socialized.[41] Although Waltz fails to develop this point, it follows his overall line of argument that the tendency for great powers to operate on the basis of common norms also needs to be treated as an aspect of internal balancing. As Waltz (1979: 128) puts it, the 'close juxtaposition of states promotes their sameness through the disadvantages that arise from a failure to conform to successful practices'.[42]

The internal balancing that occurs as the result of socialization and emulation is, therefore, very much a product of the competitive environment associated with anarchy.[43] But it also presupposes the existence of a multipolar system. Nonconformity can only be punished if there are several great powers available to punish the nonconformist. Indeed, it can be argued, the more great powers that there are operating in the system, the easier it is to bring a nonconformist into line. From this perspective, then, it appears that an expansion in the number of great powers has the potential to increase the stability of the system.[44] Although Waltz does not explore this line of argument, it is effectively overridden by his analysis of the inherent problems associated with multipolarity. Waltz recognizes that even with relatively small numbers of great powers, the problems of comprehending what is happening to the balance of power within the system increases exponentially with the addition of each new great power because of the

---

[41] According to Waltz (1979: 128) the socialization of nonconformist states 'proceeds at a pace that is set by the extent of their involvement in the system'.

[42] Buzan (1993) draws on this argument to demonstrate that a common culture is not the only basis for the emergence of common rules and practices. It may appear paradoxical that a competitive system will generate rules, but it certainly reinforces Bull's notion that the balance of power will operate differently in an international system that is mediated by an international society.

[43] This raises again the question of whether Wendt is right to argue that there is little that is social about Waltz's theory. The presumption is sometimes made that socialization involves the 'internalization of norms'. See, for example, Alderson (2001). But Theis (2003: 547) argues that sociologists have come to see this link between socialization and internalization as a mistake and that nonconformists 'do not internalize norms, rather they simply alter their behaviour to avoid sanctions'.

[44] This argument reinforces Schweller's (1996) argument that Waltz is a defensive realist. But this ignores Waltz's overall position that multipolarity is inherently unstable.

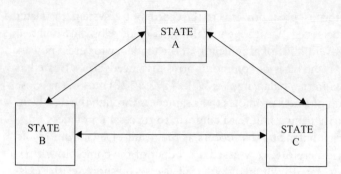

Figure 6.6 The potential for alliance formation in a tripolar system

potential the increase creates for external balancing by alliance formation. In a bipolar system, each great power only has to take account
of the power capabilities of its opposite number and there is no potential for external balancing. But in a multipolar system it is not only
necessary to focus on the power capabilities of each member of the
system, it is also essential to take account of the potential for alliance
formation. If there are three great powers in the system, then there is
a potential for three bilateral alliances to form. On the other hand,
when there are four great powers in the system, then there is a potential for six alliances to form. And when there are five great powers
in the system, then this generates the potential for ten possible bilateral alliances to be formed in total. But by adding only one extra
great power, the total number of bilateral alliances extends to 15; add
another and it goes up to 21 (see Figures 6.6 to 6.8). The total number
of potential bilateral alliances in any system is given by a very simple
formula:[45]

$$\frac{(n-1)n}{2} \qquad (n = \text{number of great powers in the system})$$

The formula reveals just how quickly the potential for alliance formation expands with every additional great power added to the system.

Despite the importance attached to alliance formation in multipolar systems, Snyder (1997) argues that it remains an understudied

[45] Waltz (1979: 135) draws on this formula, not to illustrate the point being
made here, but to reveal why bargaining becomes increasingly difficult
when the number of great powers involved increases.

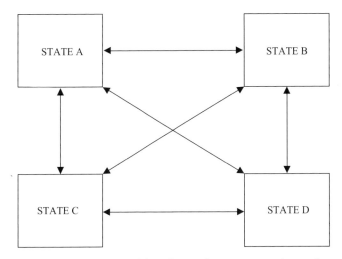

Figure 6.7 The potential for alliance formation in a four pole system

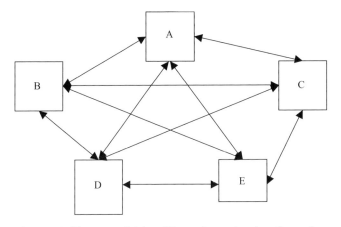

Figure 6.8 The potential for alliance formation in a five pole system

issue.[46] Nevertheless, according to Waltz (1979: 163), the prevailing view is that multipolarity is a source of stability in the international system because the potential for alliance formation introduces an element

[46] Snyder (1997) provides one of the most important attempts to develop a theoretically informed approach to alliance formation. He identifies three other attempts to develop a general comprehensive theory of alliances: Liska (1962), Holsti, Hopmann and Sullivan (1973) and Walt (1987).

of flexibility into the distribution of power.[47] This assessment is underpinned by the sociological argument that conflict can be functional
for any society when membership in competing groups overlaps. It is
argued that the resulting cross-cutting cleavages – what Simmel calls
the web of conflict – help to integrate society.[48] Waltz, by contrast,
insists that the structural constraints associated with bipolarity generate a much higher level of stability than the structural constraints
associated with multipolarity. He views the flexibility associated with
alliance formation as a source of instability that can promote war and
crises as well a high degree of insecurity. The problem is that flexibility
renders international politics much more complex, and in the process,
introduces a whole range of uncertainties. Moreover, as Waltz (1979:
165) notes, uncertainties 'about who threatens whom, about who will
oppose whom, and about who will gain or lose from the actions of
other states accelerate as the number of states increases'. The complexity and uncertainty generated by the potential for alliance formation
among the great powers has inevitable consequences for balance of
power theory. Indeed, it raises serious questions about how to identify a balance of power. As Waltz (1979: 124) admits, because 'only
a loosely defined and inconstant condition of balance is predicted, it
is difficult to say that any given distribution of power falsifies the theory'. In other words, what the balance of power theory predicts is that
by striving to maintain their own autonomy, the great powers pursue
uncoordinated strategies that constantly impact on the overall distribution of power capabilities and have the unintended consequence of
reproducing the anarchic international system.

   Waltz recognizes, therefore, that there is no single or simple definition of what is meant by the balance of power. Instead of attempting
to offer such a definition, he associates the balance of power with a
number of very different conditions. He accepts that the most 'tranquil'
and 'morally desirable condition' has sometimes been depicted as an
international system where the balance of power is defined by 'a world
of many states, all of them approximate equals in power' (Waltz, 1979:
132). Waltz attacks this formulation, however, on two grounds. First,

---

[47] This is Morgenthau's view, although as we saw in Chapter 4, he accepts
   that bipolarity could generate more stability than multipolarity.
[48] The argument stems from Simmel (1955) and was popularized by Coser
   (1956). This approach underpins Deutsch and Singer (1964) and was
   explored empirically by Singer, Bremer and Stuckey (1972).

he argues that this formulation is unrealistic because extreme inequality is an inherent feature of the state system and at the pinnacle of the power structure, 'no more than small numbers of states have ever coexisted as approximate equals' (Waltz, 1979: 132). Second, he argues that a large number of equal powers generates the potential for enormous complexity and uncertainty and, as a consequence, inevitable and persistent instability. Although inequality cannot guarantee peace and stability, it does create a context where these conditions can potentially emerge. From Waltz's perspective, the number of great powers has never reached the point where the degree of alliance flexibility is so great that it becomes impossible to conceive of the system in terms of a relatively stable balance of power.

On the other hand, Waltz accepts that even with the limited number of great powers that have co-existed within the modern European states system, there have not often been occasions when it is possible to conceive of the balance of power in terms of two evenly matched alliance systems. According to Waltz, only if power politics is played really hard will players be pressed into two rival camps. Indeed, he suggests that 'so complicated is the business of making and maintaining alliances that the game may be played hard enough to produce that result only under the pressure of war' (Waltz, 1979: 167). Even under these conditions, however, Waltz accepts that a multipolar balance of power will be required to operate in two very different ways. If there are revisionist or hegemonic states in the system, that wish to dominate the other great powers, then stability will only be preserved if there are states willing to act in a way that will 'tilt the balance against the would-be aggressors' in the international system (Waltz, 1979: 164). But the position most frequently associated with Waltz asserts that balancing involves joining forces with the weaker of two alliances systems (Waltz, 1979: 126).[49] Both of these moves, **how**ever, have the effect of defending the status quo.

Waltz accepts, however, that states do not rush to preserve the status quo. On the contrary, he identifies the existence of considerable friction in a multipolar system that discourages states from joining forces to maintain the system. Even when two or more states confront a common threat, there is no certainty that they will ally because there is a persistent tendency for states to free ride on the efforts of the first

---

[49] Waltz argues that by joining the weaker alliance a state increases its bargaining power.

state in the firing line. For the same reason, even after an alliance has been formed, there is still a constant danger that states will defect once war has broken out (Waltz, 1979: 166–7). However, Waltz draws back from the offensive realist assumption that the default position for all states is to maximize power.[50] If this was the case, Waltz (1979: 126) argues, then states would invariably join the stronger alliance and 'we would see not balances forming but a world hegemony forged'.

Nevertheless, although it is the case that throughout European history, attempts to establish world hegemony were always thwarted, Waltz insists that throughout this period, multipolarity made it extraordinarily difficult to manage the destabilizing events and conditions that characterize international politics. Indeed, from his perspective, multipolarity is, in part, the source of the problem and a series of structural problems are associated with multipolarity in any system where the logic of small numbers prevails: (i) there are too few great powers to make the effects of defection inconsequential; (ii) the flexibility of alliances keeps relations of friendship and enmity fluid; (iii) the flexibility of alliances renders uncertain any estimate by the great powers of the present or future balance of power; (iv) the actions of any one state have the potential to threaten the security of the others; (v) there are too many great powers for any of them to see for sure what is happening; (vi) there are too few states to make what is happening anywhere in the system a matter of indifference; and (vii) there are too few great powers to prevent the search for allies becoming a source of tension and hostility (Waltz, 1979: 168–76). It follows, therefore, that in any multipolar system, the balance of power theory predicts that whenever a great power increases its power capabilities, the other great powers will respond and, in the first instance, they will make 'internal efforts to strengthen themselves, however distasteful or difficult such efforts might be' (Waltz, 1979: 125). But, in the second place, when internal efforts are deemed insufficient to contend with the new distribution of power, great powers will turn to alliances to improve their power position. If bilateral alliances then start to coalesce and two coalitions emerge, Waltz argues that non-aligned great powers will either oppose the side that contains an aspiring hegemon or join the weaker side. But

[50] Waltz (1979: 126) argues 'We do not expect the strong to combine with the strong in order to increase the extent of their power over others, but rather to square off and look for allies who might help them.'

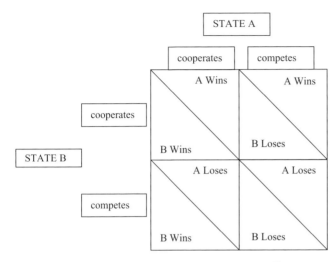

Figure 6.9 Matrix for the prisoners' dilemma game[51]

the more significant point that Waltz makes is that even if war breaks out, 'the unity of alliances is far from complete' because states 'continue to jockey for advantage and to worry about the constellation of forces that will form once the contest is over' (Waltz, 1979: 167). It follows that the structure of a multipolar system promotes a constant and high degree of uncertainty about the balance of power.

Bipolarity and the balance of power

The balance of power in a bipolar system is viewed by Waltz in a very different light to a multipolar system. He tends to view multipolarity from a zero-sum perspective and so although he acknowledges that states within an alliance may share mutual interests, he argues that these interests will tend to be negative as, for example, when states share a common enemy. Across the system, moreover, multipolarity pushes states to think in terms of winners and losers and relative rather than absolute gains. Waltz acknowledges, nevertheless, that the

---

[51] What this matrix fails to show is that A and B lose less if they both compete than if A or B cooperates and the other party competes. By the same token, A and B win less if they both cooperate than if A or B competes and the other party cooperates. It is this disparity in pay-offs that generates the dilemma.

international political system needs to be characterized in rather more complex terms – in line with the two-person 'prisoners' dilemma' game where 'if each of two players follows his own interest, both end up worse off than if each acted to achieve joint interests' (Waltz, 1979: 109; see Figure 6.9). Waltz recognizes that this model applies, in principle, even in a multipolar world, but he presupposes that it has much more relevance in a bipolar world, where the structure of the system is much more conducive to the achievement of joint gains. As a result, the two great powers are much more able to manage international affairs constructively than are the great powers in a multipolar world (Waltz, 1979: 210).

So Waltz's central argument is that a change in political structure will bring about a change in both expectations about how political actors will behave and the outcomes that their interactions will produce. The shift from multipolarity to bipolarity represents a structural change of this kind. Anarchy persists, of course, as the other key political structure and so competition remains as one of the dominant processes in the system. Indeed, in a bipolar world, Waltz argues, the zero-sum character of the competition is even more starkly apparent than in the multipolar world because the identity of the enemy is not in question (Waltz, 1979: 170–1). But having identified the continuing importance of competition, the main point that Waltz wishes to get across is that for structural reasons, competition has much less pernicious consequences in a bipolar world. In particular, its impact on the ability of the two great powers to manage international affairs is much less inhibiting.

The step level change in the ability of the great powers to manage international affairs arises from the reduction in the number of system units to two great powers and the consequential elimination of external balancing. Although Waltz accepts that alliances continue to play an important role in the bipolar world, they no longer play a structural role because the allies of the two great powers only consist of secondary states. The resources provided by these allies are useful but they are not now indispensable and alliance management becomes a much more straightforward exercise (Waltz, 1979: 169). And much more important, the complexity and uncertainty associated with external balancing drop out of the equation. The focus is now exclusively on internal balancing because the great powers recognize that 'imbalances can be righted only by their internal efforts' (Waltz, 1979: 163; see Figure 6.10). Waltz (1979: 168) argues that because calculations are easier to make, internal balancing is much more reliable and precise

Figure 6.10 The balance of power in a bipolar system

than external balancing. As a consequence, the two great powers are less likely to misjudge their relative strengths and so the level of uncertainty that is endemic with external balancing is very considerably reduced in a bipolar system, making it much easier for a stable balance of power to emerge.

The reduction of uncertainty, however, is not the only reason, according to Waltz, why bipolarity is likely to be much more stable and easy to manage than multipolarity. Although Waltz (1979: 136; 195–6) is well aware that the dangers of market failure and free riding are inherent in any anarchic system, even a bipolar one, he argues that as the number of great powers decreases, so their stake in the system and their ability and incentive to maintain the status quo rises.[52] So while Waltz (1979: 175) acknowledges that competitive processes persist in a bipolar system, he also argues that the dangers attached to this process in a nuclear world suggest that the 'condition of mutual opposition may require rather than preclude the adjustment of differences'. Moreover, because some of the structural constraints generated by multipolarity are no longer in play in a bipolar system, it is much easier for the two great powers to operate 'as sensible duopolists – moderating the intensity of their competition and cooperating at times to mutual advantage while continuing to eye each other warily' (Waltz, 1979: 203). At least two constraints associated with multipolarity are weakened in a bipolar world, according to Waltz (1979: 135). First, he argues that it is very much easier to reach agreements when there are only two parties involved because the costs of bargaining are considerably reduced while the gains are greatly expanded, provided that the duopolists are not intending to produce public goods. Second, Waltz argues that because of the distance during the cold war between the United States and the

---

[52] Market failure refers to the fact that in a market of competitive actors, there is a structural disincentive to produce public goods.

Soviet Union and the other more powerful states, the great powers can be 'concerned less with scoring relative gains and more with making absolute ones'. Both of these factors make it much easier for the great powers in a bipolar world to manage the system (see Figure 6.9).

One of the significant areas that needs to be managed, according to Waltz, is the maintenance of a stable balance of power. Such a balance can only be maintained if continuous efforts are made by the two great powers. Waltz (1979: 185) insists that 'instincts for self-preservation' will encourage them to make these efforts because the perpetuation of an international stalemate represents the 'minimum basis for the security of each of them'. Although the bipolar balance of power can only be maintained by internal balancing, Waltz (1979: 173) recognizes, by the same token, that this is a process that is very amenable to management in a way that external balancing is not. Drawing on the work of economists, Waltz assumes that in a bipolar world, the two great powers can 'learn to interpret one another's moves and how to accommodate or counter them'. He specifically cites Williamson (1968: 227) who argues that the pattern of interaction that Waltz associates with socialization leads over time to a higher level of adherence to commonly accepted practices and explicit agreements. Waltz accepts that the emergence of a learning process can be observed in all small number systems but he argues that a system consisting of two units has distinctive properties. On the one hand, tension in the system is high because the two states can do so much for and to each other but, on the other hand, because there can be no appeal to a third party, 'the pressure to moderate behaviour is heavy' (Waltz, 1979: 174). Through the process of cold war socialization, when responses by the United States were geared to the actions of the Soviet Union, and vice versa, it became possible to produce 'an increasingly solid bipolar balance' (Waltz, 1979: 171). But this is a radically different balance of power to the one that operated in the multipolar era and reflects the existence of an associational rather than an adversarial balance of power.

Waltz (1979: 171) then extends this argument and suggests that with only two states capable of acting on a world scale during the cold war, anything that happened anywhere was potentially of concern to both. Moreover, in contrast to a multipolar world, there was no diffusion of responsibility and so both promptly responded to 'unsettling events'. There was, therefore, no periphery to the system because neither great power was willing to see the other gain a strategic advantage in any part of the world (Waltz, 1979: 169). It is difficult to provide a structural explanation for this phenomenon, however, because Waltz is quite clear that the actions of secondary powers had little or no effect on the US/Soviet Union balance of power (Waltz, 1979: 171). Waltz agrees with this assessment because he argues that whereas the principal danger in a multipolar world is miscalculation, in a bipolar world it is over-reaction. By over-reaction Waltz (1979: 172) means intervening in areas where the outcome can only have local consequences. It follows that success in the periphery meant less in material terms to the bipolar powers during the cold war than in the multipolar world of nineteenth-century Europe (Waltz, 1979: 190). If this line of argument is accepted, then it has to be acknowledged that whereas there was a structural dimension to the 'great game' that was played in Central Asia in the nineteenth century, because the outcome had implications for the balance of power, the same cannot be said of American intervention in South East Asia during the cold war, the domino thesis notwithstanding. As Waltz (1979: 209) notes, the United States 'has learned, one may hope, that the domino theory holds neither economically nor militarily'. If the domino thesis had held, then Vietnam could have been assessed in balance of power terms. As it is, the US involvement in the Vietnam War requires a unit level explanation.

Conclusion

Waltz's attempt to establish a structural theory of international politics remains at the centre of contemporary debates about how to develop a theoretical understanding of international relations. He wrote *Theory of International Politics* because he believed that the effects of structure are usually overlooked or misunderstood in the study of international relations (Waltz, 1979: 175). He accepts, however, that a theory that is based on the structure of the international system can only help to explain 'some big, important, and enduring patterns' (Waltz, 1979: 70). In essence, he makes three major claims in the book. The first is that anarchy is an extremely resilient political structure and that the balance of power provides the best theoretical explanation for this phenomenon. The second claim is that the nature of international politics is very different in bipolar and multipolar systems and this is because the balance of power operates on a very different basis in these two kinds of systems. The third claim, closely related to the second, is that the international system can be more constructively managed in a bipolar system than in a multipolar system. This is because the multipolar balance of power inhibits the constructive management of international affairs. Structural explanations, therefore, can account for continuity within systems and differences between systems.

Waltz developed his balance of power theory in the context of the cold war. With the demise of the Soviet Union and the onset of the post-cold war era, there was considerable criticism levelled at international theorists in general for failing to anticipate this extraordinary development, and Waltz in particular was unquestionably tarred with this brush. However, as noted, Waltz was very clear that his theory could not account for system transformation. It can throw some light on the persistence of, and continuity within, systems and it can also help us to understand the impact of different structures on systemic patterns of behaviour. But that is the limit of what his theory can do. Nevertheless, given this orientation, Waltz's response to the end of the cold war has been anomalous, to say the least. The nub of his argument has been that, according to his theory, there will be structural pressure on the great powers to balance against the United States and we will return, at some point, to a multipolar system. But, in fact, this is a rather pale reflection, and an anaemic application of his theory. In *Theory of International Politics*, Waltz argues very robustly that it will be extremely difficult for established powers to cross the super power threshold and that theorists should not be focusing on the potential for a new multipolar world, but rather what international politics will look like if the Soviet Union falls below the super power threshold. In other words, Waltz was already anticipating the emergence of a unipolar world and the logic of his argument suggested that if unipolarity did emerge, then it would persist for some considerable time. With the elimination of the Soviet Union as a super power, therefore, Waltz was very well placed to argue that a structural transformation had taken place and to explore what this new unipolar world would look like.

Waltz had already anticipated aspects of unipolarity when he discussed the management of international affairs.[53] He argues that in

---

[53] In his discussion of great power management, of course, he fails to make reference to Bull. But, of course, Bull assumes that management is possible in a multipolar world and the whole discussion runs against the grain of Waltz's thinking.

a bipolar system where there are only two great powers and so no provision for external balancing, international affairs can be managed more constructively than in a multipolar system. In the bipolar, cold war era the balance of power was consolidated in part by coordinated actions taken by the two super powers. Joint management of the balance of power, however, seems to take us out of the realm of the international system and into the area of international society. We are now talking about an associational balance of power rather than an adversarial balance of power. Waltz accepted, however, that the Soviet Union could not adopt a management role in the non-military area and that in this context only the United States could adopt a management role. 'All nations are in the same leaky boat', he suggested, 'but only one of them wields the biggest dipper' (Waltz, 1979: 210). Waltz accepted that while his theory throws no light on how to manage problems relating to poverty, population, pollution and proliferation, it did suggest that bipolarity and, effectively in some areas, unipolarity, represented a better system than multipolarity for dealing with these problems. With the demise of the Soviet Union, Waltz missed an important opportunity to take these inchoate ideas forward.

Is there some reason why Waltz failed to move in this direction either when he wrote *Theory of International Politics* or in the subsequent post-cold war era? A possible answer is that buried in his analysis is a significant mythopoeic dimension. In other words, Waltz is not simply advancing a dispassionate argument about the structural impact of the international system, as he claims, because in practice, smuggled into his theory is a significant ideological dimension. There are two aspects to his ideological stance. The first is an aversion to war and a recognition that the main justification of the state is to ensure the security of its inhabitants. As a consequence, he believes that great powers are 'best off when the weapons they use to cope with the security dilemma are ones that make the waging of war among them unlikely' and when their cost is 'priced only in money and not also in blood' (Waltz, 1979: 187). At various points in the text of *Theory of International Politics*, Waltz (1979: 176, 185, 187) acknowledges, moreover, that with the development of nuclear weapons, military power has effectively lost its usability in great power relationships. But if this is the case, it could be argued that the whole thrust of his analysis is undermined, because it could be the inability of the great powers to use force rather than bipolarity that has encouraged the emergence of the associational balance of power. In fact, Waltz squares the circle because he believes that his argument shows that the potential dangers associated with nuclear weapons are minimized, but only in a bipolar world.[54]

The second aspect of his ideological stance emerges in the aftermath of the cold war when it becomes clear that the balance of power for Waltz is more than a structural feature of the anarchic system; he invests it with the same moral value that Europeans ascribed to it in the eighteenth and nineteenth centuries – it prevents the monopolization of power. Waltz did not need to be concerned about this possibility during the cold war and instead he focused on the fact that bipolarity opened a route to great power collaboration.[55] But with the demise of the Soviet Union and the potential consolidation of a unipolar world, Waltz, fearing the consequences of a monopolization of power by the United States, turned away from the logic of his argument in *Theory of International Politics* and resorted to the long-established myth that the threat of hegemony will always give rise to a balance of power.

[54] Waltz's (1981) subsequent argument in favour of nuclear proliferation is incompatible with the position adopted in *Theory of International Politics*. Craig (2003) argues that Waltz's position in both publications is unsustainable because it is premised on the erroneous assumption that there was no serious danger of either deliberate or accidental nuclear war during the cold war. Craig argues that documentary evidence now shows that some decision-makers did wish to use nuclear weapons, and nuclear accidents were too close for comfort.

[55] Craig (2003) argues that this move was driven by Waltz's ideological concern with the dangers posed by nuclear weapons and because of this concern Waltz had to move away from a purely structural argument and embrace a unit level variable (fear of nuclear war) to explain why the United States and Soviet Union established an associational balance of power. In fact, Waltz fails to build this move explicitly into his model. I attempt to do this in the final chapter and show that it can be done at a structural level of analysis.

7 | *John J. Mearsheimer's* The Tragedy of Great Power Politics

O NE OF THE REMARKABLE developments in the study of international politics since the cold war came to an end has been the resurgence of interest in realism. In the flush of optimism that accompanied the emergence of the post-cold war era a range of theorists assumed, or at least hoped, that the 'end of history' would include the death of realism. Instead, a new generation of realists came on to the scene and during the 1990s opened up a series of debates about the nature of realist theory. Some of this new generation followed in Waltz's footsteps, but others moved off in other directions.[1] At the start of the new millennium, John Mearsheimer, drawing on this ferment of new thinking, produced *The Tragedy of Great Power Politics*, a book that was immediately hailed as a classic that deserved to supersede the works of Morgenthau and Waltz 'in the core canon of realist literature'.[2] As in the previous chapters, it is argued here that the balance of power plays a central role in Mearsheimer's theory of international politics. Mearsheimer makes it very explicit that it is essential to draw on balance of power logic to understand international politics. But he has a very distinctive assessment of the balance of power and one that places him some distance from Morgenthau, Bull and Waltz. Their

---

[1] There are now references to 'defensive realism', 'offensive realism', 'neo-classical realism' and even 'wilful realism' (Williams, 2005). For useful reviews of the evolving approaches to realism, see Schweller and Priess (1997) and Rose (1998).

[2] This claim was made on the dust jacket by Samuel P. Huntington. But the book also elicited schizophrenic responses from potentially hostile reviewers. Gowan (2002: 47) argues that Mearsheimer's message to 'Get ready for great-power conflicts of the twenty-first century' is 'scandalous'. But although deeply critical of many aspects of Mearsheimer's analysis, particularly his failure to identify the United States as a global hegemon, he concludes that the Left has more to learn from Mearsheimer 'than any number of treatises on the coming wonders of global governance' (Gowan, 2002: 67).

213

theories all identify circumstances where great powers can move beyond zero-sum conflict and into a space where collaboration is at least possible. By contrast, Mearsheimer advances an unreservedly 'pessimistic' theory that reveals how states are pushed by the structure of the international system to pursue competitive policies towards each other and where states strive wherever and whenever possible to tip the adversarial balance of power in their own favour.[3]

Mearsheimer acknowledges, moreover, that this image of all the great powers persistently adopting a competitive posture is very much at odds with Waltz's view of the impact of the international system's structure on great powers. According to Mearsheimer (2001: 19–20), Waltz appears to develop an opposing position, whereby 'anarchy encourages states to behave defensively and to maintain rather than upset the balance of power'. So Waltz is depicted as a defensive realist in sharp contrast to Mearsheimer who identifies himself as an offensive realist. This distinction was articulated during the course of the 1990s but it was Mearsheimer who produced a fully-fledged theory to underpin offensive realism and one that can stand comparison with Waltz's *Theory of International Politics*. There are, however, good grounds for thinking that the distinction rests on a false dichotomy.

As argued in the previous chapter, the depiction of Waltz as a defensive realist reflects a misreading of his text. So, if we move away from the generic metaphorical scales that have been used to capture what is meant by the balance of power and think instead of the international system as a treadmill, then what Waltz argues, in effect, is that states are like rats on a treadmill. To survive, a state has to tread at whatever speed the mill is moving or risk being thrown off. Waltz's theory suggests that states have relatively little control over the speed of the treadmill in a multipolar system and the speed will vary across time. However, if the number of states on the treadmill is reduced to two, then there is a possibility that these two states can collaborate to reduce the speed of the treadmill or bring it to a stop, or even put it into reverse. But if the treadmill metaphor is applied to Mearsheimer, then

---

[3] However, it is easy to exaggerate this difference. There is nothing, necessarily, benign about great power collaboration – which is why the partition of Poland proves to be so problematic for some balance of power theorists like Morgenthau, but not Bull. By the same token, Mearsheimer's view can be seen to possess a more optimistic twist because his analysis suggests that the structure of the system helps to inhibit the threat of hegemony.

he is seen to be suggesting that great powers will tread as fast as they possibly can in the hope that they can move the mill faster than their rivals can tolerate. Reducing the number of great powers in the system has no impact on this process. When there are only two great powers in the international system, there is still exactly the same incentive to eliminate the rival state. Waltz, by contrast, argues that unmitigated rivalry is a possible but not inevitable outcome.

The treadmill metaphor supports the idea that the offensive/defensive distinction is not helpful for understanding the relationship between Mearsheimer and Waltz. But it is important to note, however, that the metaphor fits Waltz's theory much more effectively than it fits Mearsheimer's. This is because the two theories operate on very different foundations. Snyder (2002) observes that Waltz and Mearsheimer develop quite distinct theories, but he concludes that they are, in practice, complementary, with Waltz providing a theory that explains the behaviour of status quo states and Mearsheimer with a theory that explains the behaviour of revisionist states. Apart from the contentious assessment of Waltz as a defensive realist, Snyder also fails to take account of the very different approaches that Waltz and Mearsheimer bring to the task of theory building. Although they both claim to be interested in developing a structural theory of international politics, and both define the structure of the international system in terms of anarchy and the distribution of power, their competing approaches to theory building push them in very different directions so that the balance of power plays out in the two theories in very different ways. The aim of this chapter is to highlight the role that the balance of power plays in Mearsheimer's theory of international politics and to show how his theory transforms the conventional or certainly the Waltzian image of the international system and reveals that it is, inherently, a regionally based system. In other words, Mearsheimer's theory demonstrates that it is not possible to understand the international system without first acknowledging that it is made up of a number of distinct regional balances of power.

Of course, Mearsheimer is not the first theorist to draw attention to regional balances of power. As noted in Chapter 5, Bull distinguishes between the general balance of power and regional balances of power and he then argues that the general balance of power takes precedence. But Mearsheimer approaches this issue from a completely different perspective and one that reveals that there is no general balance of power except in the sense that there exists a systemic relationship between the regional balances of power. On closer inspection, this is an extremely important and innovative move and one that has, potentially, significant implications for our understanding of both modern and world history. Mearsheimer uses his theory to provide an account of the international system over the past two hundred years and his approach enables him to move away from conventional Eurocentric accounts of the modern international system that privilege the idea of a European balance of power. Instead, Mearsheimer provides an account that embraces Europe, but gives equal weight to developments in the western hemisphere and, in the process, reveals a very different pattern of international politics to the one that evolved in Europe at the same time. Moreover, it is a pattern that the Waltzian theory cannot begin to accommodate. But the approach not only moves us away from a Eurocentric perspective, it also holds the potential to provide a distinctive entry point into the analysis of world history. So far, international relations theory has had virtually no impact on the study of world history – in sharp contrast to Wallerstein's world systems framework (Buzan and Little, 2000).[4] Waltz's conception of the international system has simply not been taken on board in the study of world history. However, on the face of it, Mearsheimer's theoretical framework, because of its regional focus, seems to offer a much more promising vehicle for studying international systems in the pre-European era of world history.

Mearsheimer, however, is primarily concerned with the more recent past, as well as the future. In contrast to the three theorists examined in previous chapters, Mearsheimer developed his theory in the context of the post-cold war era. He has, therefore, had the opportunity to accommodate the implications of this dramatic shift in the balance of power. His response, on first sight, however, is surprising. Mearsheimer does not identify the international system that emerged after the cold war in unipolar terms. On the contrary, the theory presupposes that unipolarity is incompatible with a regionalized approach to international politics because, Mearsheimer argues, the structure of the international system makes it extremely difficult, if not impossible, for a global hegemon to emerge. So the United States is identified as a regional hegemon rather than a unipolar power or a global hegemon. Mearsheimer's

---

[4] But see now the work of Eckstein (2006; 2007).

thinking about hegemony, however, has been challenged by theorists who broadly accept the theoretical position associated with offensive realism. On the one hand, it is argued that even before the start of the cold war, the United States was pushing for global hegemony, and so offensive realism needs to accommodate this fact. On the other hand, it is argued that the emergence of the United States as a regional hegemon is attributable to factors that are never going to be repeated. As a consequence, Mearsheimer's argument that the United States must start now to deter China from developing as a regional hegemon builds on a false premise. Both of these critiques reveal that Mearsheimer's theory is much more sensitive to the assessment of individual case studies than Waltz's. But, as a consequence, whereas Waltz acknowledges that his theory can only throw light on systemic processes, Mearsheimer insists that his theory helps to illuminate the foreign policy orientation of individual states.

Because of these two very different positions, it is unsurprising that Waltz and Mearsheimer conclude their analyses in very different ways. Waltz ends by arguing that although his theory says nothing about how the international system should be managed, it does make clear that it is very much easier for great powers to collaborate and manage a bipolar system than it is for great powers to regulate a multipolar system. By contrast, Mearsheimer concludes by arguing that offensive realism shows unequivocally why the United States must do all it can to hinder the development of China. This is a highly contentious position to take and provides a reason, on its own, for rejecting the theory underpinning offensive realism. But it is important to acknowledge before going into the details of the theory that Mearsheimer does not, in fact, sponsor rampant aggression. On the contrary, whereas liberals tend to focus on the benign aspects of the international system, American realists, in general, are prone to draw attention to factors that reveal the international system as a very dangerous place in which to operate. As a consequence, they invariably counsel caution. Before the 2003 invasion of Iraq, for example, Mearsheimer, drawing directly on his theory, argued strenuously in public that the war was unnecessary and would lead to very counterproductive consequences. In particular, he predicted that, in the event of war, apart from the fact that the United States would then have to occupy Iraq for many years at horrendous cost, it would also make it more difficult for the United States to deal with the problems of nuclear proliferation and global terrorism.[5] From Mearsheimer's perspective, as the events unfolded, they demonstrated the merits of his theory and led him to conclude that Paul Wolfowitz, who was Deputy Secretary of Defence at the time, and often seen as the architect of the Iraq war, adhered to a theory that was 'deeply flawed'.[6]

This chapter is divided into three sections. The first section identifies and examines the distinctive features of Mearsheimer's approach to theory building. It also points out a major and unresolved tension that underpins this approach. The second and longest section sets out and assesses the essential features of Mearsheimer's model and reveals the centrality of the balance of power in his thinking. It also demonstrates that although he draws on some of the key features of Waltz's model, because of Mearsheimer's approach to theory building, he takes his theory in a radically different direction and one that renders the model much more susceptible to modification and development. The third section then examines two attempts to modify the theory and examines the implications of these modifications for the balance of power.

Theory building

Mearsheimer has two clear advantages over the other three theorists being considered in this book. First, as already noted, he honed his theory in the decade after the cold war came to an end. As a consequence, he was in a position to ensure that his theory had sufficient flexibility to embrace and accommodate the essential features of the international system that evolved after the collapse of the Soviet Empire. But more important from a theory building perspective is the fact that Mearsheimer was able to consider and respond to the impressive metatheoretical developments that have taken place in the field of international relations over the past quarter of a century. Although it has always been acknowledged that the world that international decision-makers confront is extraordinarily complex, there is now a

---

[5] Mearsheimer developed this line of argument in an op-ed written with Stephen Walt for the *New York Times*, 2 February 2003. He was also one of 33 academics who paid for an advertisement in the *New York Times*, opposing the war, in the fall of 2002.

[6] See the interview between John Mearsheimer and Lia Bastarache http//int.usamnesia.com/Mearsheimer-1.htm.

growing awareness not only that theorists have to take this complexity into account but also that there are difficult philosophical issues that have to be confronted when endeavouring to explore any kind of social reality. Wendt (1999) has, perhaps, done more than any other international relations theorist to put these philosophical issues on the table, although, of course, he has done so in a way that is not to everyone's satisfaction.[7] Mearsheimer gives only a passing nod to these issues, but there is no doubt that the aim of the theory is to present an unassailable case in favour of a materialist approach to theory building and one that cannot be unpicked by social constructivists. In going down this road, however, he also turns his back on the approach to theory building followed by Waltz.

Waltz and Mearsheimer approach the task of theory building from very different directions. Mearsheimer (2001: 9) starts from the position that 'there is no escaping the fact that we could not make sense of the complex world around us without simplifying theories'. It follows, as a consequence, that whether or not they are aware of it, all students and practitioners of international politics have recourse to theories and models in order to understand the 'real world'. Waltz also accepts that the world is infinitely complex but he puts a different gloss on this point and insists that because of this infinite complexity, it is not possible for human beings to apprehend the world in a direct or unmediated fashion. As Waltz (1979: 5) notes, if it was possible to apprehend the world directly, then 'we would have no need for theory'. It is not entirely clear that Mearsheimer would dispute this Kantian or idealist epistemological position taken by Waltz. Certainly, they both agree that theories are simplifying devices that encourage us to focus on some aspects of reality at the expense of others. Both eschew the idea of a general theory that can explain everything and acknowledge the need for multiple theories that can explain different aspects of the complex world that we live in. Nevertheless, despite these areas of agreement, Waltz and Mearsheimer apparently move off in different directions.

These two theorists part company over the question of theoretical assumptions. Mearsheimer (2001: 30) states unequivocally that 'a theory based on unrealistic or false assumptions will not explain much

---

[7] See 'Forum on Alexander Wendt', *Review of International Studies* (2000) 26:1, 123–80.

about how the world works'.[8] But Waltz (1979: 7) works from the opposing position that explanatory power is gained 'by moving away from "reality", not by staying close to it' and this necessarily involves making 'unrealistic' assumptions about the world. Waltz accepts that departing from reality can only be justified, however, if there is an explanatory pay-off, although he reiterates that if we are interested in explanation rather than description then there is no alternative to building the explanation on the basis of 'unrealistic' assumptions. There are two problems with this debate. First, it is conducted within a positivist framework. In other words, the examples used to justify the use of 'unrealistic assumptions' are almost invariably drawn from the natural sciences.[9] Although Mearsheimer does not use this line of argument, he is a positivist and it is not unreasonable to question whether it is appropriate to develop explanations about the social world on the basis of procedures that work in the natural sciences. Second, there is no agreement on what constitutes an 'unrealistic assumption'. So, for example, Waltz (1979: 91) argues that in any microtheory, the motivation of actors is assumed, and he acknowledges that when he assumes that states aim to survive, he is making a 'radical simplification'. Mearsheimer, however, endeavours to make this assumption more realistic, by assuming that states aim to survive by maximizing power. However, whereas it is generally accepted that it is uncontentious to suggest that states aim to survive (it is 'trivially true', according to Wendt), Mearsheimer's assumption is certainly considered by some theorists to be totally unrealistic. Ironically, this is not a problem for Waltz, indeed, it could be considered as one of the strengths of Mearsheimer's theory, although obviously it does pose a potential problem for Mearsheimer. He, of course, denies that it is an unrealistic assumption.

Nevertheless, as the next section attempts to demonstrate, Mearsheimer's theory reflects a model of the international system that is much closer to the real world than Waltz's.[10] It endeavours

---

[8] Mearsheimer is refuting the argument developed by the economist Milton Friedman (1953) who argues that 'the more significant the theory, the more unrealistic the assumptions' as well as Waltz (1979: 5–6).

[9] Waltz (1979: 5–6) notes, for example, that when Newton made the assumption that mass concentrates at a point, he knew perfectly well that mass does not concentrate at a point.

[10] This, of course, is a deeply problematic statement if you start from the premise that we do not have access to the 'real' world.

to ground the model in terms of material/geographical factors that Waltz excludes. By accommodating geographical factors, however, Mearsheimer not only renders the model more realistic, but it also has the effect of raising issues that from his perspective cannot be accommodated within a social constructivist model. Mearsheimer (2001: 368) is a well-known critic of social constructivism and he is profoundly sceptical of the view that state behaviour 'is largely determined by how individuals think and talk about international politics'. He disputes the idea that it is possible to move the United States into a peaceful and cooperative world by simply changing the prevailing international discourse and he insists that the longstanding anarchic structure of the international system necessarily shapes the way that decision-makers think and act in international politics. Mearsheimer presupposes, therefore, that his theory provides the most effective account of how international decision-makers think and act. But there is a tension in Mearsheimer's thinking that ironically he chooses to highlight at the end of his book. The tension, however, is apparent from the start, when he accepts that practitioners have no alternative but to operate on the basis of a theory of international politics. This is, in fact, a very significant concession to the social constructivists because it opens up an important role for ideas in international politics.

At the end of *The Tragedy of Great Power Politics*, moreover, Mearsheimer accepts that practitioners may not adhere to his theory and he acknowledges that the United States possesses a culture that is particularly prone to be 'hostile' to realist ideas and, as a consequence, to disregard realist prescriptions. But if the United States is not operating on realist principles, then this has very significant implications for Mearsheimer's theory. He endeavours to establish wiggle-room by arguing that it would be a mistake for the United States to persist in its policy of constructive engagement with China and that 'structural imperatives' will probably force the United States to conform to realist prescriptions. But if this is the case, then it really does not matter whether or not American policy-makers subscribe to realist theory. It appears that Mearsheimer's position implicitly accepts Waltz's argument that actors are socialized by the structure of the system. Moreover, his discussion of the United States' failure to balance against a rising China provides a significant riposte to his own comment on Waltz that 'it is not clear why states need to be socialized to balance against aggressors' (Mearsheimer, 2001: 166). States will need to be socialized when they subscribe to ideas that inhibit them from identifying other states as aggressors. But if the dominant state in the system does subscribe to the idea that there are alternatives to balancing strategies, then it is not difficult to push the argument further, and suggest that if the United States can eschew balancing tactics then is it not also possible to encourage China to subscribe to ideas and practices that eschew aggression? Of course, Mearsheimer is not going to accept this line of argument because of the significance that he attaches to structural forces. But there is, nevertheless, an unresolved tension between the importance that he attaches to structural forces, on the one hand, and the theories adhered to by practitioners, on the other.

Mearsheimer's conception of the international system

Waltzian features of the system

Although the approaches that Mearsheimer and Waltz adopt to theory building eventually lead them along very different tracks, they start from a number of significant common assumptions. Indeed, given the proximity of their initial positions, it is surprising how far apart they eventually move. In the first place, like Waltz, Mearsheimer (2001: xi) accepts that it is great powers that 'shape the international system' and so, as a consequence, he also accepts that great powers necessarily provide the focal point for a theory of international politics. However, Mearsheimer operationalizes this central concept in a different way to Waltz, who argues that great powers need to score on all fronts (size of population, area, military, economy and so on). So for Waltz (1979: 131) when identifying great powers, it is essential to acknowledge that the economic, military and other capabilities cannot be 'sectored and separately weighed'. By contrast, Mearsheimer (2001: 55) argues that 'a state's effective power is ultimately a function of its military forces and how they compare with the military forces of rival states'. He assumes, in other words, that military power can be sectored out, weighed and then used to identify the great powers in the international system. However, Mearsheimer also accepts that when considering the balance of power, states adopt both a short-term and a long-term perspective. In the short term, at any given moment, the balance of power reflects the distribution of military power possessed by all the great powers. But, at the same time, it is also recognized that in the long term there is a close relationship between military power and what Mearsheimer (2001: 55) calls 'latent power', which is largely based on a 'state's wealth and the overall size of its population'. It follows, therefore, that whatever the distribution of military power is at a particular point in time, great powers must also keep a close eye on latent power, because it will determine the balance of power in the future. It is Mearsheimer's assessment of latent power that leads him to express concern about China. His assumption is that in the future, the balance of power will tilt in China's favour. But despite these differences in how to identify which states qualify as great powers, Waltz and Mearsheimer agree that power needs to be defined in terms of capabilities, not outcomes, and that the focus for any structural theory of international politics needs to be on great powers.

Waltz and Mearsheimer also agree that great powers are overwhelmingly concerned with their own survival, because there is no organization – or night watchman, as Mearsheimer puts it – that great powers can turn to if they run into problems. The international arena is, in other words, a self-help system. In the final analysis, great powers have to rely on their own resources. But at this juncture, there is a parting of the ways, because whereas Waltz does not attempt to specify the level of resources that great powers draw on to ensure their survival, Mearsheimer insists that states will aim to maximize their power in order to ensure their survival. In making this move, Mearsheimer is responding to the criticism developed during the 1990s that Waltz's analysis presupposes that every state in the anarchic international system favours the status quo. As Schweller (1996: 91) puts it: 'If states are assumed to seek nothing more than their own survival, why would they feel threatened? Why would they engage in balancing behaviour? In a hypothetical world that has never experienced crime, the concept of security is meaningless.' For Schweller, these are rhetorical questions and it is clear to him that Waltz has led the discipline down a trail with no exit. He argues that it is essential to re-introduce the notion of conflicting state interests propagated by classical realists as well as the distinction that they drew between revisionist and status quo states.

This 'neoclassical' move, of course, erodes the distinction that Waltz makes between structural and reductionist explanations. But this is not a move that Mearsheimer wants to make. He accepts Waltz's argument that there are substantial benefits to be reaped by establishing a structural framework to explain international politics. Moreover, he acknowledges the force of Waltz's argument that the structure of the international system can be defined by anarchy on the one hand and the distribution of power on the other. The combination of these two structural factors generates chronic insecurity for great powers. For example, a key consequence of anarchy is that states are inherently uncertain about the intentions of other states. It follows that a dynamic economy within one state then becomes a source of concern for surrounding states because of the possibility that the resulting economic growth will be translated into military power in the future, thereby precipitating a shift in the balance of power at a later point in time. Uncertainty about how states will deploy their resources in the future, therefore, is another closely related source of insecurity in the international system. From Mearsheimer's perspective, moreover, the uncertainty generated by the structure of the international system makes it necessary to extend Waltz's theoretical assumption that the minimum goal of all states is survival. Whereas Waltz only assumes that in an anarchic arena the survival of every state is potentially at risk, Mearsheimer takes the argument one stage further and assumes that the only way for states to deal with the constant risk to their survival is to maximize their own power. But it is left underspecified what it would mean for a state to maximize its military power. Certainly the United States is a long way from maximizing its military power.

As far as Mearsheimer is concerned, therefore, the logic of anarchy compels every great power to adopt an aggressive stance in the international system. He makes this assumption in order to circumvent Schweller's assertion that Waltz's theory unravels because of its status quo bias. Mearsheimer also wants to maintain a structural level of explanation, however, and so he cannot adopt the reductionist tactic that allows Schweller to take account of the fact that the international system consists of revisionist and status quo states. Instead he assumes that the structure of the international system pushes all great powers to become power maximizers and, as a result, they all have revisionist aims. Nevertheless, although this move starts to distance Mearsheimer from Waltz, there is still some remaining common ground. In particular, Mearsheimer (2001: 338–44) acknowledges that the distinction Waltz draws between bipolarity and multipolarity is useful and that it is necessary to distinguish the behaviour of states in these structurally differentiated systems. In particular he accepts that war is more likely in a multipolar system than in a bipolar system and he draws, for example, on Waltz's argument that states are more likely to miscalculate in a multipolar system. He also notes that in a bipolar world there is only provision for internal balancing. But, on the other hand, his assumption that states are power maximizers undercuts Waltz's argument that great powers can manage the international system more effectively in a bipolar system than in a multipolar system. Indeed, Mearsheimer necessarily bypasses the issue of management altogether. Whereas the overall thrust of Waltz's argument is that there was greater scope for managing the international system during the cold war than in any previous period, the underlying message that Mearsheimer wants to present is that the anarchic structure of the international system makes it impossible to discount the possibility of future great power wars. It becomes extremely dangerous, as a consequence, for great powers to dispense with balance of power logic. What Mearsheimer means by balance of power logic is that great powers must constantly monitor the changing distribution of military and latent power and wherever and whenever possible pursue strategies that will shift the balance of power in their own favour. While Waltz does not assume that states are pushed by the structure of the system to expand at the expense of other states, he certainly accepts that this is a possible scenario for any anarchic system. But he also presupposes that the actions of each state will operate as negative feedback and maintain the overall equilibrium or balance of power. Although Mearsheimer also accepts that international anarchy is likely to persist, he does not follow the route mapped out by Waltz to account for this phenomenon. Despite the presence of some Waltzian features, Mearsheimer establishes an overarching framework to account for the persistence of anarchy that is radically different from Waltz's.

Geography and the international political structure

What really pulls Mearsheimer apart from Waltz is the link that he establishes between geography and the international political structure. Waltz can accept that this link may make Mearsheimer's model more 'realistic' and provide a more accurate description of the international system, but he nevertheless self-consciously eschews moves of this kind because he is committed to the methodological position that descriptive accuracy comes at the expense of the explanatory value of a model. Waltz is only interested in developing a deductive model of international politics that should apply equally well whether we are focusing on nineteenth-century Europe or fifth-century Greece.[11] As a consequence, Waltz's model assumes that the only structural difference between the multipolar political system that operated in Europe during the nineteenth century and the bipolar political system that emerged after the end of the Second World War is the reduced number of great powers in the system. The very different geographical scope of the two systems is not considered to have any structural impact on the behaviour of the states within those two systems. So does Mearsheimer derive any significant benefits from the introduction of a geographical dimension apart from providing a more accurate picture of the world? There are at least three potential and inter-related benefits and they come very clearly into focus if we contrast the way that Waltz and Mearsheimer view the last two centuries from an international politics perspective. First, the geographical dimension opens up the idea that regionalism is an inherent feature of the structure of the system; second, Mearsheimer finds that he has no alternative but to investigate the impact of unipolarity on state behaviour; and third, Mearsheimer's approach shows how the structure of the system has differential effects on the foreign policy orientation of states depending upon their geographical location. If closer investigation reveals that these potential benefits can be realized, then it follows that the effect of geography on the conceptualization of the international system is indeed very significant.[12]

Geography, however, is a very broad church and, in fact, Mearsheimer focuses essentially on only one feature: the distinction between land and sea. He takes this feature on board because, from his perspective, it has a fundamental impact on balance of power logic. It is not possible, in other words, to understand the structural consequences of anarchy and the distribution of power in the international

---

[11] Some specialists on the ancient world have unquestionably found a Waltzian perspective useful. See Strauss (1991) and Eckstein (2007).

[12] There is a growing interest in the 'geography of power' in social theory. See Allen (2003). Sayer (2004: 255) notes that although theorists like Foucault and Deleuze have enriched our spatial vocabularies, they have promoted a 'vision of a somewhat undifferentiated spatiality'. He goes on to argue that 'it is not merely that geography contingently makes a difference to the exercise of power, but that power is necessarily spatial from the start'. Although Mearsheimer is coming from a very different direction and is not concerned with social theory there is no doubt that he establishes a model that embraces spatial differentiation.

system if these two factors have not embraced the land/sea dichotomy. It follows that the political structure is mediated by this dichotomy and once the international system is viewed from this perspective, it becomes apparent that to come to terms with balance of power logic it is necessary to distinguish between insular and continental states. As a consequence, Mearsheimer contests Waltz's fundamental assumption that the structure of the international system has a uniform effect on all the constituent great powers. His model aims to demonstrate that insular and continental great powers respond differently to the balance of power.

Mearsheimer (2001: 114) attributes the difference to what he calls the 'stopping power of water' and his contention is that 'large bodies of water sharply limit an army's power-projection capability'. He does not deny, of course, that an effective navy can transport men and equipment across oceans, but he insists that it is extremely difficult to mount an effective invasion from the sea against the opposition of a well-prepared great power. Indeed, while he accepts that the British have over the centuries mounted large numbers of raids against other states, his historical survey reveals that there were no successful amphibious assaults against great powers carried out in modern Europe, from the putative founding of the state system in 1648 to the middle of the nineteenth century when sailing boats began to give way to steam ships. Although he accepts that steam ships have made it easier, in principle, to carry out amphibious assaults, he argues that the development of air power complicates the issue. The few successful amphibious assaults that took place in the twentieth century were accompanied by substantial air superiority and are not seen, therefore, to challenge the basic proposition that great powers separated by large stretches of water have not, historically, posed a significant threat to each other.[13] As a consequence, the stopping power of water not only inhibits war but also inhibits the consolidation of a security dilemma between such states.[14]

Not everyone has been convinced by the stopping power of water thesis. Rosecrance (2002: 149), for example, notes that water did not stop twentieth-century Japan from attacking the largest land powers:

[13] Even with air superiority, the 1944 Normandy landings, although ultimately successful, were extremely costly in terms of men and materiel.

[14] Mearsheimer's position is bolstered by Levy's (2001a; 2001b) argument that an expansion of power by a sea-based great power is considered to be less threatening than the expansion in power by a land-based power. See also Levy and Thompson (2003).

Russia, China, and the United States.[15] On the other hand, the Japanese
never attempted an amphibious assault on the United States and they
were hoping that the difficulties of defeating Japan would encourage the United States to reach a settlement. The Japanese attacks on
Russia and China are more problematic and do represent anomalies for Mearsheimer. Nevertheless, Mearsheimer does present more
than enough evidence to accept that a useful distinction can be drawn
between insular and continental great powers. States such as Russia,
France and Prussia/Germany are all identified as continental great powers in the nineteenth century because they co-existed on the same large
body of land. They possessed large land armies and the capacity to
invade each other. European history over the past two hundred years
suggests that these are the most dangerous states in the system because
they have initiated most of the wars of conquest, although Mearsheimer's account suggests that they almost invariably attack other
continental great powers and eschew attacking insular great powers.

Mearsheimer postulates that an insular great power occupies a territory that is surrounded by water and that does not contain any other
great powers. Both the United States and Britain are seen to fit this definition, despite the enormous differences between these two states. But
whereas Britain is unarguably an island, the United States is identified
as an insular great power because ever since it became a great power
in the course of the nineteenth century, it has occupied a territory surrounded by water that embraces other states but none that can mount
a realistic challenge to the United States. The key point Mearsheimer
wants to make is that if, for example, North America had divided into
four or five states during the nineteenth century, which is what the
British and the French wanted to happen, and if these states had all
been of equal strength, then they would all have been continental great
powers and there would have been no insular states in the Americas. As
it is, because the United States succeeded in dominating the continent,
not only are there no continental great powers in the Americas, but
the United States can also, as a consequence, be identified as an insular
great power and, in terms of the international system's political structure, it can then be compared to the position occupied by Britain.[16] It

---

[15] See also Gowan (2002) and Layne (2002: 43), who make similar arguments.

[16] The labels adopted by Mearsheimer are open to misinterpretation. The
United States and the former Soviet Union can be identified as continental

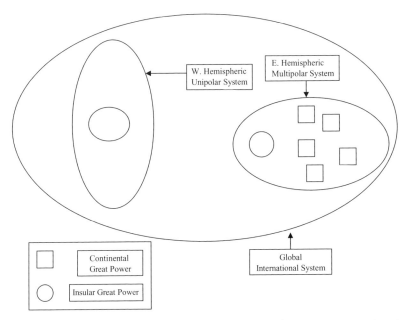

Figure 7.1 Mearsheimer's view of the mid-nineteenth-century international system[17]

follows, however, that Mearsheimer promotes a very different image of the nineteenth century to the one that Waltz draws upon (see Figure 7.1). It makes clear that Waltz is drawing on a regional system and the crucial question is whether or not there was a systemic relationship in existence between the two hemispheric systems. Mearsheimer does not discuss the issue in depth but his model unquestionably presupposes that although there was a global system in existence, structural forces within the two hemispheres were undoubtedly much stronger. There are also important foreign policy implications that flow from the model that will be discussed in the next section.

> great powers because they embraced the bulk of a continent. However, Mearsheimer's definitions make the distinction between continental and insular powers quite clear.
>
> [17] Although overly simplified, the diagram reveals the essential features of Mearsheimer's model and it has the heuristic value of opening up questions about the nature of the relationship between the two hemispheres. The British philosopher Bryan Magee (1999: 161–6), discussing his education at Yale University, describes the 'genius for teaching' displayed by Arnold Wolfers. Magee describes how Wolfers put an even simpler

Mearsheimer's stopping power of water thesis, therefore, extends beyond the distinction between insular and continental great powers. In particular, the thesis creates space for postulating the existence of two co-existing hemispheric systems that arguably became increasingly independent across the two hundred years that Mearsheimer draws upon. Although the United States played a crucial role in developing the discipline of international relations theory during the course of the twentieth century, when thinking about the nineteenth century, the focus has tended to be on the Eurasian system and on theories like the balance of power, with a strong Eurocentric bias (Levy, 2004). Mearsheimer, however, lays down the foundations for a different way of approaching international relations in the modern world. What his model suggests is that by the start of the nineteenth century, as the formal links established between the Eurasian hemisphere and the western hemisphere over the previous three hundred years began to break down, it becomes increasingly appropriate to view these two hemispheres as independent political systems, with distinctive regional dynamics developing within them.[18]

International Relations theorists have largely ignored how international relations in the western hemisphere developed as well as the relationship between the two hemispheres.[19] Although the details are only lightly sketched by Mearsheimer, the basic message is very clear. While it proved impossible for any single state to establish a hegemony in the Eurasian hemisphere, by the end of the nineteenth century, the United States did establish itself as a regional hegemon in the western hemisphere. This outcome in the western hemisphere is very significant for Mearsheimer's model because of its presumption that all great powers are interested in becoming a hegemon. A hegemon is defined as 'a state that is so powerful that it dominates all the other states in the

diagram than Figure 7.1 (combining polarity and geography) on the blackboard and how he then got his students to discuss the foreign policies that would be available to the different actors in the system.

[18] This is a rather different geopolitical formulation to Mackinder's famous heartland thesis developed at the start of the twentieth century. Mackinder (1904) argued that Eurasia was a closed system until the sixteenth century when contacts began to be established with the oceanic arena. At that juncture, Eurasia became an open system.

[19] There is no doubt that this is beginning to change. See Steele (2005) and Little (2007a).

system' (Mearsheimer, 2001: 40). Such a state is so far out in front in terms of military hardware and manpower that there is no other state that can put up a serious fight against it and so it becomes the only great power in the system. If the international system is regarded as fully integrated, in line with Waltz's model, then there is only scope for one hegemon in the system. But Mearsheimer's stopping power of water thesis opens the potential, in the first instance, for two largely independent hemispheric security systems. For reasons that Mearsheimer never makes clear, however, this is not quite how he operationalizes his model. While he accepts that the whole of the western hemisphere can be treated as a region, he insists that it is possible to identify several distinct regions in the Eurasian hemisphere, although, in fact, he only makes reference to Europe and Northeast Asia.[20] Mearsheimer needs to postulate the existence of different regions in Eurasia, however, because it helps to account for the asymmetrical developments within the two hemispheres. But even if it is accepted that the western hemisphere can be treated as a region whereas Eurasia divides into a number of separate regions, the asymmetry between the western hemisphere and Eurasia still leaves anomalies for Mearsheimer's model that need to be examined.

Focusing on the western hemisphere, Mearsheimer's model makes it clear that all the great powers on the hemisphere should have been interested in achieving hegemony. He stipulates, however, that it was the United States that had the overarching goal during the nineteenth century of 'achieving hegemony in the Western Hemisphere' (Mearsheimer, 2001: 236). Yet at the start of 1800, the British Empire, the Spanish Empire, the French Empire – after the acquisition of Louisiana from Spain – and even the Russian Empire (with its toehold in Alaska) had a presence on North America. In effect, this was a multipolar system, but in Mearsheimer's terminology, it was an unbalanced rather than a balanced multipolar system because it contained a potential hegemon. To qualify as a potential hegemon, a great power must possess, by a reasonably large margin 'the most formidable army as well as the most latent power among all the states located in its region' (Mearsheimer, 2001: 45). As it happens, the United States used surprisingly little force to become the hegemonic power in North America. Louisiana was

---

[20] Buzan and Waever (2003) by contrast establish a very sophisticated framework for examining regional security.

purchased from France in 1803 and Florida from Spain in 1819. Texas petitioned to join the United States after achieving independence from Mexico in 1836 and the state was annexed by the United States in 1845. Oregon was ceded by the British in 1846. So, only California was acquired by force from Mexico in 1848. By the end of the 1840s, therefore, the expansion across the continent was virtually complete. Mearsheimer (2001: 244) cites the head of the Census Bureau of the time, who noted that US territory now dwarfed European great powers such as France and Britain and was the equal of the Roman empire. In 1867, further expansion took place when Alaska was purchased from the Russians.

The ease with which the United States was able to expand represents an anomaly for Mearsheimer's model. Confronted by a potential hegemon, the European states should have united to prevent US expansion. But it has been argued that tensions among the European states made it remarkably easy for the United States to pursue a strategy of expansion.[21] Indeed, it can be argued that it is inappropriate to view North America at the start of the nineteenth century as a multipolar system because the European territories were an ocean away from their home bases. On the other hand, this line of argument then makes it more difficult to account for the persistence of Canada in the face of the longstanding desire by some in the United States to acquire this territory.[22] Another anomaly for Mearsheimer is the failure of any of the Europeans to intervene in the American civil war, despite their hope that a balance of power could be re-established on North America.[23] Schweller (2006) sees this as a clear case of 'underbalancing'. Mearsheimer (2001: 245) acknowledges that if the Confederacy had succeeded in establishing independence for the South there would have been 'profound' consequences for the balance of power in the western hemisphere because the United States would not have become a regional hegemon (nor, as noted above, an insular great power) and, even more important, the Europeans would then have opportunities to 'increase their political presence in the Western Hemisphere'. Moreover, as discussed below, Mearsheimer's model also suggests that the

[21] See Kutolowski (1965). It was much easier for the United States to establish its hegemonic status than for the Qing Empire to overtake its continental neighbouring states. See Hui (2004; 2005).

[22] For a discussion of the issue, see Stuart (1988).

[23] For a discussion see Merk (1966).

presence of two great powers in North America would have discouraged either from becoming involved in Eurasian conflicts. So a different outcome to the American Civil War could potentially have had profound ramifications for the course of twentieth-century world history.

Theorists in International Relations, however, have not only ignored historical developments in North America but, until very recently, they have also ignored developments in South America. Despite Mearsheimer's interest in the idea of a largely independent western hemisphere, his focus of attention is on North America and there is little discussion of the process whereby the United States became a hemispheric hegemon or the implications that flow from this position for international relations in South America. Yet a good case can be made that Mearsheimer's model provides a useful basis for theorizing how international relations in South America evolved. Fifty years ago, Burr (1955; 1965), a diplomatic historian, established a balance of power model to account for the development of international relations in South America during the nineteenth century. His model closely corresponds to Mearsheimer's, with the drive for hegemony occupying centre stage.[24]

Burr, however, is not only interested in hegemony but also in the evolution of the international system in South America. His starting position is that it took decades for an international system to extend across the continent after independence was achieved and the Europeans retreated across the Atlantic. The evolution of the international system was delayed primarily because it proved very difficult to establish fully fledged states. Most of the nascent states encountered difficulties when they attempted to form stable governments and these governments often had only a very vague notion of territorial limits, with the result that boundary disputes were to become a distinctive feature of international relations in South America, right up to the present day. Communications across the continent also meant that, initially, two regional international systems were established on either side of the continent and they operated almost independently of each other in the first instance (Burr, 1955: 44). In both systems, however, foreign policy-makers discussed international relations in terms of the balance of power and equilibrium, although Burr notes that the dominant states

---

[24] For an alternative theoretical framework that focuses on the western hemisphere, see Kelly (1986; 1997).

were determined to establish a balance of power that placed them in a position of hegemony. Persistent friction within both regional systems led to the formation of intersecting alliances that began to pull the two regions together and to the consolidation of a continental-wide international system. By exploiting tensions among the other South American states, Chile was then able to establish itself as a hegemon across South America.

At the end of the nineteenth century, however, it was becoming increasingly difficult for Chile, and Argentina, its nearest competitor, to sustain the financial burden imposed by the arms race in which they were engaged. In 1902, as a consequence, the two states agreed to set aside their differences and establish a *rapprochement*. A very different pattern of behaviour developed among the South American states in the twentieth century and, indeed, the system has been identified as a 'pacific union' (Cohen 1994: 215–16).

Mearsheimer, however, fails to identify or discuss this change. Instead, he observes that by the start of the twentieth century, the United States had emerged as a great power in the global international system and because it dwarfed all of the states in Central and South America, the resulting power differential enabled the United States to establish itself as a regional hegemon. Although Burr does not extend his analysis into the twentieth century, Mearsheimer's assessment is unquestionably compatible with his line of argument. Burr asserts that all the South American states were well aware of their potential vulnerability during the nineteenth century to intervention from the United States and the European great powers. Despite these concerns, Burr (1955: 39–40; 1965: 7–8) argues that the South American states were to a large extent protected by the 'rivalries' among the European states and between them and the United States. When the European states are taken out of this equation at the start of the twentieth century, however, then the South American states clearly become much more vulnerable to pressure from the United States. As a consequence, it can certainly be hypothesized that the pattern of largely peaceful behaviour that emerged among the South American states in the twentieth century is the product of the structural change in the global international system. Although Mearsheimer fails to explore this possibility, it remains the case that by introducing a geographical dimension into his model it becomes possible to contemplate radically different patterns of behaviour in different regional systems. This is one of the central insights that flows from Mearsheimer's model. To capitalize on this insight, however, Mearsheimer recognizes that it is necessary to extend the focus of analysis and embrace a foreign policy dimension.

The foreign policy dimension

The explicit introduction of a foreign policy dimension into Mearsheimer's model further differentiates his approach from that of Waltz. The key question is whether a structural theory of international politics can also serve as the basis for a theory of foreign policy. Waltz is adamant that his theory is only intended to explain international outcomes, for example, whether international management is easier to achieve in a bipolar or a multipolar system; it cannot explain why a state fails to pursue a balancing strategy. Elman (1996a; 1996b) has challenged this assessment and argues that Waltz's theory can be used to account for the foreign policies of individual states. Indeed, the whole point of the theory, he insists, is to demonstrate that the foreign policies of great powers will be affected by changes in the structure of the international system. Although Waltz (1996) does not dispute this point in principle, he insists that his theory will not carry you very far in practice because it was never designed to account for the foreign policies of individual states. Waltz accepts that in practice there may be occasions when great powers fail to balance and, indeed, there could even be occasions when the drive for hegemony may be successful. But in this event, his theory will have failed and a theory of foreign policy will be required to account for the failure. What Waltz insists is that his theory shows why there are balancing responses by states and why the outcome of these responses ensures the reproduction of the anarchic structure of the international system.

Waltz's response circumvents the critique made by Schroeder (1994b) that states often fail to pursue balancing strategies, but it then confronts a more significant problem that from a world historical perspective, balancing has often failed to prevent the emergence of a hegemon.[25] Waltz's theory is unable to explain balancing success

---

[25] See the case studies in Kaufman, Little and Wohlforth (2007) which reveal that from a world historical perspective the balance of power has regularly failed to prevent the emergence of hegemons.

but not balancing failure. Although Mearsheimer (2001: 422) does not adopt a world historical perspective, he does take account of the possibility that hegemony can emerge within an international system and in doing so, he constructs a model that can be used to 'explain both the foreign policy of individual states and international outcomes'. He is able to do this because of the link that he establishes between geography and the structure of the international system. Whereas Waltz only makes provision for a balancing response to changes in the structure of the international system, Mearsheimer argues that there are a range of strategic options that are available to great powers and he seeks to demonstrate that the option that they choose will be significantly affected by the way that their geographical position intersects with the systemic distribution of power.

According to Mearsheimer, great powers have two main strategic aims; one relates to the acquisition of power and the other relates to the restraint of potential hegemons. Historically, he argues, one of the most effective ways of increasing power is by means of war. In advancing this position, Mearsheimer contests the assertion that going to war does not pay.[26] Although this is a controversial position, if, for the sake of argument, it is accepted, then the foreign policy dimension can be brought into focus. Central to Mearsheimer's position is the impact of the stopping power of water thesis on the foreign policy orientation of states. Large stretches of water very substantially reduce the possibility of insular and continental great powers initiating war against each other. It is continental great powers, therefore, that are most likely to promote war for gain, but Mearsheimer's model indicates that they will only direct their troops against other continental great powers.[27]

The crux of Mearsheimer's position is that great powers have always been willing to go to war in order to shift the balance of power in their favour. Satiated or status quo great powers that have no incentive to improve their power position are, he insists, a rare phenomenon in

[26] Norman Angell provides the classic argument that although wars might still occur, countries will never benefit from them. See Angell (1910). For a recent assessment of war in the contemporary world, see Jones (2006).
[27] Mearsheimer also identifies blackmail (where great powers threaten war in order to obtain a gain), bait and bleed (where a great power encourages two of its rivals to go to war), and bloodletting (where a great power helps to sustain a war between two of its rivals) as related strategies used by great powers to promote their own position in the international system.

international politics; most great powers are revisionist states and he surveys international history over the past two hundred years to substantiate this proposition.[28] The major exception, Mearsheimer argues, is the United States, and it has transformed into a status quo state only because, on the one hand, it has achieved regional hegemony while, on the other, it knows that because of the stopping power of water it is unable to establish global hegemony. But Mearsheimer also asserts that a regional hegemon will want the next best thing to establishing a global hegemony, which is ensuring that there are no other regional hegemons in the system. It follows that although one great power may be able to establish regional hegemonic status, it will be extraordinarily difficult for any other great power to emulate this achievement because any potential hegemon that emerges in another region will inevitably confront the opposition of the established regional hegemon. Mearsheimer vehemently denies, therefore, that wars between great powers are now a redundant or anachronistic feature of world politics. War – even nuclear war – remains a possible strategy for great powers.[29] This line of argument, however, has the effect of eroding Mearsheimer's assumption that a regional hegemon will favour the status quo. As Mearsheimer (2001: 145–7) admits himself, 'states have a powerful incentive to be nuclear hegemons' and, as a consequence, 'great powers seek nuclear superiority over their rivals'. Regional hegemons are unable to escape this logic and so it is anomalous to identify them as unequivocal status quo great powers.

The nuclear arms race represents a form of internal balancing. But Mearsheimer identifies two very different manoeuvres that have been deployed historically by great powers to restrain potential hegemons. One is external balancing and the other is buckpassing. Here again, the intersection of geography and systemic structure plays a crucial role in determining which strategy a great power adopts. When confronted by a potential hegemon, according to Mearsheimer, buckpassing will

---

[28] Matthew Rendall (2006) argues, however, that Mearsheimer's case selection is biased and that he 'focuses on history's bully boys' and then looks in more detail at 'particularly aggressive periods in their histories'. See also Snyder (2002: 161).

[29] See Mearsheimer's (2001: 367) claim that 'war between nuclear armed great powers is still a serious possibility'. He does not go as far as saying that nuclear war is a 'serious possibility', but it would have to be a possible outcome in the event of a war between nuclear armed states.

always be the preferred strategy. In other words, whenever possible, any great power will always avoid directly confronting a potential hegemon. Instead it will prefer to buckpass and get another great power to confront the potential hegemon and thereby get the buckcatcher to sustain the cost of eliminating the danger posed by the potential hegemon. An obvious risk inherent in this strategy is of the buck being dropped and a failure to restrain the hegemon. Given this scenario, the great power that has chosen to sit out the confrontation and observe the anticipated defeat of the hegemon suddenly finds itself in a much more vulnerable position than it might otherwise have been in. It could, potentially, have been in a much stronger position by adopting an external balancing strategy. Nevertheless, Mearsheimer's model also demonstrates that it is very much easier and safer for an insular great power than a continental great power to buckpass.[30] Even if a continental buckcatcher fails to hold a potential hegemon at bay, the insular great power is still protected by the stopping power of water. Mearsheimer identifies the strategy of the insular great power as offshore balancing.[31] It is not a strategy that is unique to the United States, but can also be linked to the familiar idea of Britain as the 'balancer' in the European states system.[32] The idea also resonates with examples from world history. Realists have often made reference to the Greek city states system, but fail to note that the Greeks were operating in a much broader Mediterranean system that included Persia. Persia unsuccessfully attempted to conquer the Greeks at the start of the fifth century BCE, but by the end of the century had adopted the position of an offshore balancer and developed Mearsheimer's strategy of bait and bleed during the course of the Peloponnesian War (431–404 BCE. See Figure 7.2).[33]

By intersecting geography and the political structure of the international system, Mearsheimer is able to say more about the foreign

---

[30] See Baugh (1987) and Gray (1992).

[31] The idea of offshore balancing is most closely associated with Christopher Layne (1997). He disputes the way that Mearsheimer employs the term. See next section.

[32] See Sheehan (1989; 1996: 65–71). It also has much in common with what Buzan and Waever (2003: 456) call a 'swing power' which they apply to the United States, 'which is engaged in several regions other than its own but not permanently wedded to any of them'.

[33] For an assessment of Greek–Persian relations during the fifth century BCE see Little (2007b).

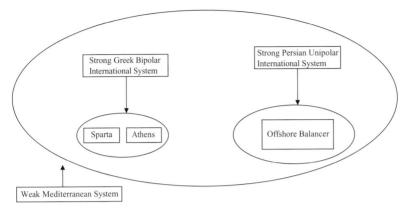

Figure 7.2 Greek–Persian relations in the fifth century BCE

policy orientation of great powers than Waltz.[34] In particular, he is able to show why the foreign policy orientations of the great powers diverge when confronted by a shift in the balance of power. Like Waltz, Mearsheimer presupposes that the structure of the international system requires great powers to monitor the balance of power at all times, but with the introduction of a geographical dimension he can begin to specify more precisely how great powers will respond to changes in the balance of power. But it is important not to exaggerate the significance of this difference. After all, Waltz specifies that in a bipolar system only internal balancing strategies are available and that, in contrast to multipolar systems, buckpassing is not an option.[35] The geographical dimension, however, does allow Mearsheimer to say more about which states are likely to buckpass in a multipolar system. But at the end of the day Mearsheimer cannot say a lot more about foreign policy than Waltz can. Although his theory allows him to say which states are likely to buckpass, a neoclassical realist, like Schweller (2006), is undoubtedly right when he argues that structural theorists like Waltz and Mearsheimer cannot answer the more interesting question of why states fail to balance when they are self-evidently in danger of being overwhelmed.

[34] Waltz, however, subscribes to a different conception of foreign policy analysis to Mearsheimer (and Elman, 1996a). Waltz argues that foreign policy analysis is needed to explain the goals that states set themselves and why they sometimes fail to respond to structural pressures.

[35] See Mearsheimer (2001: 338–46) for a discussion of the difference between bipolar and multipolar systems.

Reassessing hegemony

In contrast to Waltz, Mearsheimer constructed his theory with full knowledge of at least the initial consequences that flowed from the end of the cold war. As argued in the previous chapter, the logic of Waltz's position as expressed in *Theory of International Politics* should have been that with the collapse of the Soviet Union, bipolarity gave way to a unipolarity that will persist for some considerable time into the future. This is not how Waltz chose to view the post-cold war era.[36] It is also not how Mearsheimer wanted to theorize international politics. Like Waltz, he wanted to view the post-cold war era in multipolar terms. Unlike Waltz, however, he was able rethink his realist premises and present them in a way that challenges the widely held views that the post-cold war world is characterized by either unipolarity or American global hegemony. As Layne (2002/3: 123) notes, 'Mearsheimer takes on both of these "givens"'.[37] He insists that power politics still prevail in the post-cold war era and that the great powers 'still care deeply about the balance of power and are determined to compete for power among themselves for the foreseeable future' (Mearsheimer, 2001: 361). Although he accepts that the two main regional power centres on Eurasia – Europe and North East Asia – are stable at the moment, this is largely because the US presence is helping to maintain stability.[38] But his model predicts that with the demise of the Soviet Union and its elimination as a potential hegemon, US troops will be withdrawn from both regions.[39] But the model also predicts that in the future, balance of power logic will continue to encourage potential hegemons to aim for regional hegemony, although

[36] Waltz (2000b) insists that unipolarity is already giving way to multipolarity. But he accepts that an alliance of great powers will be required to balance the United States. But such an alliance would not, at least in terms of his own theory, challenge unipolarity. Contrast with Wohlforth's (1999) view that unipolarity ends if the unipolar state can be balanced.

[37] For Mearsheimer (2001: 381), they seem to be one and the same thing. He notes 'some might say that the post-cold war is unipolar, which is another way of saying that the United States is a global hegemon'.

[38] Mearsheimer (2001: 379–80) links this position to 'pacifer logic' which he relates to the US role as 'offshore balancer'.

[39] This is because the United States is an offshore balancer and it only intervenes when a potential hegemon is threatening to establish a regional hegemony.

the logic also reveals that it is irrational for them to aim for global hegemony.

Both of these assessments have come under attack from different wings of the realist camp. Elman (2004) argues that Mearsheimer extends his argument too far because a fully explicated balance of power logic reveals that regional hegemony is not a realistic option for any great power to pursue in the contemporary world. By contrast, Layne (2002/3; 2006) insists that, contrary to Mearsheimer, the United States has not been operating as an offshore balancer, but, on the contrary, it has pursued a grand strategy of primacy or global hegemony since the end of the Second World War and it has continued to do so since the end of the cold war. Mearsheimer's approach to theory building, therefore, proves to be susceptible to modification and development in ways that have significant implications for an assessment of the balance of power.

The basic thrust of Elman's position is that a more fully specified version of offensive realism demonstrates that Mcarsheimer is mistaken when he suggests that the United States achieved regional hegemony despite the opposition of other great powers in the international system. Elman (2004: 563) argues that, on the contrary, the United States was only able to achieve regional hegemony because of 'an improbable absence of either local or extraregional balancers'. Because it is unlikely that these advantageous conditions will occur again, there is no real incentive for great powers in the contemporary era to aim for regional hegemony. Elman is able to develop this line of argument by extending the geographical dimension that distinguishes between insular and continental great powers, on the one hand, and regional and extraregional great powers on the other. These geographical factors are seen to have a major impact on the overall structure of the international system. According to Elman, therefore, Mearsheimer under-specifies the range of structural conditions that great powers can confront. Once the range has been fully specified it then becomes possible to extend the foreign policy dimension of Mearsheimer's theoretical framework.[40]

---

[40] Elman (2004; 2005) elaborates these different positions on the basis of an explanatory typology. When the various structural positions are cross-tabulated, there are twenty possible situations that a state could confront. Seven of these have no empirical referents and one is excluded on theoretical grounds, leaving twelve possible structural situations that

Elman focuses on the structural situation where a continental great power in a multipolar region is acting in another region containing only one great power. The case study that he then uses to assess his theoretical analysis is the French decision to sell Louisiana to the United States in 1803, thereby more than doubling the size of this emerging great power, and representing possibly the most important step taken by the United States towards regional hegemony. Elman asserts that there was no other indigenous great power in North America that could effectively challenge the United States. Despite possessing extensive territory in the western hemisphere, he treats France, Britain and Spain as extraregional powers and this geographical factor has a very significant impact on the way the international system structured their responses to the expansion of the United States.

Working theoretically and deductively, Elman reasons that confronted by the only indigenous great power in another region that is also intent on expansion, an extraregional continental great power will respond differently from an extraregional insular great power. Although the continental great power will have concerns, because the expanding great power could eventually act as an offshore balancer and thwart its own attempts at regional hegemony in the future, its response will be dictated by what is happening in its own region. In other words, continental powers are much more concerned about their immediate neighbours than developments in other regions and will only engage in balancing activities when circumstances are favourable in their own region. But even under these favourable circumstances, although Elman does not make this point, there will also be a desire to buckpass to one of the other continental great powers. By contrast, and this runs against Mearsheimer's position, Elman argues that an insular great power would welcome the establishment of a hegemonic great power in another region, because it could then operate as an offshore balancer in the future and, as a consequence, would serve as a balancer of last resort in the insular great power's own region.

The decision by Napoleon to sell Louisiana to the United States poses a problem for Mearsheimer's theory, according to Elman, but

a state could find inself in. Elman, moreover, only considers the situation where there are two regions. But the typology could be even further extended if additional regions in the system are brought into play. As noted, Mearsheimer identifies Europe and North East Asia as separate regions on the Eurasian hemisphere.

it can be resolved by an expanded version of the theory, which indicates that pressure on states by the structure of the international system varies more substantially than Mearsheimer acknowledges. What Elman reveals is that there was no effective opposition to the expansion of the United States at the start of the nineteenth century partly because local forces were too weak and partly because extraregional balancing failed to emerge because of the exigencies in Europe. His focus is specifically on France, and he demonstrates convincingly that France's extraregional policy was subordinated to local power considerations. Although Elman does not investigate Britain's foreign policy, his assumption that its structural position encouraged this insular great power to acquiesce in the expansion of the United States because of a future offshore balancing potential is unconvincing. This scenario presupposes an extraordinary prescience on the part of the British and it would seem more likely that they too were preoccupied with regional power considerations. It is certainly the case that by the 1840s both the British and the French were becoming increasingly concerned with the way that the power of the United States was growing.[41] Nevertheless, Elman's approach is important because it demonstrates that Mearsheimer's theory is amenable to extension in ways that push it even further from Waltz's theory, not because of the emphasis on offensive motivation but because the inclusion of the geographical dimension creates the potential for an expansion in the foreign policy framework.

The extended framework of offensive realism developed by Elman has important contemporary implications because it indicates that although the United States was able to achieve regional hegemony, this is not an option that has been available to any subsequent great power. Elman acknowledges that although Germany, Japan and the Soviet Union attempted to establish regional hegemony in the twentieth century, they were not successful because their attempts were blocked by the United States and other great powers in the region. Elman insists that the structural forces that operated in the twentieth century will continue to operate in the twenty-first century and forestall any potential regional hegemon from consolidating its position. As a consequence, he disputes Mearsheimer's assessment that if China's economy continues to develop, then 'for sound strategic reasons

---

[41] See the discussion of the British and the French preference for a number of different power centres on North America in Chapter 1.

other states in the system from developing countervailing forces and soft power to legitimize its hegemony. Layne then presents a substantial amount of evidence in support of his argument that during the post-cold war era, the United States has consistently pursued a grand strategy that has opposed a return to global multipolarity and has aimed instead at global hegemony.[45] He goes on to argue, however, that this was not a new move, but simply represented an implementation of the US strategy that had been in place since 1945. The strength of Layne's argument is that it explains why the United States has retained a military presence in Europe and North East Asia. If Mearsheimer's theory was correct, then as an offshore balancer, the United States should have started to withdraw and leave the great powers in Eurasia to balance among themselves. Mearsheimer (2001: 390) argues that although the logic of offensive realism predicts this outcome, it has not yet happened partly because of inertia and partly because it has taken time to work out the implications of the 'new architecture' for US interests. Layne hopes that Mearsheimer's analysis is correct because he considers off-shore balancing to be a preferable option to attempting to sustain a policy of hegemony. But he is convinced that the widespread acceptance of the putative benefits associated with hegemony will prevent the logic of offshore balancing from coming into effect.

Conclusion

Despite the very different models that Waltz and Mearsheimer have constructed, both are unpersuaded that the contemporary international system can be characterized as unipolar and operating under US hegemony. Neither accepts that the United States is so militarily powerful that it can dominate all the other states in the system, and neither believes that the United States is in a position to prevent other great powers from building up their military capabilities. From

---

[45] The case against multipolarity was made, for example, by the Pentagon in a classified document prepared in 1992 by Paul Wolfowitz (Gellman, 1992). It argued that the United States should make a concerted effort to preserve its global military supremacy. It stated that it was not in the interest of the United States 'to return to earlier periods in which multiple military powers balanced one against another in what passed for security structures, while regional, or even global peace hung in the balance' (cited in Layne, 2002/3: 137).

Mearsheimer's perspective, a hegemon 'is the only great power in the system'. But whereas he accepts that the United States is the only great power in the western hemisphere, he strongly disagrees with the presumption that China and Russia do not have the 'wherewithal to stand up to the United States' (Mearsheimer, 2001: 258).[46]

It is clear that they are not alone in drawing this conclusion. A report from the National Intelligence Council (2004) argues that the alliances and relationships that provided the foundations for US power during the cold war will probably alter dramatically in future decades. On the one hand, the 'likely emergence of China and India as new major global players – similar to the rise of Germany in the nineteenth century and the United States in the early twentieth century – will transform the geopolitical landscape, with impacts potentially as dramatic as those of the previous two centuries'. On the other hand, it is also accepted that the EU, rather than NATO, 'will increasingly become the primary institution for Europe, and the role which Europeans shape for themselves on the world stage is most likely to be projected through it'. Confronted by this changing landscape, the report argues that it is possible to envisage a range of possible responses from the US 'enhancing its role as balancer between contending forces to Washington being seen as increasingly irrelevant'.[47] What is not envisaged is the persistence of a putative US hegemony.

Given the common interest that Waltz and Mearsheimer have in developing a structural theory of international politics and their shared assumptions about the nature of international politics, the marked differences in their two models are striking.[48] The differences can to some extent be explained by reference to the dramatic changes that occurred in international politics in the era after Waltz produced his text and before Mearsheimer wrote his. But it is also the case that their mythopoeic concerns are, in practice, quite different. Waltz produced

---

[46] It is revealing that the United States, having rented an airbase in Uzbekistan in 2001, was asked to leave in 2005 when the government decided to turn to Russia and China for investment (Osborn, 2005a). See also the joint military exercises between Russia and China carried out in August 2005 (Osborn, 2005b).

[47] National Intelligence Council (2004) 'Mapping the Global Future', downloaded at www.dni.gov/nic/NIC_globaltrend2020.html on 6 December 2006.

[48] For an assessment of these differences see Mearsheimer (2006a; 2006b).

a book that demonstrated that the United States was operating under optimum conditions for preserving a stable international system within which an attempt could be made to solve the difficult international problems that confronted the international community. But to maintain stability and to solve the problems, future collaboration between the two super powers, especially on the nuclear front, was considered to be essential. From Waltz's perspective, therefore, with the development of nuclear weapons, the nature of international politics has undergone a transformation because great power war is no longer a practical option.

Mearsheimer insists that because it is not possible for great powers to signal benign intentions they have no alternative but to operate on worst case assumptions. And so the possibility of war, even nuclear war, persists. Whereas Waltz's model gives rise to an ideological argument that the United States must acknowledge and accommodate the interests of other great powers in the system, Mearsheimer's model generates the ideological argument that because emerging great powers will endeavour to damage US interests in the future, the United States has no alternative but to prepare for this eventuality. Mearsheimer's model, therefore, precludes the possibility of a desirable future international order. From his perspective, however, the United States has an enormous structural advantage because of its capacity to operate as an offshore balancer. He is quite clear that 'the United States ought to be the offshore balancer, not the world's policeman' (Mearsheimer, 2006a: 114); it would be even better if it could achieve nuclear superiority. But there is no vision of the future for the anarchic international system. The logic of the adversarial balance of power is inexorable and for Mearsheimer that will always remain the tragedy of great power politics.

PART IV

Conclusion

8 | A composite view of the balance of power for the twenty-first century

T HE MAIN AIM of this book has been to suggest that the balance of power has played a more interesting and complex role in international relations theory than is generally recognized. Yet it is not only critics of the balance of power who have provided an inadequate assessment of the concept, balance of power theorists themselves often fail to assess the work of earlier balance of power theorists adequately, or provide distorted accounts of the earlier assessments of the concept. The four theorists examined in this book all attempt to set themselves apart from other theorists. As a consequence, there has been an unintended but nevertheless persistent and pervasive tendency to underplay or over-simplify what others have had to say about the balance of power.

As we move into the twenty-first century, there are no signs of change on this front. In a recent survey of the literature, prior to making his own major contribution, Schweller (2006: 4), for example, traces the idea of an international balance of power back to the Renaissance where it is viewed as a 'metaphorical concept' that treats balancing behaviour as a response 'driven by a law of nature'.[1] He then goes on to argue that this conception of the balance of power 'still infuses most discussions of how the theory operates'. This is not an idiosyncratic view and Schweller, moreover, has no difficulty finding quotations from previous balance of power theorists such as Morgenthau and Waltz to illustrate his assessment. Nevertheless, the overall thrust of this book undermines Schweller's basic assumption that contemporary balance of power theorists presuppose that the balance of power represents a natural law and that, as a result, they subscribe to a view of the international arena as a machine 'created and kept in motion by the

---

[1] As noted in Chapter 3, however, in Guicciardini's history, the balance of power provides us with the basis for a counterfactual analysis rather than a law of nature.

divine watchmaker'.[2] Although all four of the theorists examined here are interested in structural constraints, none of them come close to viewing international politics in purely deterministic terms. Perhaps more surprising, however, are the contrasting but interrelated ways that they do approach the balance of power.

What I want to do in this final chapter is to identify the points of contact between the four models examined in Chapters 4 to 7 and to explore the implications of trying to develop a more integrated approach to the balance of power than the attempts made by any of the individual theorists discussed here. Necessarily, this examination is carried out against the background provided by both the theoretical debates that are currently going on in the field of international relations as well as the prevailing assessments of the balance of power in the contemporary international arena. These two factors, of course, are not unrelated. Thompson (2006: 1–2), for example, argues that international change and turmoil 'dramatize analytical puzzles', but he then expresses some surprise that the unexpected and sudden emergence of unipolarity has not led to more systemic analysis. Schweller, however, is not surprised by this development and, indeed, he has played a leading part in trying to steer realism away from systemic and structural analysis and towards domestic politics explanations. A major puzzle for realists, according to Schweller (2006: 2), is the fact that unipolarity has 'not provoked global alarm to restore a balance of power'. But he sees the phenomenon of 'underbalancing' not as an aberration but as a habitual feature of international politics, and this gives rise to his intriguing hypothesis that 'only strong and unified states can effectively adapt to structural-systemic incentives, even when they are quite compelling and intense' (Schweller, 2006: 130).[3]

---

[2] Schweller (2006: 4) takes this quotation from Morgenthau (1973: 203) who prefaces this quotation by noting that the metaphor was 'appropriate to the way of thinking in the sixteenth, seventeenth, and eighteenth centuries'. But as noted in footnote 1, Guicciardini certainly did not think in these terms.

[3] There are interesting similarities between Guicciardini and Schweller. Guicciardini (1984: 1) argues that it was 'foolish errors and shortsighted greed' that prevented the balance of power operating, whereas Schweller (2006: 10) argues that it was divisions within the domestic system and that 'the underbalancing state brings about a war that could have been avoided'. Both, as a consequence, use the balance of power as the basis for a counterfactual argument about what could have happened.

But the move to explain international politics from a domestic politics perspective has not been the only response to the emergence of unipolarity. There is no doubt that the end of the cold war provided an enormous fillip to the emergence of constructivist approaches to international politics. Rightly or wrongly, constructivists were able to make a plausible case that established thinking in International Relations not only failed to anticipate the end of the cold war, but, more importantly, it was also unable to account for the transformation, even retrospectively. The implications of social constructivism, moreover, are far-reaching. From a social constructivist perspective, many of the long-established debates in the social sciences, between, for example, rationalism and reflectivism, materialism and idealism, structure and agency, facts and values, and holism and individualism, all build on false dichotomies. It follows that social constructivists are prone to see themselves occupying the middle ground and, indeed, possessing the capacity to build bridges that make it possible for advocates of the competing positions to make contact with each other and engage in a dialogue. They consider that they have dealt a fatal blow to the established view that in conducting international relations states are driven by objective interests that are defined by the material circumstances that underpin the state. Constructivists postulate that although interests do take account of these material circumstances, they are also profoundly influenced by normative and ideational factors. Because norms and ideas are amenable to dramatic transformation, social constructivists argue that international relations, in theory and practice, can be subject to profound change. But they also insist that for change to take place there must be a shift in the established intersubjective and epistemic understanding of the world and this requires a degree of cognitive evolution that is often not easily achieved.[4]

The interpretation of a text can never be innocent or neutral and there is no doubt that the emergence of constructivism and the debate in the literature about unipolarity have influenced my reading of the texts examined in Chapters 4 to 7, even though three of them were

---

[4] Although Wendt (1999) is perhaps the most influential constructivist in the field, he is often attacked for presenting constructivist ideas in a way that can be co-opted by mainstream social science. Adler (2005) is perhaps the best-known advocate for holding, or as he puts it 'seizing' the middle ground.

written in the putatively bipolar era of the cold war and none was written by a constructivist. In the first section of this chapter, the distinctive features of the balance of power that emerge from a comparison of the four texts are identified and the similarities and differences between the texts are then discussed. In the second section, the four authors are located in the context of a broader set of debates about the balance of power that can be identified in the literature. In the third section, I attempt to establish a composite picture of the balance of power. Then in the final section I look at the implications of the composite picture for the future of the theory and practice of international relations.

Comparing and contrasting approaches to the balance of power

The theorists discussed in the previous four chapters all approach the balance of power from rather different perspectives. Morgenthau is interested in the way that the operation of the balance of power has changed across time. But his specific concern when he wrote *Politics Among Nations* was with the rise of nationalistic universalism in the twentieth century, in conjunction with the steady erosion during the nineteenth century of the factors that had helped to maintain what I label an associational balance of power. Morgenthau feared that these developments would give free rein to the systemic forces associated with an adversarial balance of power. Although he accepted that it was possible, through the creation of a global world society, to establish the necessary preconditions for the formation of a world government that could eradicate international war, he did not see these preconditions emerging in the near future. It is unlikely, therefore, that he would have viewed the emergence of the United States as a global hegemon with equanimity and unquestionably he would have viewed evidence of untrammelled US unilateralism with alarm.

Bull's approach to the balance of power, and indeed his approach in general, has much more in common with Morgenthau than is generally recognized.[5] For example, despite the centrality of the balance of power to their assessments of international politics, both acknowledge

---

[5] For a more extended discussion of the links between classical realism and the English school, see Little (2003).

the potential importance of world society in the future.[6] At the time Bull wrote *The Anarchical Society*, however, he was cautiously optimistic that the United States and the Soviet Union could co-exist and, indeed, that the existence of nuclear weapons helped to stabilize relations between the two super powers, although at the expense of establishing order on a more positive basis. But, like Morgenthau, Bull accepts that states can use the balance of power competitively to promote their own interests as well as cooperatively to help to preserve a society of states. However, he associates this distinction much more explicitly than Morgenthau does with the idea of an ontological divide between a system and a society, although he is primarily interested in interaction among the institutional dimensions of international politics and how this interaction affects and is in turn affected by both the adversarial and associational balance of power. By contrast, Morgenthau is more concerned with the way that the persistent change that characterizes international politics impacts on the relationship between the associational and the adversarial balance of power.

While Morgenthau and Bull both want to capture some of the complexity associated with the two dimensions of the balance of power, Waltz, by contrast, wants to strip away any extraneous detail and he does so by focusing exclusively on the ideas of anarchy and polarity. As a consequence, he develops a much clearer picture than either Morgenthau or Bull about what it might mean to talk about an international system as opposed to an international society. For Waltz, the balance of power emerges, in the first instance, as an unintended consequence of states endeavouring to survive in the anarchic international system. Although Waltz seems to acknowledge the existence of an international society, it is essentially a recessed concept that is never clearly articulated and because the international system is privileged in Waltz's approach, the international society is subordinated to the international system. It is ironic, therefore, that he argues at the end of the book that in the context of bipolarity, an adversarial balance of power was giving way to an associational balance of power.

Finally, Mearsheimer, focusing exclusively on the idea of an international system, but from a foreign policy as well as a structural

---

[6] However, neither developed the concept of world society in detail. This was one of Buzan's (2004a) central aims in his influential attempt to extend the English school framework.

perspective, privileges geography over polarity. In other words, when he considers the international system, he presupposes that we cannot understand what is happening at the global dimension without taking the regional dimension into account. Mearsheimer, therefore, develops a position that runs counter to Morgenthau, Bull and Waltz who all assume that the global balance of power takes precedence over regional balances of power. By contrast, Mearsheimer argues that hegemony or unipolarity can emerge at the regional level and it is primarily, or perhaps only, geography which prevents the emergence of global hegemony or unipolarity. From Mearsheimer's perspective, then, the United States only succeeded in becoming a regional hegemon because of favourable historical circumstances, but because it has now achieved this status, there are structural pressures that should encourage the United States to prevent a hegemon from emerging in another region. It follows that in contrast to the more usual realist position, Mearsheimer is not just suggesting that other states will eventually start to balance against the United States, but that global geography inhibits any state from occupying a position of worldwide hegemony and it is this factor that is ultimately responsible for preserving a global balance of power.

What emerges from an assessment of the four balance of power theorists, therefore, is that they can be compared along three distinct dimensions (see Figure 8.1). First, they vary in terms of the importance that can be attached to the system/society distinction for understanding the balance of power. Although Bull formally draws attention to the significance of the distinction for our understanding of the balance of power, Morgenthau makes more effective use of the divide by arguing explicitly that the long-established (associational) balance of power was giving way to a new (adversarial) balance of power in the twentieth century. Waltz, by contrast, only draws on the distinction implicitly, while it plays no role at all in Mearsheimer's thinking.

Polarity, on the other hand, plays a significant role in the way that all four theorists approach the balance of power. Bull associates polarity with complexity. A system becomes more complex every time an additional pole or centre of power emerges. Morgenthau initially makes the argument that multipolarity is more stable than bipolarity on the grounds that it generates higher levels of uncertainty and therefore encourages caution. But Morgenthau goes on to acknowledge that two actors in a bipolar system could, in principle, cooperate and establish

	System/society divide	Polarity	Geographical dimension
Morgenthau	+ + +	+ +	+ +
Bull	+ +	+ +	+ +
Waltz	+	+ + +	
Mearsheimer		+ + +	+ + +

+	Indicates the significance of the dimension for a theorist

Figure 8.1 How four theorists assess the importance of divergent dimensions of the balance of power

an extremely stable system. For both Bull and Morgenthau, therefore, although a significant dimension of the balance power, polarity fails to outweigh the importance that they attach to the system/society distinction.

For Waltz, however, polarity is of overriding importance for his model of the balance of power because this is the factor that changes the structure of the system and as the structure of the system changes, so too does its impact on the constituent members of the system. His model not only reveals that the balance of power is much more stable in a bipolar system than in a multipolar system but it also explains why the potential for cooperation is greater in a bipolar system. Waltz's failure to explore the structural implications of unipolarity, as a consequence, leaves a substantial gap in his analysis.

Polarity is also of crucial importance in Mearsheimer's analysis, although it is impossible to disentangle this dimension from the third dimension that focuses on a global/regional divide. Mearsheimer distinguishes between polarity at the regional and the global level. He accepts that regional systemic pressures are not necessarily sufficient to prevent the emergence of a regional hegemon because states within a region so frequently fail to pursue a balancing foreign policy option. From Mearsheimer's perspective, therefore, effective balancing is much more likely to be carried out by an extraregional, offshore balancer, especially if that state is a hegemon within its own region. When we bring the global/regional divide into focus, moreover, Waltz appears at the opposite end of the spectrum to Mearsheimer because he wants to exclude the geographical dimension from his analysis. Morgenthau and Bull, on the other hand, both acknowledge the need to take geography into account and subscribe to a common image of the European international society expanding across the globe. But contrary to Mearsheimer, in the contemporary world, both see a sharp distinction between global and regional levels of analysis and they privilege the global balance of power over regional balances of power. In other words, they see the global balance of power overarching or embracing regional balances of power, whereas Mearsheimer views the global balance of power in terms of the interaction among the different regions.

Figure 8.1 provides a summary of this section, although the weightings of the dimensions ascribed to each theorist should be treated as indicative rather than definitive.

Even so, Figure 8.1 does suggest that the approaches of all four theorists to the balance of power are more complex than is often acknowledged and although the profile of each theorist is distinctive there is a considerable amount of overlap in the use made of the three dimensions. The degree of overlap raises the question of whether or not it is possible to establish a composite model of the balance of power on the basis of the three dimensions.

Balance of power debates

Before attempting to establish a composite model of the balance of power, however, it is necessary to locate the four theorists in the context of a broader set of debates about the balance of power. What Figure 8.1 does not fully reveal is the changes of emphasis in the orientation of the literature on the balance of power since the end of the Second World War. These changes are illustrated in Figure 8.2. During that period, there have been five key developments in how theorists in international relations have approached the balance of power. Each of these developments is the product of more broad-ranging changes in the literature that have impinged directly on balance of power thinking and have also been the source of a significant debate. For the first thirty years, balance of power thinking was ostensibly dominated by classical realism, as exemplified by Morgenthau. Almost as soon as the balance of power was identified as the central theoretical concept in the field, however, it came under attack for being an incoherent concept.[7] More specifically, as noted in Chapter 4, ever since Morgenthau presented his theory of the balance of power, critiques of his work habitually offer assessments that are based on extremely attenuated accounts of how Morgenthau actually viewed the concept.

Ironically, these attenuated assessments have been reinforced by linking Morgenthau to a second approach to the balance of power that emerged during this period. Alongside classical realism, a behavioural approach developed that is intended to introduce a much more systematic and scientific methodology into the study of international relations. The balance of power seems to be an ideal theory on which to use these methods because, on the face of it, the concept is so amenable to quantification. It is possible to trace how quantified measures of the distribution of power in the international system change year by year and the same can be done for the number of alliances in existence at any one time, as well as the number of wars that are occurring. Moreover, it became possible, as a consequence, through the aggregation of data, to provide an overall or holistic picture of the international system that shows, for example, whether the distribution of power in the system concentrates or diffuses across the system over time. It is also possible to correlate changes in the concentration of power with changes in the patterns of alliance formations and the number of wars in the system.[8]

The motivation and behaviour of individual states, however, inevitably get washed out of this systemic picture and, unsurprisingly, classical realists and diplomatic historians have often been particularly hostile to this development. Yet Vasquez (1983) successfully promoted the view that the behaviouralists are effectively working with a realist model of the world. But, in fact, this assessment underestimates the distinctively systemic view that the behaviouralists generate, on the one hand, as well as the complexity of Morgenthau's approach, on the other.

Despite the fact that some of the distinctively societal aspects of Morgenthau's thinking are foregrounded in Bull's approach to the balance

---

[7] For one of the earliest critiques of the balance of power, see Haas (1953).
[8] For a characteristic example of this kind of research, see Singer, Bremer and Stuckey (1972).

of power, the similarities between the two theorists are rarely noted. Moreover, although there is now widespread interest in English school thinking, the emphasis is on their idea of norm-driven explanations, and the more pluralistic dimension of Bull's thinking that is captured by the system/society divide is largely overlooked. As a consequence, this aspect of classical realism and English school thinking is radically underplayed.

A third significant development in the orientation of balance of power thinking was precipitated by Waltz at the end of the 1970s. What he wanted to do was to show how the uncoordinated but rational actions of states reproduce an anarchic international system. As a consequence, it can be inferred that he wanted to eliminate the sense of mystery that is often attached to the idea of the balance of power being the product of a natural law. From Waltz's perspective, the balance of power persists as the result of states responding to pressure that derives from the structure of the international system. In other words, Waltz identifies a structural but non-observable mechanism that generates the behaviour that is attributed to the existence of a natural law. By going down this route, the balance of power is defined exclusively in terms of a competitive relationship that forms among the poles of power in the system. It follows that the complex of factors that Morgenthau and Bull associate with the balance of power are reduced down to the single factor of competitive polarity. From one perspective, therefore, Waltz simply re-packaged a rather familiar conception of the balance of power as a natural law, but from another perspective he clarified what is meant by the structure of the international system and demonstrated how changes in the polarity or structure of the system give rise to and explain the very different responses by the constituent states. As demonstrated in Chapter 6, Waltz's structural approach to international politics has come under sustained and persistent attack from the moment that he articulated his position, and there are few signs that the debate is running out of steam.[9]

Within a few years, however, even realists began to reject the parsimony of Waltz's approach and they expressed a growing interest in a set of variables that began to open up a foreign policy framework. Initially, these moves were couched as modifications of Waltz's approach,

---

[9] For a survey of some of the early critiques, see Keohane (1986). Molloy (2006) reveals that Waltz continues to generate controversy.

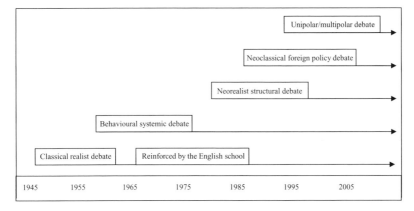

Figure 8.2 The emergence of balance of power debates after the Second World War

as with Walt's (1987) shift from a focus on the balance of power to a concern with a balance of threat. But twenty years later, as already noted, Schweller's (2006) explanation of underbalancing is premised on the need to focus on the internal constitution of the state. But this 'neoclassical' approach emerged even before the end of the cold war. So when critics argued that international relations theory, in general, and realism, in particular, had failed the discipline because it was unable to account for this historical transformation, realism was already positioned to provide a robust response.

An important consequence of this movement away from Waltz's structural approach to explanation is that instead of relating the balance of power to the reproduction of the anarchic international system, attention is now often focused on the specific foreign policy responses of individual states and 'balancing' is associated with a very specific kind of foreign policy behaviour. Schweller (2006: 10), for example, distinguishes between balancing, underbalancing, overbalancing, and nonbalancing. But over the last twenty years, balancing has been examined in the context of a growing range of alternative responses or strategies. These include, among others: bandwagoning, buckpassing, chainganging, distancing, hiding, grouping, baiting, bloodletting and boondoggling.[10] Critics of the balance of power argue that not only

[10] See Schweller (1994) on bandwagoning; Christiansen and Snyder (1990) on buckpassing and chainganging; Schweller (1998) on distancing;

are all these strategies available, but that states are much more likely to follow these strategies than either internal or external balancing. But from Waltz's perspective, there is generally enough balancing to ensure that anarchy is reproduced and that if there is not, then this cannot be explained at the structural level and it is necessary to drop down to a foreign policy level of analysis. Whereas Waltz invariably tries to maintain the distinction between structural analysis and foreign policy analysis, his neoclassical critics are effectively dissolving the distinction.[11] The growth of the neoclassical approach to realism has unquestionably meant that Waltz has been pushed onto the back foot and there is much more scepticism about the utility of the distinction than there was before the end of the cold war.

The end of the cold war precipitated a new development in the balance of power literature and provided the source for a new debate. Initially, some neorealist structuralists argued that unipolarity would precipitate balancing and a return to multipolarity. But there were always realists who saw unipolarity as the norm rather than the exception. So it is unsurprising that realists returned to this argument and insisted that there is no reason to suppose that unipolarity is necessarily unstable or that it will rapidly give way to multipolarity.[12] Realists, like Waltz, however, remained critical of this argument and they insisted that no matter how benign a hegemonic power might seem to be in the first instance, over time they will start to pursue policies that other states in the international system find unacceptable. As discussed in Chapter 6, whether right or wrong, this mythopoeic position is certainly not compatible with the structural logic that Waltz developed in *Theory of International Politics*.

Although Waltz (2000a) persists with the argument that unipolarity is inherently unstable and will eventually give way to multipolarity, other structural realists have acknowledged that there is a need to

Schroeder (1994b; 2003) on hiding and grouping, Mearsheimer (2001) on baiting and bloodletting; and Kaufman, Little and Wohlforth (2007) on boondoggling.

[11] Although not a neoclassical realist, this line of critique is very apparent in Elman's debate with Waltz (1996). For a very articulate discussion of the implications of Waltz's position as well as the general failure of theorists in International Relations to appreciate the significance of his position, see Humphrey (2006).

[12] For a survey of this debate, see Kapstein and Mastanduno (1999).

develop a more profound understanding of the prevailing structure –
in line with Waltz's original injunction. The resulting debate reveals
that the task of understanding unipolarity is a good deal more complex
and contentious than Waltz appears willing to acknowledge. Wohlforth
(1999) makes the important point that the structure of the contemporary international system is very distinctive and that in contrast to the
hegemonic powers of the nineteenth and twentieth centuries, there is
no state that can challenge the United States now or in the near future.
As a consequence, 'structural pressures' on the United States are weak.
But as we saw in Chapter 7, offensive realists have added geographical factors into the structural equation. For Mearsheimer, the effect of
this move is essentially to regionalize the international system, because
although regional hegemony becomes a plausible goal for great powers to pursue (as the United States did in the western hemisphere),
geographical factors make it impossible for great powers to achieve
global or extraregional hegemony. Since the end of the Second World
War, according to Mearsheimer, the United States has played the role
of offshore balancer, ensuring that no other great power (specifically
the Soviet Union and China during the cold war) became a regional
hegemon.

Layne (2006) has launched a powerful attack on this line of argument, buying into Wohlforth's view of unipolarity and then extending it
to argue that the United States has achieved extraregional hegemony in
the three most important regions in the world: Europe, East Asia, and
the Middle East. He also accepts that structural pressures are weak
and that it is not possible to develop an understanding of US grand
strategy using a structural perspective. Instead he adopts a neoclassical realist perspective that focuses on the interaction between the
domestic sources of foreign policy in conjunction with the structure
of the international system. So US grand strategy is accounted for in
terms of the orientation of US economic policy and ideology as well
as the distribution of power in the international system. Layne then
uses Mearsheimer's structural understanding of the system to make the
counterfactual argument that the United States does have the option of
employing an offshore balancing strategy and it would be wise to pursue this option because, in the long haul, the drive for global hegemony
will fail.

Disputes about unipolarity, however, are not restricted to the orientation of US grand strategy. The disagreements also extend to accounts

Figure 8.3 International systems with one strong state

of what the other states in the system are doing. Pape (2005), for example, insists that what they can do is structurally constrained and that it is not possible to discuss their position without having a precise understanding of the distribution of power within the system. He draws a sharp distinction between balance of power systems and hegemonic systems. He argues that in a balance of power system as opposed to a hegemonic system, the unipolar super power is 'still not altogether immune to the possibility of balancing by most or all of the second-ranked powers acting in concert' (Pape, 2005: 11, see Figure 8.3). Drawing on Waltzian ideas about the difficulties of achieving coordination in a multipolar system, Pape then goes on to argue that it is even more difficult for second-ranked powers in a unipolar system to act in concert and establish a military alliance that is directed at the super power. Pape suggests that while hard balancing is very difficult to achieve, soft balancing is much easier to bring off. In a unipolar system, while hard balancing necessarily requires the formation of military alliances, soft balancing uses the coordination of non-military policy instruments 'to delay, frustrate and undermine' the unilateral activity of the super power. Soft balancing, therefore, involves international institutions, economic statecraft and diplomatic initiatives.

Interest in soft balancing expanded rapidly as a consequence of the widespread opposition to the essentially unilateral decision in 2003 by the United States to intervene in Iraq. It was argued that the very widespread support for the US grand strategy that prevailed after the end of the cold war was seen to be in danger of fragmenting. Though there is no consensus yet among the great powers in favour of 'hard balancing' the United States by establishing a countervailing military alliance, it is argued that there is now evidence of the great powers agreeing on less extreme 'soft balancing' measures, to encourage the United States to rein in its unilateralism (Pape, 2005; Paul, 2004; 2005; Walt, 2005). Critics, however, are unconvinced that 'soft balancing' is a helpful concept. Brooks and Wohlforth (2005) argue that there are better explanations for the measures being discussed that have nothing to do with balancing the United States. Along the same lines, Lieber and Alexander (2005: 110) argue that 'soft balancing' is indistinguishable from 'routine diplomatic friction' and is, as a consequence, fundamentally different from traditional balancing. From their perspective, therefore, 'soft balancing' is a case of 'concept stretching' (Sartori, 1970) which occurs when a theorist extends an established term to cover a completely different phenomenon.[13]

Although Figure 8.2 indicates that the five debates about the balance of power initiated in the era since the end of the Second World War are proceeding on separate tramlines, there is, as indicated above, some overlap. Indeed, it can be argued that the three most recent debates have all merged and they can now be viewed as one complex and inter-related ongoing debate. This is not surprising, since the separate debates all start from the common assumption that states are self-interested units operating within a competitive environment. There is also a limited engagement with the more behavioural literature.[14] By contrast, theorists working within these debates have displayed no interest in engaging with the approaches to the balance of power advanced by Morgenthau and Bull. But as I argued in Chapters 4 and 5, both theorists worked within a framework that created space for a more expansive conception of the balance of power. The aim of the next section is to explore this space and to examine the implications of developing a more composite model of the balance of power.

Widening the dimensions of the balance of power

The balance of power is usually discussed in terms of polarity, but the intention of this section is to extend the dimensions of the concept by also taking into account a geographical dimension as well as the distinction that the English school draws between system and society. Once all three of these dimensions are embraced, it then becomes apparent why it is inadequate to try to understand the balance of power simply in terms of polarity. Moreover, because the three dimensions are intimately inter-related, they also precipitate a very distinctive view of the international arena.

---

[13] I am grateful to Stuart Kaufman for drawing this reference to my attention.
[14] See, for example, Thompson's (2006) very illuminating application of behavioural research to a series of propositions drawn from the emerging literature on unipolarity.

The system/society divide is privileged in this discussion. This is partly because it has important knock-on consequences for how we think about both polarity and the geographical dimension but also because there are substantial and growing differences among English school theorists about the utility of the distinction. As noted in Chapter 5, it can be argued that there is a consensus within the English school for moving away from the distinction, despite the importance that both Bull and Watson attached to it. Buzan (2004a), for example, identifies the international system as a type of international society that is governed by power politics. It operates at one end of a spectrum of international societies. But in a critique of Buzan, Dunne (2005) argues in favour of retaining an analytical distinction between system and society. He starts to make the case on two grounds, first in order to distinguish between anomic and social interactions; and second to accommodate a distinction between the social and the material world.

But these distinctions fail to establish clear blue water between Dunne and Buzan. After all, Buzan employs the first distinction that Dunne advances, treating the international system as an anomic world that operates on the basis of power political practices. Buzan insists, however, that these practices are necessarily social practices and so the world of power politics has to be viewed as a particular kind of international society. A power political arena is then located on a continuum of international societies that runs from one extreme where states share no common norms and values through to what Buzan labels a convergence international society where all the states subscribe to the same norms and values. Buzan also acknowledges, however, the need to accommodate the distinction between social and material factors, although he accepts Wendt's constructivist argument that almost everything that we want to explain about international politics needs to be dealt with from a social rather than a material perspective.

What Buzan loses in making this move is Bull's notion that the international system represents the foundation on which any international society builds. Buzan, however, does not think that this foundation amounts to very much. And indeed, at first sight, it is difficult to disagree with him. Bull formally defines a system as a 'constellation' of states that interact and monitor each other's activity. But this is a necessary feature of any society and it is certainly not self-evident what is gained by extracting this element out and identifying it as a system.

But as we showed in Chapter 5, Bull does make quite a lot more of the distinction than this, and distinguishes between a kind of Hobbesian international system (Buzan's power political international society) and an international system that is mediated by the existence of a rule-governed international society. Bull, however, fails to develop this distinction and so it is still difficult to rely on him to make further progress.[15] What I want to do in this section, therefore, is to tie the system/society distinction to the idea that the balance of power can be related to two very different dynamics: one linked to an adversarial balance of power and the other linked to an associational balance of power. The assumption is that these two dynamics co-exist but that they are never equally prominent. As a consequence, it is not the case that the international system provides the foundations for the international society, but rather, if one is in the foreground, then the other is in the background. Whichever dynamic is in the background, however, provides the basis for a counterfactual analysis of current developments.

One way forward to clarify what is meant by an international system is to focus on the models developed by Waltz and Mearsheimer. They are both primarily concerned with the idea of an international system and downgrade the significance that the English school attaches to the idea of an international society. From their perspective, the international system is derived from material factors that impose structural pressures on states to pursue balancing strategies and so they explicitly aim to develop an understanding of the balance of power without taking account of international society. In doing so, Waltz highlights the impact of polarity and Mearsheimer also brings geographical factors to centre stage. Both polarity and geography are treated by Mearsheimer and Waltz as material forces that have an independent impact on how statesmen behave.

Waltz's theory of the balance of power shows why bipolarity is much more stable than multipolarity. At the heart of the argument is the assumption that in a bipolar system, the two states rely solely on their own resources to survive. So if one state starts to increase expenditure on armaments and the other state wishes to ensure that it can survive in

---

[15] The importance of the distinction for both Bull and Watson is discussed in some detail in Vigezzi (2005). Some of the key articles where Watson (2007) looks at the concept have now been reprinted, along with Watson's latest thinking.

the future, then it has no alternative but to follow suit. This argument presupposes, of course, that the other state can keep up. In fact, as we saw in Chapter 6, Waltz recognized in 1979 that it would be difficult for the Soviet Union to keep pace with the United States. Built into his theory, therefore, is the potential for an account of how bipolarity can collapse into unipolarity, although Waltz did not pursue the argument. As noted earlier, Waltz's failure to bring unipolarity into focus represents an anomaly in his thinking. It has been left to subsequent theorists to explore the implications of unipolarity.[16]

Waltz's discussion of multipolarity is similarly incomplete. He argues that under these structural and material conditions, states not only resort to internal balancing, but they also engage in external balancing, forming alliances with each other. But he argues that even with a limited number of states forming alliances it is very easy to miscalculate. As a consequence, there is a constant danger that balancing will fail to take place. Waltz insists, however, that even though the structure is much less stable than under conditions of bipolarity, there is sufficient flexibility to ensure that anarchy is reproduced. It is difficult to refute this line of argument in the European context because a system of independent sovereign states has persisted throughout modern history. Waltz, however, makes the argument that this is a persistent feature across world history, whereas a systematic survey of world history reveals that multipolarity has frequently given way to unipolarity or hegemony.[17] Indeed, Watson (1992; 2007) makes the argument that hegemony rather than anarchy represents the norm in international relations from a world historical perspective. Waltz could have acknowledged that his theory provides the basis of an explanation for the collapse of multipolar systems as well as multipolar system reproduction. But although he is well placed to develop this argument, it too has been left to others to make the running.[18]

---

[16] Wohlforth (1999) and Pape (2005) provide very different but sophisticated accounts of behaviour in a unipolar system.

[17] This is a longstanding criticism of Waltz's work. See Buzan, Jones and Little (1993) and Buzan and Little (2000).

[18] Hui (2004; 2005) provides one of the most interesting accounts of how a potential hegemon can manipulate a multipolar system to its own advantage and overcome the resistance of the other states. For a series of case studies and theoretical reflections on this theme, see Kaufman, Little and Wohlforth (2007).

What this line of argument suggests is that the systemic mechanisms associated with a material conception of the balance of power are not a foolproof way of preserving anarchy. For Morgenthau and Bull this is not a surprising conclusion. They recognized that the purely self-interested and uncoordinated actions of states can never guarantee stability or produce order. But unlike Waltz, Mearsheimer also acknowledges that the balancing mechanisms associated with polarity are insufficient to account for the persistence of the modern system of independent states. From his perspective, geography introduces differential amounts of friction into the international system and thereby helps to account for the survival of independent states. Whereas Waltz simply ignores geography, Mearsheimer argues that it has the effect of putting states under different levels of material constraint.

Despite its limitations, Mearsheimer's approach also allows him to explore the balance of power from a foreign policy perspective and to explain, for example, why it is easier for some states (specifically insular states) to leave the task of balancing a hegemon to others. Insular states become offshore balancers that can potentially delay the decision to resist an aspiring hegemon. But perhaps even more important, the distinction creates space for Mearsheimer to introduce a regional and hemispheric dimension to his analysis of the balance of power. Bull, of course, also makes room for a regional dimension, but he concludes, at least in the context of the cold war, that regional balances are unequivocally subordinate to the global balance of power. Mearsheimer, however, adopts a very different position and one that privileges regions and hemispheres. Whereas Waltz argues that the exemplar for his mulipolar system is nineteenth-century Europe, Mearsheimer presents a very different structural model, which views the continent as part of a much broader system. It is a model moreover, as we saw in Chapter 7, that also poses interesting questions for Mearsheimer's theory. In particular, why did the European great powers fail to do anything to stop the United States from becoming a hemispheric hegemon? To answer this question, however, it is necessary to have a better understanding of the system/society relationship.

From an English school perspective, the idea of an international society has traditionally presupposed the existence of states that share common interests and values and are willing to be bound by agreed rules and to operate on the basis of common institutions. But there is also a presumption, expressed most clearly by Bull, that the international society is sustained by the balance of power and is underpinned by an international system. What he fails to do is to clarify the relationship that exists between the balance of power and both the international system and the international society. At first sight, it might seem that Bull's image of the international society being underpinned by the international system can be mapped onto the social/material distinction, with the international system being defined by material factors and the international society being defined by social factors. Making this move, however, is questionable because although the discussion so far has given priority to the international system, there are good grounds for thinking that the international society must be privileged over the international system. In other words, there is a fundamental problem with the idea that the international system underpins international society. The nature of the problem has been highlighted by Ruggie (1998: 25), who criticizes the theoretical stances adopted by both neorealists and neoliberals because they focus on 'regulative rules that coordinate behaviour in a pre-constituted world'. So, for example, states are taken for granted in these theories and there is no attempt to understand how international reality is constituted in the first instance.

The neorealist literature, exemplified by Waltz and Mearsheimer, certainly treats the international system as a given, and the balance of power is regarded as a mechanism that maintains this pre-constituted world. But neither Waltz nor Mearsheimer give any thought to how this order was established in the first place. By contrast, both Morgenthau and Bull are interested in how international reality is constituted and how the constitution of this reality has changed across time. Moreover, both also acknowledge that balance of power thinking has historically played a crucial role in constituting and reconstituting the prevailing international order. But to understand this role it is necessary to move beyond the conception of an international system and embrace the conceptions of an international society and an associational balance of power.

There is growing support for the idea that the evolution of the modern international society can most effectively be traced through the history of the major international peace settlements that have taken place over the last four hundred years, because it is recognized that decision-makers are necessarily very sensitive to how the structure of the international society is being constituted or re-constituted at these junctures.[19] So, for example, the 1648 peace settlement formulated at Westphalia is now regarded as important not because it established the foundations of the contemporary international society but because it consolidated the principle that international developments could only be legitimized by common agreement. Although balance of power thinking played no more than an informal role at Westphalia, during the Utrecht settlement of 1713–14 maintaining the balance of power was formally espoused as a legitimate principle of international society 'that should take precedence over competing norms' (Clark, 2005: 81). What this meant in practice was that the major parties to the agreement accepted that they needed to moderate their demands so as to ensure that the legitimate security interests of all the parties were satisfied. On this basis it was possible to establish a consensus about the territorial settlements. It was the general acceptability of the distribution of power that created the basis for the 'just equilibrium' and explains why this associational balance of power had such an important constitutive role to play in the international society that emerged from the Utrecht peace settlement. The same concern with building a just equilibrium on the basis of consensus prevailed in 1815 at the Congress of Vienna, thereby ensuring that the distribution of power that emerged from the territorial agreements carried legitimacy. But it was also agreed at Vienna that it was the responsibility of the newly constituted directorate of great powers to manage future changes in this legitimized balance of power.

As both Morgenthau and Bull acknowledge, the European international society emerged out of the complex society that had formed and evolved during the medieval era. As a consequence, it is simply anachronistic to presume that a society of sovereign states emerged fully fledged in 1648 at Westphalia. Nevertheless, an investigation of the major peace treaties reveals that the concept of an associational balance of power played a crucial role in helping to consolidate the idea of an international society that consisted of states that mutually recognized each other's sovereign rights, and also the idea that the great powers had the responsibility of managing the society and maintaining a stable distribution of power. Morgenthau and Bull also make clear, however, that how states are constituted and the practices employed to maintain

---

[19] See, for example, Holsti (1991), Osiander (1994), Ikenberry (2001), Bobbitt (2002) and Clark (2005).

a stable society of states have changed across time and that both of these developments are intimately linked to the associational balance of power that underpinned the European international society. For both theorists, the intersubjective agreement among European statesmen, displayed most clearly at the major eighteenth- and nineteenth-century peace settlements, that international order depended upon an agreed distribution of power that maintained a sense of security among all the great powers, represented the bedrock on which the European international society could build.

This assessment of an associational balance of power and its relationship with the European international society is complicated by three inter-related factors. First is Europe's relations with the non-European world, second is Europe's relations with the western hemisphere, and third is the relationship that Bull, explicitly, and Morgenthau, implicitly, establishes between system and society. Bull presupposes that in the nineteenth century the European international society operated within a global international system. Although there is no simple and straightforward way of articulating the relationship between Europe and the rest of the world, Bull's formulation unnecessarily complicates the relationship between system and society. A more coherent position, consistent with Keene (2002), accepts that the Europeans established a social relationship with the non-European world, but that a different set of rules and values underpinned Europe's relations with the non-western world (see Figure 8.4). The difference is very evident at the 1884–5 Berlin Africa Conference. As Uzoigwe (1988: 541) notes, for the first time in history 'a concert of one continent gathered together to plan how to share out another continent without the knowledge of the latter's leaders'. Wesserling (1988: 533) adds that 'Politically speaking, the role of the Berlin Conference was not to do the partitioning itself, but to draw the attention of the world to this process and legitimize it.'

In practice, of course, there was nothing new about partitioning territory. As noted in Chapter 4, partitioning territory is often depicted as a characteristic practice in seventeenth- and eighteenth-century balance of power politics. But with the growth of nationalism in Europe, partitioning was a practice that was much more difficult to accomplish in nineteenth-century Europe. But not in Africa. The Berlin Conference illustrates very clearly that although Africa was part of a global international society, the Europeans were operating on the basis of

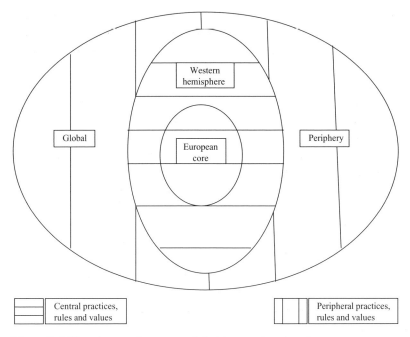

Figure 8.4 The nineteenth-century global international society

very different practices, rules and values to those that they applied to themselves. By contrast, when we turn to the western hemisphere in the nineteenth century, and in particular to Europe's relations with the United States, it is clear that the Europeans accepted that the practices, rules and values that operated within Europe had been extended to the western hemisphere. Although Britain and France would have preferred to see North America divided into a number of states, they were resigned to the continental expansion of the United States, and the Europeans in general accepted the legitimacy of this expansion and acknowledged that the United States was an emergent great power. The Europeans, in other words, did not consider that the establishment of the continental-wide United States posed a threat to the distribution of power on which international society rested. As a consequence, when the civil war in the United States broke out in 1861, the Europeans, following the British and French lead, chose to observe the dictates of customary international law (Little, 2007a).

This assessment, as we saw in Chapter 7, represents an anomaly for Mearsheimer, but it also raises the question of the system/society divide in Morgenthau and Bull's thinking and the relationship that this divide has with the view of system that Waltz and Mearsheimer entertain. The assumption that underpins the society side of the divide is that by the eighteenth century there was an established consensus within Europe that acknowledged the value of maintaining a society of sovereign states and it was also recognized that to sustain this society, the legitimate security interests of all the great powers had to be met. It is this fundamental consensus about the need for an agreed distribution of power that provides one of the essential features of the European international society. However, these foundations also embrace a systemic or adversarial assessment of the balance of power. The systemic assessment presupposes a general recognition within the international society that if a great power pursues a policy that challenges the security of another great power, then the inter-subjective consensus will start to break down and the great powers will revert to self-help strategies. There will, as a consequence, be some pressure on states to pursue balancing strategies, and this pressure increases with the identification of a great power that aims to overturn the foundations of the international society.

What is important about this formulation is that the systemic dimension is encompassed by the social dimension. In other words, the dynamics defined by the adversarial balance of power operates within the context of an international society. At the same time, it is the inter-subjective awareness of the potential for the adversarial dynamics to come into play that produces the disincentive for states to move away from the established associational balance of power. This line of argument, therefore, is only partially compatible with Kissinger's (1964: 173; 1994: 77–9) assertion that the stability that prevailed after the 1815 Vienna settlement was attributable to the great power consensus in favour of the status quo, in conjunction with the recognition that the status quo was underpinned by a balance of power. The argument being made here is that the status quo was designed to promote the security of the great powers, but it was also underpinned by an awareness that any attempt to change the associational balance of power by force would generate self-help measures and the dynamics associated with an adversarial balance of power. These dynamics, however, would eliminate any possibility of unconditional victory and hence inevitably lead to the establishment of a new associational balance of power.

The key point about this formulation, therefore, is that during the eighteenth and nineteenth centuries there was a presumption that when the consensus broke down, it could in principle be re-established. Throughout this period, however, the territorial interests of the European great powers across the globe were in constant flux and, as a consequence, so too was the balance of power and the security interests of the great powers. So, in practice, the consensus on which the associational balance of power rested always did break down because of the inherent dynamism of the international environment. As a consequence, the significance of the associational balance of power is open to question. Even the nineteenth-century Concert of Europe that rested on the associational balance defined by the Vienna settlement has been dismissed as a myth (Kagan, 1997).[20] But this assessment underestimates the extent to which there was broad inter-subjective agreement about the merits and durability of the international society of states and the recognition that if the consensus surrounding the associational balance of power broke down, states could still rely on the mechanisms defined by the adversarial balance of power to survive and reconstitute the associational balance of power. There was, therefore, a strong incentive to try to implement change on a consensual basis.

From the perspective of Morgenthau and Bull, however, the system/society distinction becomes more contentious in the twentieth century because both acknowledge that the emergence of a fundamental division between the United States and the Soviet Union had the effect of undermining the basis for a common international society. The Soviet Union was, in fact, socialized into acknowledging the fundamental rules and practices of the global international society, but in the aftermath of the Second World War both the super powers established themselves as hegemons in sub-global international societies that began to elaborate distinctive rules and practices that threatened to undermine the rules and practices of the global international society. Tensions between the two super powers can be traced back to the formation of the Soviet Union. This new state was not represented at

[20] A close reading of diplomatic history, in conjunction with an interest in theory, has failed to resolve the issue. Schroeder (1994a) argues that there was an institutional transformation in the international arena after 1815, whereas Kagan (1997) insists that the great powers were not interested in operating on a consensus basis and simply pursued their own short-term interests. For a more nuanced view, see Rendall (2000; 2002; 2006).

the Versailles settlement in 1919 and so there was no possibility of establishing an international consensus on that occasion.

Although it can be argued that the outcome of the Second World War resulted in a settlement informally established by the two super powers, Clark (2005: 144) concludes that on the basis of the available evidence 'the argument that the division of Europe into spheres was consensually reached at the time does not appear very convincing'.[21] But even if the division was consensually agreed, the consensus unequivocally broke down soon after the Second World War and the adversarial or systemic forces came into play. The United States and the Soviet Union accused each other of having imperial or hegemonic ambitions, although both states insisted that they intended to observe the fundamental rules of the extant international society. In practice, both super powers proceeded to bend these rules in the process of promoting an international society within their own sphere of influence that reflected their own norms and values.[22] Waltz insists that there were no systemic pressures driving the two super powers to become involved in areas beyond their own spheres of influence. But this argument ignores the complex interaction between system and society. Both super powers wanted to expand the domain of the international society that was centred on them. As a consequence, the resulting competition between the United States and the Soviet Union had a substantial impact on the decolonization process and their interactions in these areas in the subsequent post-colonial period.

Figure 8.5 attempts in a rather crude way to use the system/society distinction to map the cold war, although using Mearsheimer's view of the system rather than Waltz's conception of a system. What emerges is

[21] The 'spheres of influence' deal, contemplated during World War Two, which had the effect of dividing Europe, was widely condemned (Reis, 1981; 1978).

[22] One of the clearest example of transforming the rules of the global international society came with the establishment of President Johnson's Doctrine, enunciated in 1965 to justify the landing of troops on the Dominican Republic. The Americans argued that communists could precipitate 'internal aggression' and the United States had the right to go to the assistance of a government under such an internal communist threat. Three years later, the exact same justification, almost word for word, was echoed back to the Americans by President Brezhnev in his Doctrine, formulated to justify the intervention by the Warsaw Pact countries into Czechoslovakia. See Franck and Weisband (1971) and Keal (1983).

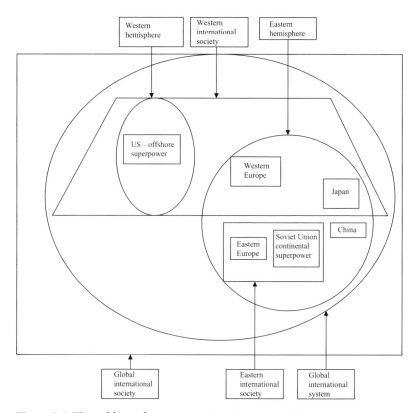

Figure 8.5 The cold war from a system/society perspective

that the alliance systems that the United States established with Japan and western Europe reinforced an emerging western international society that built upon and promoted common norms and values. These two developments went hand in hand. If we remove the societal dimension, and think purely in systemic terms, then counterfactual questions arise: what would have happened if the United States, operating in line with Mearsheimer's conception of an offshore balancer, had withdrawn from its alliance commitments once Japan and western Europe had recovered economically, and why, given its offshore status, did it fail to do so? An adversarial balance of power theory predicts that if the United States had withdrawn, then Europe and Japan would have been compelled to respond, either by internal balancing, with nuclear weapons, or by external balancing, linking with each other and/or possibly China. From a Waltzian perspective, the resulting multipolar

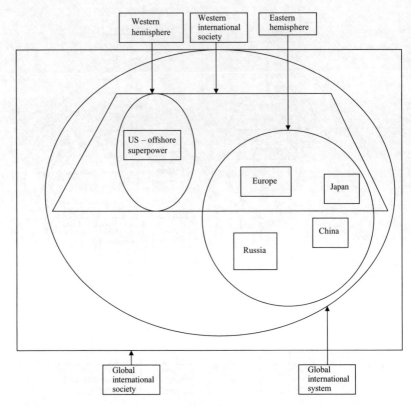

Figure 8.6 The post-cold war era from a system/society perspective

outcome would be much less stable than the bipolar situation where the adversarial balance of power was maintained by the United States and the Soviet Union. The danger of instability could provide a sufficient explanation for the continued presence of the United States in Eurasia. But bringing the societal dimension into focus offers a different, albeit reinforcing line of argument. Withdrawing from Eurasia would not only have raised the danger of instability, but it would also have signalled a lack of interest in defending the norms and values linked to the western international society. It would have encouraged further nuclear proliferation and that runs against the norms and values not only of the western international society, but the global international society as well. But perhaps the most significant point that emerges from Figure 8.5 is that to define the cold war era as bipolar represents a one-dimensional and over-simplified view of the structure of the international arena.

If we now turn, briefly, to examine the post-cold war era from a system/society perspective, again using Mearsheimer's framework to characterize the international system (see Figure 8.6), then very little changes from the picture of the cold war presented in Figure 8.5, except that Russia has replaced the Soviet Union and the latter's attempt to build an international society has turned to dust with eastern Europe now rapidly consolidating its position within the western international society. However, if we remove the societal dimension for a moment, and focus on the systemic perspective, then once again a number of counterfactual questions arise. Why has the United States not withdrawn from Eurasia and why is there so little evidence of balancing against the United States? As in a systemic assessment of the cold war, the continued presence of the United States on Eurasia appears anomalous. It was frequently forecast in the aftermath of the cold war that the United States would disband the North Atlantic Treaty Organisation (NATO), whereas in practice its membership has increased. By the same token, the demise of the Soviet Union leaves the United States in a much stronger position than it occupied during the cold war. An adversarial balance of power theory predicts, therefore, that the great powers of Eurasia will begin to balance internally and externally against the United States.

Reintroducing the societal dimension, however, puts a very different gloss on the post-cold war setting, certainly from the perspective of members of the western international society who share common norms and values. The arguments against the United States withdrawing from Eurasia during the cold war continue to hold in the post-cold war era. It would reflect a lack of solidarity with other members of the western international society and potentially encourage them to think in terms of an adversarial balance of power. Given this perspective, it would be irrational for these states either to request the United States to withdraw from Eurasia or to balance against the United States. At the same time, there is very little incentive for either Russia or China to balance against the United States, since there is no evidence to suggest that the United States poses a threat to their existence. The United States, for example, has made no move to exploit internal unrest within Russia and has shown no signs of wanting to get involved in China's troubled relationship with Taiwan. Although there are many issues that divide the major powers, their interactions with each other are constrained by the basic norms and rules that underpin the global international society.

Reassessing the balance of power

In one of the most devastating critiques of realism that has ever been made, Guzzini (1998) argues that realist theorists, from Morgenthau onwards, have endeavoured without any success to translate the maxims of nineteenth-century diplomatic practice into general social scientific laws. The balance of power unquestionably plays a central role in these maxims as well as in the models of the four theorists examined in this book. My central argument, however, completely runs against the grain of Guzzini's thesis. Although it is unquestionably the case that the four theorists are influenced by the longstanding metaphorical and mythical thinking associated with the balance of power, the models that they develop are quite distinct and, in practice, the metaphorical and mythical thinking has only provided a springboard which has propelled each theorist along a rather different trajectory. In other words, the positivist account of how scientists move from metaphors to models provides a more accurate assessment of how the four theorists have proceeded than Guzzini's idea that they are all engaged in an unsuccessful act of translation. This is true, despite the fact that Morgenthau and Bull were both profoundly sceptical of attempts to apply positivist methods to the study of international relations.

Although the four theorists proceed in rather different directions, they do start from a common interest in accounting for the persistence of an international arena of independent states and they each adopt a top-down approach to the task. As a consequence, they are drawn to the balance of power metaphor because it generates a structural assessment of power that requires them to recognize that power is not only a central feature of international politics, but it is also a product of the system of which the states form a part. But the four theorists also acknowledge that the way that power diffuses through the system is not straightforward and is mediated by other factors that have changed across time. As a consequence, all four theorists acknowledge that the balance of power is a dynamic feature of international politics. It is at this juncture that the theorists start moving in different directions, because they place a different emphasis on the factors that can potentially affect the diffusion of power through the system. The aim of the previous section was to explore the possibility of establishing a composite assessment of the balance of power. While offering no more than a thumbnail sketch of the composite view, three overarching implications with potentially important ramifications seem to follow. First, the composite view widens the scope for thinking about the balance of power; second, it only provides a research framework and not a more comprehensive theory; and third, it confronts any attempt to establish a balance of power theory on a more restricted basis with significant problems.

For example, despite the fact that Mearsheimer's emphasis on the 'stopping power of water' has run into fierce criticism, it does nevertheless highlight the potential importance of the geographical dimension because it creates scope for considerable friction in the way that power is seen to diffuse through the system. So although the 'stopping power of water' may be a very blunt tool, it undoubtedly raises questions about the relationship between the western and Eurasian hemispheres and to what extent this factor has affected balance of power calculations over the past three or four centuries. Initially, the western hemisphere was defined in terms of European spheres of influence, but by the nineteenth century, the United States began to enter European balance of power calculations. By the 1860s, Lord Russell, the British Foreign Secretary during the American Civil War, was acutely conscious of the long-term consequences of victory for the North and saw that a Russo-American agreement had the capacity to produce a new balance of power in the world with these two states establishing primacy on the world stage. Ultimately, he argued, they could establish two spheres of influence, one in the East and the other in the West (Crook, 1974: 285). It is evidence of this kind that Mearsheimer can draw upon in support of his argument that by this point North America was considered invulnerable to successful invasion by the Europeans; and it is central to his argument that the United States remains invulnerable. The implications of having an invulnerable great power in the system for possibly the past 150 years have certainly not been explored by international relations theorists and Mearsheimer's identification of the United States as an offshore balancer during this period at least has the effect of helping theorists to break out of the Eurocentric straitjacket.

By taking the geographical dimension seriously, it also opens up the intriguing notion that the international arena should be viewed as a set of inter-linked regions rather than a fully integrated system. Mearsheimer is certainly not alone in thinking that the notion of regions is much more important than has generally been acknowledged by international relations theory.[23] But perhaps this has always been the case. Although many theorists in international relations have noted the acuteness and sophistication of the account of the Peloponnesian War given by Thucydides, his failure to assess what Persia was doing for much of the war is regarded by at least one scholar as 'a scandal' (Cawkwell, 1997: 17). From Mearsheimer's perspective, of course, Persia was without doubt operating as an offshore balancer and its failure to get directly involved is entirely to be expected. There are certainly problems with such an account (Little, 2007b), but it nevertheless draws attention to the fact that regions have always operated in the context of broader systems.

Despite opening up new avenues of thinking, when we turn the clock back and look at the approach to the balance of power adopted by Morgenthau and Bull, Mearsheimer's assessment looks one-dimensional. Indeed, it is clear that more recent attempts to develop a more rigorous conception of the balance of power have taken place at the expense of stripping away the complexity of the more traditional concept. But in doing so, they have generated problems for themselves which do not arise when a more composite view of the balance of power is adopted. The problems come from two different directions. For Mearsheimer, given the collapse of the Soviet Union, it is anomalous that the United States has not yet pulled out of Europe and Japan. For Waltz, given the disparity in power between the United States and all the other great powers, the anomaly is the failure of the Eurasian great powers to balance against the United States. Both Waltz and Mearsheimer, however, are only looking at international politics in terms of an adversarial balance of power. But this perspective presupposes that to understand international politics we only need to think in terms of an international system. By also taking account of an international society, as Morgenthau and Bull do, then it has to be acknowledged not only that the diffusion of power is affected by the norms and rules that constitute this

[23] For radically different, although equally interesting, approaches see Buzan and Waever (2003); and Katzenstein (2005).

society but also that these norms and rules have changed across time, building on a consensus that is defined by an associational balance of power.

Perhaps the most surprising implication of the composite view of the balance of power is the way that the significance of polarity gets downgraded. For Waltz, of course, polarity is the most crucial feature of the balance of power. Moreover, polarity provides the basis for one of the dominant narratives of how the international system changed across the course of the twentieth century, with multipolarity giving way to bipolarity and then finally unipolarity at the end of the century. The composite view of the balance of power challenges this account, because by highlighting the hemispheric divide it places the United States in a unique position in the western hemisphere and leaves the Eurasian hemisphere defined by multipolarity throughout the twentieth century. As we saw in Chapter 6, however, the picture that Waltz paints is rather different from the one that is generally associated with him because of his argument that with the emergence of bipolarity, the way is opened for a shift from an adversarial balance of power through to an associational one, with competition giving way to collaboration. The fundamental problem with Waltz's exclusive focus on polarity, therefore, is his failure not only to articulate the implications of unipolarity, but also to acknowledge and account for the potential for multilateral collaboration. But such a move would require him to extend his discussion of the balance of power beyond polarity.

Finally, what does the composite view have to say about the future of the balance of power? As we saw in Part III, the four theorists respond in very different ways to this issue. Only Mearsheimer thinks that, from a balance of power perspective, the future will resemble the past. Only he thinks that the potential still exists for great powers to use force to establish hegemony. Just as the United States used its power to establish control over North America and hegemony over the whole hemisphere, so Mearsheimer believes that China will follow suit in its region if the balance of power shifts in its favour. By contrast, the models developed by the other three theorists all point in the opposite direction and reveal that the future will not resemble the past. The crucial difference relates to the role of war in great power relations. Morgenthau, Bull and Waltz all acknowledge that in the past a great power would, in the final analysis, go to war with another great power to defend its vital interests. But when both super powers acquired nuclear weapons with second strike capability, and mutually assured destruction, there was a growing conviction that war between nuclear powers is no longer a rational strategy.

None of the three theorists, however, followed through on the full implications of this insight for their conception of the balance of power. Waltz's starting position is that anarchy is a structure that generates competitive relationships and, as a consequence, states will forego gains from collaboration rather than risk another state gaining a relative advantage by reneging on a collaborative agreement. But having established this position, Waltz then endeavours to show that in a bipolar structure, the move from competition to collaboration is possible. The future consequence of the model is clear: there were no insuperable structural constraints preventing the United States and the Soviet Union from collaborating on the task of solving global problems. However, Waltz failed to examine how the elimination of war as a rational strategy for promoting vital interests opposed by another great power affected his argument about the balance of power. We need to return to this issue.

In contrast to Waltz, neither Morgenthau nor Bull accepted that multipolar conditions necessarily imposed structural constraints on collaboration among the great powers. Both argued that the historical record demonstrated that the European states were able to develop a growing body of norms and rules and that by the nineteenth century the European great powers acknowledged a responsibility to manage the evolving international society. But from the perspective of Morgenthau and Bull, with the emergence of the United States and the Soviet Union not only as the dominant great powers but also as ideological adversaries, any possibility of developing a more integrated international society was stymied. Moreover, with the recognition after the Second World War that any future great power war would be irretrievably catastrophic, Morgenthau concluded that the only rational way forward in the long term was the establishment of a world government that rested on an associational balance of power. By contrast, although Bull examined a wide range of alternative futures and recognized that the future could be very bleak indeed, he concluded that the promotion of a stable and peaceful international society of states still represented the most optimistic vision for the future. Moreover, he also accepted that future great power war was highly unlikely, although he recognized that the ideological cleavage made any further progress on international order difficult and he focused on the promotion of justice rather than order because he believed that this was an issue that straddled the ideological divide. But like Waltz and Morgenthau, Bull also failed to explore the implications for his approach to the balance of power of his belief that great power war is no longer a rational strategy.

There are, however, two obvious but important implications. The first is that great powers will in the future rely on their own resources to establish their security. If the United States ended its alliance with Japan or Europe, then both would extend their own military resources to restore the balance of power. The second conclusion that follows axiomatically from the first is that external balancing is now redundant. A military alliance between China and Russia would not enhance their level of security or shift the balance of power in their favour. This line of argument is only partly to do with nuclear weapons. It is also the consequence of the growing acceptance that war between any of the great powers cannot be rationally contemplated. Neither China nor Russia consider that they are under any existential threat from the United States and so forming an alliance would not change the balance of power. But if this is the case, then it can be questioned whether it is still meaningful to talk of an adversarial balance of power. The generic metaphor presupposes that the distribution of power can potentially change. If the flow of power through the system is halted, then it is no longer possible to identify a military balance of power among the great powers. Bull moved somewhere towards this conclusion when he argued that it was necessary to draw a categorical distinction between deterrence and the balance of power.

If the global adversarial balance of power is becoming redundant, then should it not also follow that the global international system will disappear and security concerns will only register at the regional level? The composite view of the balance of power is certainly compatible with the idea of the global international system moving down to the regional level. But it also identifies the existence of a global international society. Here the assumption has been since the nineteenth century that there should be evidence of collective great power management. During the cold war, the ideological schism prevented management of this kind. Since the end of the cold war, what we have seen is evidence of the United States operating increasingly on a unilateral basis to establish an international order defined by the United

States. Although the composite view of the balance of power challenges the familiar unipolar image of the contemporary international arena, it is also compatible with the idea that the United States is in a unique position to pursue a unilateral foreign policy on a global basis. It is this factor that keeps the global international system in play, with the United States being the only country with global reach and a willingness to use force unilaterally to deal with perceived threats to its interests. Moreover, since the 9/11 terrorist attacks on the United States, this trend has accelerated.

But there have been two inter-related developments that have significant consequences from the perspective of the composite view of the balance of power. First, the United States is finding it increasingly difficult to establish the legitimacy of its actions not only within the global international society but also within the western international society. Second, it is proving no easier in the twenty-first century for external forces to achieve military victory in unconventional wars than it has been in previous centuries and invariably civilians bear the heaviest costs, making legitimacy for future unilateral actions difficult to achieve. As Clark (2005: 252) acknowledges, legitimacy requires consensus, but consensus must accommodate the underlying distribution of power. In other words, legitimacy can only be established on the basis of an associational balance of power and requires an agreement that is tailored to maximize consent. From Bull's perspective, the use of force by the United States and the Soviet Union in the context of the cold war operated within the international system and could never be legitimized in the global international society, although Soviet actions were invariably legitimized within the eastern international society and American actions were generally although not invariably legitimized in the western international society.

From the US perspective, therefore, establishing global legitimacy for its actions has never been a major priority. But as the cold war recedes into the distance and the idea of a condominium of great powers that no longer operate on the basis of an adversarial balance of power begins to take hold, then it will become increasingly difficult for the United States to sustain this position. The emerging great powers are interested in using international society to elevate and promote their own positions. China, for example, is one of the few states to maintain an embassy in almost every country with which it has diplomatic relations. As the idea of an adversarial balance of power fades into the background, the idea of the United States as an offshore balancer will also appear anachronistic. Europe and Japan will begin to play independent roles at the global level. At the same time, the importance of an associational balance of power, requiring the great powers to build consensus, will become increasingly important. The reference to the balance of power in President Bush's 'Introduction' to the 2002 *National Security Strategy*, discussed in Chapter 3, is indicative of the fact that the United States wants to lead from the front, but is aware of the emerging condominium and that the absence of an adversarial balance of power will have significant consequences for the future of world politics.

The historical record of successful great power management of the international society does not always lead to self-evidently desirable results, as the legitimization of African partition illustrates. Nevertheless, it remains the case that there are a whole host of global problems, from the dangers posed by the existence of nuclear weapons, to the threats that human activity poses to the global environment that seem likely to get worse rather than better if the great powers fail to collaborate. In other words, great power collaboration is not only an essential ingredient of legitimacy, but also a necessary ingredient for the successful resolution of some global problems.[24] If it is true that the adversarial balance of power that has always preoccupied the great powers in the past is beginning to atrophy, then one of the impediments to the establishment of an associational balance of power is in the process of being removed. It is far from clear that Waltz is right to link polarity to ease of collaboration. But in any event, the historical record indicates that the European great powers did succeed in building an international society on the basis of an associational balance of power. Although some do see the existence of this society as part of the problem, given that it does exist and is unlikely to disappear in the near future, the knowledge that it can overcome as well as precipitate collective action problems provides a glimmer of hope for the future.

---

[24] For a discussion of the difficulties associated with deciding what constitutes a successful solution to a global problem and why the solution for some represents the problem for others, see McKinlay and Little (1986).

Bibliography

Adler, Emanuel (1992), 'The Emergence of Cooperation: National Epistemic Communities and the International Evolution of the Idea of Nuclear Arms Control', *International Organization* 46(1), 101–45.

Adler, Emanuel (2005), *Communitarian International Relations: The Epistemic Foundations of International Relations*, London: Routledge.

Alderson, Kai (2001), 'Making Sense of State Socialisation', *Review of International Studies* 27(3), 415–33.

Alexandroff, Alan, Richard Rosecrance and Arthur Stein (1977), 'History, Quantitative Analysis and the Balance of Power', *The Journal of Conflict Resolution* 21(1), 35–56.

Allen, John (2003), *Lost Geographies of Power*, Oxford: Blackwell.

Almeida, João Marques de (2006), 'Hedley Bull, "Embedded Cosmopolitanism" and the Pluralist-Solidarist Debate', in Richard Little and John Williams, eds., *The Anarchical Society in a Globalized World*, Houndmills: Palgrave Macmillan.

Armstrong, David (1993), *Revolution and World Order: The Revolutionary State in International Society*, Oxford: Clarendon Press.

Armstrong, David (2006), 'The Nature of Law in an Anarchical Society', in Richard Little and John Williams, eds., *The Anarchical Society in a Globalized World*, Houndmills: Palgrave Macmillan.

Anderson, M. S. (1970), 'Eighteenth-Century Theories of the Balance of Power', in R. Hatton and M. S. Anderson, eds., *Studies in Diplomatic History*, London: Harlow Longmans.

Anderson, M. S. (1993), *The Rise of Modern Diplomacy 1450–1919*, London: Longman.

Angell, Norman (1910), *The Great Illusion: A Study of the Relation of Military Power in Nations to their Economic and Social Advantage*, London: Heinemann.

Aron, Raymond (1966), *Peace and War: A Theory of International Relations*, trans. Richard Howard and Annette Baker Fox, London: Weidenfeld & Nicolson.

Art, Robert J. (1999), 'Force and Fungibility Reconsidered', *Security Studies* 8(4), 183–9.

Asch, Solomon E. (1955), 'On the Use of Metaphors in the Description of Persons', in Heinz Werner, ed., *On Expressive Language*, Worcester, Mass.: Clark University Press.

Bacon, Francis (1904), *The Essays*, London: Macmillan.

Baldwin, David A. (1989), *Paradoxes of Power*, New York and Oxford: Blackwell.

Baldwin, David A. (1993), ed., *Neorealism and Neoliberalism: The Contemporary Debate*, New York: Columbia University Press.

Baldwin, David A. (1999), 'Force, Fungibility and Influence', *Security Studies* 8(4), 173–83.

Baldwin, David A. (2004), 'Power and International Relations', in Walter Carlsnaes, Thomas Risse, and Beth A. Simmons, eds., *Handbook of International Relations*, Thousand Oaks: Sage Publications Ltd.

Ball, Terence (1975), 'Models of Power: Past and Present', *Journal of the History of the Behavioural Sciences* 11: 211–22.

Ball, Terence (1988), *Transforming Political Discourse: Political Theory and Critical Conceptual History*, Oxford: Basil Blackwell.

Barbour, Ian G. (1974), *Myths, Models and Paradigms: A Comparative Study in Science and Religion*, San Francisco: Harper and Row.

Barbour, Ian G. (1998), *Religion and Science: Historical and Contemporary Issues*, London: SCM Press.

Barnes, Trevor J. (1996), *Logics of Dislocation: Models, Metaphors and Meanings of Economic Space*, New York: Guilford Press.

Barthes, Roland (1972), *Mythologies*, trans. Annette Lavers, New York: Noonday Press.

Barthes, Roland (1974), *S/Z: An Essay*, trans. Richard Miller, New York: Hill and Wang.

Baugh, Daniel A. (1987), 'British Strategy During the First World War in the Context of Four Centuries: Blue-Water Versus Continental Commitment', in Daniel M. Masterson, ed., *Naval History: The Sixth Symposium of the U.S. Naval Academy*, Wilmington, Del.: Scholarly Resources.

Beale, H. (1956), *Theodore Roosevelt and the Rise of America to World Power*, Baltimore: John Hopkins Press.

Beer, Francis A. and Christ'L De Landtsheer (2004a), eds., *Metaphorical World Politics*, Lansing: Michigan State University Press.

Beer, Francis A. and Christ'L De Landtsheer (2004b), 'Introduction. Metaphors, Politics and World Politics', in Francis A. Beer and Christ'L De Landtsheer, eds., *Metaphorical World Politics*, Lansing: Michigan State University Press.

Bennett, D. Scott and Allan C. Stam (2004), *The Behavioral Origins of War*, Ann Arbor: University of Michigan.

Black, Jeremy (1990), *The Rise and Fall of the European Powers 1679–1793*, London: Edward Arnold.

Black, Max (1962), *Models and Metaphors: Studies in Language and Philosophy*, Ithaca: Cornell University Press.

Black, Max (1979), 'More about Metaphors', in Andrew Ortony, ed., *Metaphor and Thought*, Cambridge: Cambridge University Press.

Black, Max (1990), *Perplexities: Rational Choice, the Prisoner's Dilemma, Metaphor, Poetic Ambiguity and Other Puzzles*, Ithaca: Cornell University Press.

Blau, Peter M. (1964), *Exchange and Power in Social Life*, New York: Wiley.

Bobbitt, Philip (2002), *The Shield of Achilles: War, Peace and the Course of History*, London: Penguin Books.

Booth, Ken and Nicholas J. Wheeler (2007), *The Security Dilemma: Fear, Cooperation and Trust in World Politics*, Houndmills: Palgrave Macmillan.

Bourke, Joanna (2004), 'New Tales from the Trenches', *The Independent* Review Section, Friday, 3 September, p. 23.

Brookes, Adam (2005), 'US Watches China Warily', news.bbc.co.uk/1/hi/world /americas/4342527.stm, last downloaded 7 December 2005.

Brooks, Stephen G. and William C. Wohlforth (2005), 'Hard Times for Soft Balancing', *International Security* 30(1), 72–108.

Brown, Richard H. (1976), 'Social Theory as Metaphor: On the Logic of Discovery for the Sciences of Conduct', *Theory and Society* 3, 169–97.

Bull, Hedley (2002), *The Anarchical Society: A Study of Order in World Politics*, 3rd edn, Basingstoke: Macmillan.

Bull, Hedley and Adam Watson (1984) eds., *The Expansion of International Society*, Oxford: Oxford University Press.

Burr, Robert N. (1955), 'The Balance of Power in Nineteenth Century South America: An Exploratory Essay', *Hispanic American Historical Review* 35, February, 37–60.

Burr, Robert N. (1965), *By Reason or Force: Chile and the Balancing of Power in South America*, Berkeley: University of California Press.

Butterfield, Herbert (1966), 'The Balance of Power', in H. Butterfield and M. Wight, eds., *Diplomatic Investigations: Essays in the Theory of International Politics*, London: Allen and Unwin.

Buzan, Barry (1993), 'From International System to International Society: Structural Realism and Regime Theory Meet the English School', *International Organization* 47(3), 327–52.

Buzan, Barry (2004a), *From International to World Society: English School Theory and the Social Structure of Globalization*, Cambridge: Cambridge University Press.

Buzan, Barry (2004b), *The United States and the Great Powers: World Politics in the Twenty First Century*, Cambridge: Polity.

Buzan, Barry (2006), 'Rethinking Hedley Bull on the Institutions of International Society', in Richard Little and John Williams, eds., *The Anarchical Society in a Globalized World*, Houndmills: Palgrave Macmillan.

Buzan, Barry and Richard Little (2000), *International Systems in History: Remaking the Study of International Relations*, Oxford: Oxford University Press.

Buzan, Barry and Ole Waever (2003), *Regions and Power: The Structure of International Security*, Cambridge: Cambridge University Press.

Buzan, Barry, Charles Jones and Richard Little (1993), *The Logic of Anarchy: Neorealism to Structural Realism*, New York: Columbia University Press.

Byers, Michael (1999), *Custom, Power and the Power of Rules: International Relations and Customary International Law*, Cambridge: Cambridge University Press.

Byers, Michael (2000), *The Role of Law in International Politics: Essays in International Relations and International Law*, Oxford: Oxford University Press.

Callahan, W. (2004), 'Nationalizing International Theory: Race, Class and the English School', *Global Society* 18(4), 305–23.

Cantor, Paul (1982), 'Frederich Nietzsche: The Use and Abuse of Metaphor', in David S. Miall, ed., *Metaphor: Problems and Perspectives*, Brighton: Harvester Press.

Cassirer, Ernst (1946), *The Myth of the State*, New Haven: Yale University Press.

Cassirer, Ernst (1966), *The Philosophy of Symbolic Forms, Vol 2, Mythical Thought*, New Haven: Yale University Press.

Cawkwell, George (1997), *Thucydides And The Peloponnesian War*, London: Routledge.

Checkel, Jeffrey T. (2004), 'Social Constructivisms in Global and European Politics', *Review of International Politics* 30(2), 229–44.

Chilton, Paul A. (1996), *Security Metaphors: Cold War Discourse from Containment to Common House*, New York: Peter Lang.

Christiansen, Tomas J. and Jack Snyder (1990), 'Chain Gangs and Passed Bucks: Predicting Alliance Patterns in Multipolarity', *International Organization* 44(2), 137–68.

Clark, Ian (1989), *The Hierarchy of States: Reform and Resistance in the International Order*, Cambridge: Cambridge University Press.

Clark, Ian (2005), *Legitimacy in International Society*, Oxford: Oxford University Press.

Claude, Inis L. (1962), *Power and International Relations*, New York: Random House.

Clegg, Stewart R. (1989), *Frameworks of Power*, London: Sage Publications.

Cohen, Raymond (1994), 'Pacific Unions: A Reappraisal of the Theory that "Democracies" Do Not Go to War with Each Other', *Review of International Studies* 20(3), 205–6.

Coser, Lewis A. (1956), *The Functions of Social Conflict*, London: Routledge & K. Paul.

Craig, Campbell (2003), *Glimmer of a New Leviathan: Total War in the Realism of Niebuhr, Morgenthau and Waltz*, New York: Columbia University Press.

Crosby, Alfred W. (1986), *Ecological Imperialism: The Biological Expansion of Europe 900–1900*, Cambridge: Cambridge University Press.

Dahl, Robert, A. (1957), 'The Concept of Power', *Behavioral Science* 2(3), 201–5.

Dahl, Robert A. (1968), 'Power' in David A. Sills, ed., *International Encyclopedia for the Social Sciences* Vol 12: 405–15, New York: Free Press.

Dallmayr, Fred R. (1984a), *Language and Politics: Why Does Language Matter to Political Philosophy*, Notre Dame, Ind: University of Notre Dame Press.

Dallmayr, Fred R. (1984b), *Polis and Praxis: Exercises in Political Theory*, Cambridge: Massachusetts Institute of Technology.

Davidson, D. (1979), 'What Metaphors Mean', in S. Sacks, ed., *On Metaphor*, Chicago: University of Chicago Press.

Dehio, L. (1962), *The Precarious Balance: Four Centuries of the European Power Struggle*, trans. Charles Fullman, New York: Vintage Books.

Dehio, L. (1967), *Germany and World Politics in the Twentieth Century*, trans. Dieter Persner, New York: W. W. Norton.

Deleuze, Gilles and Felix Guattari (1987), trans. Brain Massumi, *A Thousand Plateaus: Capitalism and Schizophrenia*, Minneapolis: University of Minnesota Press.

Der Derian, James (1998), 'The Scriptures of Security', *Mershon International Studies Review* 42(1), 117–22.

Desch, Michael C. (1998), 'Culture Clash: Assessing the Importance of Ideas in Security Studies', *International Security* 23(1), 141–70.

Deutsch, Karl W. (1963), *The Nerves of Government*, Glencoe: Free Press.

Deutsch, Karl W. and David Singer (1964), 'Multipolar Power Systems and International Stability', *World Politics* 16(3), 390–406.

Donnelly, Jack (2000), *Realism and International Relations*, Cambridge: Cambridge University Press.

Doty, Roxanne Lynn (1996), *Imperial Encounters: The Politics of Representation in North–South Relations*, Minneapolis: University of Minnesota Press.

Draaisma, Douwe (2000), *Metaphors of Memory: A History of Ideas About the Mind*, trans. Paul Vincent, Cambridge: Cambridge University Press.

Draaisma, Douwe (2005), *Why Life Speeds Up as You Get Older: How Memory Shapes Our Past*, Cambridge: Cambridge University Press.

Dunne, Tim (1998), *Inventing International Society: A History of the English School*, Basingstoke: Macmillan.

Dunne, Tim (2005), 'System, State and Society: How Does It All Hang Together?', *Millennium* 34(1), 157–70.

Duverger, Maurice (1972), *The Study of Politics*, trans. Robert Wagoner, Sunbury-on Thames: Thomas Nelson and Sons.

Eccleshall, Robert (1984), 'Introduction: The World of Ideology', in Robert Eccleshall, *et al.*, *Political Ideologies*, London: Hutchinson and Co.

Eckstein, Arthur M. (2006), *Mediterranean Anarchy, Interstate War, and the Rise of Rome*, Berkeley: University of California Press.

Eckstein, Arthur M. (2007), 'Intra-Greek Balancing, the Mediterranean Crisis of ca. 201–200 B.C. and the Rise of Rome', in Stuart J. Kaufman, Richard Little and William C. Wohlforth, eds., *The Balance of Power in World History*, Basingstoke: Palgrave Macmillan.

The Economist (2006), 'The European Union in the World: Abroad Be Dangers', 26 August, 29–30.

Edelman, Murray (1971), *Politics As Symbolic Action: Mass Arousal and Quiescence*, Chicago: Markham Publishing Company.

Edkins, Jenny and Maja Zehfuss (2005), 'Generalising the International', *Review of International Studies* 31(3), 451–71.

Egerton, George W. (1983), 'Collective Security as Political Myth: Liberal Internationalism and the League of Nations in Politics and History', *International History Review* 5(4), 496–524.

Elman, Colin, Miriam Fendius Elman and Paul W. Schroeder (1995), 'History vs. Neorealism: A Second Look', *International Security* 20(1), 182–95.

Elman, Colin (1996a), 'Horses for Courses: Why Not Neorealist Theories of Foreign Policy?', *Security Studies* 6(1), 7–53.

Elman, Colin (1996b), 'Cause, Effect and Consistency: A Response to Kenneth Waltz', *Security Studies* 6(1), 58–61.

Elman, Colin (2004), 'Extending Offensive Realism: The Louisiana Purchase and America's Rise to Regional Hegemony', *American Political Science Review* 98(4), 563–76.

Elman, Colin (2005), 'Explanatory Typologies in the Qualitative Study of International Politics', *International Organization* 59(2), 293–336.

Emerson, Ralph Waldo (1903), 'The Poet', in R. W. Emerson and W. E. Forbes eds., *Complete Works*, Moston: Houghton.

Eubanks, Philip (2000), *A War of Words in the Discourse of Trade: The Rhetorical Constitution of Metaphor*, Carbondale: Southern Illinois University Press.

Fierke, Karin (1996), *Changing Games, Changing Strategies: Critical Investigations in Security*, Manchester: Manchester University Press.

Fink, Z. S. (1945), *The Classical Republicans: An Essay in the Recovery of a Pattern of Thought in Seventeenth Century, England*, Evanston: Northwestern University Press.

Finnegan, R. B. (1972), 'The Field of International Relations: The View From Within', *Towson State Journal of International Affairs* 7, 1–24.

Flood, Christopher G. (2002), *Political Myth: A Theoretical Introduction*, London: Routledge.

Folz, Robert (1969), *The Concept of Empire in Western Europe from the Fifth to the Fourteenth Century*, trans. S. A. Ogilvie, London: Edward Arnold.

Franck, Thomas J. and Edward Weisband (1971), *World Politics: Verbal Strategy Among the Superpowers*, New York: Oxford University Press.

Freedman, Lawrence (1981), 'NATO Myths', *Foreign Policy* 45 (Winter), 48–68.

Friedman, Milton (1953), *Essays in Positive Economics*, Chicago: Chicago University Press.

Friedrich, Carl Joachim (1938), *Foreign Policy in the Making: The Search for a New Balance of Power*, New York: W. W. Norton and Co.

Friedrich, Carl Joachim (1980), *Man and Government: An Empirical Theory of Politics*, New York: McGraw-Hill Book Company, Inc.

Fry, Greg and Jacinta O'Hagan (2000), 'Contending Images of World Politics: An Introduction', in Fry and O'Hagan, eds., *Contending Images of World Politics*, Houndmills: Macmillan.

Geertz, Clifford (1993), 'Ideology as a Cultural System', in *The Interpretation of Cultures: Selected Essays*, London: Fontana Press.

Gellman, Barton (1992), 'Keeping the US first', *Washington Post*, 11 March, zfacts.com/metaPage/lib/9203-Wolfowitz.pdf, last downloaded 7 December 2006.

George, Alexander L. (1983), *Managing US–Soviet rivalry: Problems of Crisis Prevention*, Boulder, Colo.: Westview Press.

Gilbert, Felix (1965), *Machiavelli and Guicciardini: Politics and History in Sixteenth Century Florence*, Princeton: Princeton University Press.

Gilmore, Myron P. (1952), *The World of Humanism 1453–1517*, New York: Harper.

Glaser, Charles Louis (1997), 'The Security Dilemma Revisited', *World Politics* 50(1), 171–201.

Goddard, Stacie E. and Daniel H. Nexon (2005), 'Paradigm Lost? Reassessing Theory of International Politics', *European Journal of International Relations* 11(1), 9–61.

Gong, Gerrit W. (1984), *The Standard of Civilization in International Society*, Oxford: Clarendon Press.

Goodman, Nelson (1976), *Languages of Art*, 2nd ed., Indianapolis: Hackett Publishing Company.

Gowan, Peter (2002), 'A Calculus of Power', *New Left Review* 16, (July/August), 47–67.

Graham, M. W. (1948), *American Diplomacy in the International Community*, Baltimore: John Hopkins Press.

Gray, Colin S. (1992), *The Leverage of Seapower: The Strategic Advantage of Navies in War*, New York: Free Press.

Griffiths, Martin (1999), *Fifty Key Thinkers in International Relations* London: Routledge.

Gruber, Lloyd (2000), *Ruling the World: Power Politics and the Rise of Supranational Institutions*, Princeton: Princeton University Press.

Guicciardini, Francesco (1984 [1561]), *The History of Italy*, Sidney Alexander trans. and ed., Princeton: Princton University Press.

Gulick, Edward Vose (1967, [1955]), *Europe's Classical Balance of Power*, New York: W. W. Norton and Co.

Guzzini, Stefano (1993), 'Structural Power: The Limits of Neorealist Power Analysis', *International Organization* 47(3), 443–78.

Guzzini, Stefano (1998), *Realism in International Relations and International Political Economy: The Continuing Story of a Death Foretold*, London: Routledge.

Guzzini, Stefano (2004), 'The Enduring Dilemmas of Realism in International Relations', *European Journal of International Relations* 10(4), 533–68.

Guzzini, Stefano (2005), 'The Concept of Power: A Constructivist Analysis', *Millennium* 33(3), 495–521.

Haas, Ernst B. (1953), 'The Balance of Power: Prescription, Concept or Propaganda', *World Politics* (4), 442–77.

Hacohen, Malachi Haim (1996), 'Leonard Krieger: Historicization and Political Engagement in Intellectual History', *History and Theory* 35: 80–130.

Haddon, Mark (2003), *The Curious Incident of the Dog in the Night-time*, London: David Fickling Books.

Haldén, Peter (2006), *Compound Republics as Viable Political Systems: A Comparison of the Holy Roman Empire of the German Nation and the European Union*, Phd Thesis, Florence: European University Institute.

Hale, J. R. (1966), 'Introduction', in Francesco Guicciardini, *History of Italy and History of Florence*, trans. C. Grayson, Chalfont St Giles: New English Library.

Hall, Ian (2006), 'Diplomacy, Anti-Diplomacy and International Society', in Richard Little and John Williams, eds., *The Anarchical Society in a Globalized World*, Houndmills: Palgrave Macmillan.

Halliday, Fred (1999), *Revolution and World Politics: The Rise and Fall of the Sixth Great Power*, Basingstoke: Macmillan.

Halliday, Fred (2005), *100 Myths about the Middle East*, London: Saqi Books.

Haslam, John (2002), *No Virtue Like Necessity: Realist Thought in International Relations*, New Haven: Yale University Press.

Haywood, Clarissa Rile (2000), *Defacing Power*, Cambridge: Cambridge University Press.

Heidegger, Martin (1971), *On the Way to Language*, Peter D. Hertz, trans., New York: Harper and Row.

Herz, John H. (1959), *International Politics in the Atomic Age*, New York: Columbia University Press.

Herz, John H. (1969), 'The Territorial State Revisited: Reflections on the Future of the Nation-State', in James N. Rosenau, ed., *International Politics and Foreign Policy*, New York: Free Press.

Heywood, Andrew (2003), *Political Ideologies: An Introduction*, 3rd edn, Houndmills: Palgrave Macmillan.

Hindess, Barry (2006), 'Bringing States Back In', from Review Symposium on Steven Lukes' Power: A Radical View, in *Political Studies Review* 4(2), 115–23.

Hinsley, F. H. (1963), *Power and the Pursuit of Peace*, Cambridge: Cambridge University Press.

Hirschbein, Ron (2005), *Massing the Tropes: The Metaphorical Construction of American Nuclear Strategy*, New York: Praeger.

Hobson, John M. and J. C. Sharman (2005), 'The Enduring Place of Hierarchy in World Politics: Tracing the Social Logics of Hierarchy and Political Change', *European Journal of International Relations* 11(1), 63–98.

Hoffmann, Stanley H. (1960), ed., *Contemporary Theory in International Relations*, Englewood Cliffs: Prentice Hall, Inc.

Hoffmann, Stanley (1977), 'An American Social Science: International Relations', *Daedalus* 106 (Summer), 41–60.

Hoffmann, Stanley (2002), 'Foreword to the Second Edition: Revisiting *The Anarchical Society*', in Hedley Bull, *The Anarchical Society: A Study of Order in World Politics*, 3rd edn, Basingstoke: Macmillan.

Holbraad, Carsten (1970), *The Concert of Europe: A Study in German and British International Theory*, London: Longman.

Hollis, Martin and Steve Smith (1990), *Explaining and Understanding International Relations*, Oxford: Clarendon.

Holsti, K. J. (1991), *Peace and War: Armed Conflicts and International Order*, Cambridge: Cambridge University Press.

Holsti, K. J. (2004), *Taming the Sovereigns: Institutional Change in International Politics*, Cambridge: Cambridge University Press.

Holsti, Ole R., P. Terrence Hopmann and John D. Sullivan (1973), *Unity and Disintegration in International Alliances: Comparative Studies*, New York: John Wiley & Sons.

Hopkins, Raymond F. and Richard W. Mansbach (1973), *Structure and Process in International Politics*, New York: Harper and Row.

Hostetler, Michael, J. (1997), 'The Enigmatic Ends of Rhetoric: Churchill's Fulton Address as Great Art and Failed Persuasion', *Quarterly Journal of Speech* 83(4), 416–28.

Hui, Victoria Tin-bor (2004), 'Towards a Dynamic Theory of International Politics: Insights from Comparing Ancient China and Early Modern Europe', *International Organization* 58 (Winter), 175–205.

Hui, Victoria Tin-bor (2005), *War and State Formation in Ancient China and Early Modern Europe*, Princeton: Princeton University Press.

Humphrey, Adam R. C. (2006), *Kenneth Waltz and the Limits of Explanatory Theory in International Relations*, DPhil Thesis, University of Oxford.

Huntington, Samuel, P. (1999), 'The Lonely Superpower', *Foreign Affairs* 78(2), 35–49.

Hurrell, Andrew (1993) 'International Society and the Study of International Regimes', in Volker Rittberger, ed., *Regime Theory in International Relations*, Oxford: Clarendon.

Hurrell, Andrew (2002), 'Foreword to the Third Edition: *The Anarchical Society* 25 Years On', in Hedley Bull, *The Anarchical Society: A Study of Order in World Politics*, 3rd edn, Basingstoke: Palgrave Macmillan.

Hutson, J. H. (1980), *John Adams and the Diplomacy of the American Revolution*, Lexington: University of Kentucky Press.

Ikenberry, John G. (2001), *After Victory: Institutions, Strategic Restraint, and the Rebuilding of Order after Major Wars*, Princeton: Princeton University Press.

Ikenberry, John G. (2003), ed., *America Unrivalled: The Future of the Balance of Power*, Ithaca and London: Cornell University Press.

James, Alan (1993), 'System or Society', *Review of International Studies* 19(3), 269–88.

Jackson, Robert (2000), *The Global Covenant: Human Conduct in a World of States*, Oxford: Oxford University Press.

Jervis, Robert (1997), *System Effects: Complexity in Political and Social Life*, Princeton: Princeton University Press.

Jones, Charles A. (2006), 'War in the twenty-first century: An Institution in Crisis', in Richard Little and John C. Williams, eds., *The Anarchical Society in a Globalized World*, Basingstoke: Palgrave Macmillan.

Jones, Charles A. (2007) 'The Americas: 1400–1800', in Stuart J. Kaufman, Richard Little and William C. Wohlforth, eds., *The Balance of Power in World History*, Basingstoke: Palgrave Macmillan.

Kagan, Korina (1997), 'The Myth of the European Concert: The Realist–Institutionalist Debate and Great Power Behavior in the Eastern Question, 1821–41', *Security Studies* 7(2), 1–57.

Kaplan, Morton A. (1962), *System and Process in International Politics*, New York: Wiley.

Kapstein, Ethan B. and Michael Mastanduno (1999), eds., *Unipolar Politics: Realism and State Strategies After the Cold War*, New York: Columbia University Press.

Katzenstein, Peter J. (2005), *A World of Regions: Asia and Europe in the American Imperium*, Ithaca: Cornell University Press.

Kaufman, Stuart J., Richard Little and William C. Wohlforth (2007), 'Conclusion', in Stuart J. Kaufman, Richard Little and William C. Wohlforth, eds., *The Balance of Power in World History*, Basingstoke: Palgrave Macmillan.

Kautsky, John H. (1965), 'Myth, Self-fulfilling Prophecy, and Symbolic Reassurance in East–West Conflict', *Journal of Conflict Resolution* 9(1), 1–17.

Keal, Paul (1983), *Unspoken Rules and Superpower Dominance*, Basingstoke: Macmillan.

Keene, Edward (2002), *Beyond the Anarchical Society: Grotius, Colonialism and Order in World Politics*, Cambridge: Cambridge University Press.

Kelly, Phil (1986), 'Escalation of Regional Conflict: Testing the Shatterbelt Concept', *Political Geography Quarterly* 5: 161–80.

Kelly, Phil (1997), *Checkerboards and Shatterbelts: The Geopolitics of South America*, Austin: University of Texas Press.

Keohane, Robert O. (1986), ed., *Neorealism and Its Critics*, New York: Columbia University Press.

Keohane, Robert O. and Joseph Nye (1977), *Power and Interdependence*, Boston: Little Brown.

Kihlstrom, John F. (2004), 'Joseph Jastrow and his Duck – or is it a Rabbit', http://ist-socrates.berkeley.edu/~kihlstrm/JastrowDuck.htm, last downloaded 7 December 2006.

Kingsbury, Benedict (2002), 'Legal Positivism as Normative Politics: International Society, Balance of Power and Lassa Oppenheim's Positive International Law', *European Journal of International Law* 13(2), 401–36.

Kissinger, Henry (1964), *A World Restored*, New York: Grosset & Dunlap.

Kissinger, Henry (1994), *Diplomacy*, New York: Simon & Schuster.

Kittay, E. F., and A. Lehrer (1981), 'Semantic Fields and the Structure of Metaphors', *Studies in Language 5*, 31–63.

Kohnstamm, Max (1992), 'Time to Recall What European Union Is All About', in *International Herald Tribune* 12 May, www.iht.com/articles/1992/05/12/edma_1.php, last downloaded 7 December 2006.

Kövecses, Zoltán (2002), *Metaphor: A Practical Introduction*, Oxford: Oxford University Press.

Krasner, Stephen D. (1999), *Sovereignty: Organized Hypocrisy*, Princeton: Princeton University Press.

Krieger, Leonard (1968), 'Power and Responsibility: The Historical Assumptions', in Leonard Krieger and Fritz Stern, eds., *The Responsibility of Power: Historical Essays in Honor of Hajo Holborn*, London: Macmillan.

Kratochwil, F. (2000), 'Constructing a New Orthodoxy? Wendt's *Social Theory of International Politics* and the Constructivist Challenge', *Millennium* 29(1), 73–101.

Kroker, Arthur (1984), 'Modern Power in Reverse Image: The Paradigm Shift of Michel Foucault and Talcott Parsons', in John Fekete, ed., *The Structural Allegory: Reconstructive Encounters with the New French Thought*, Manchester: Manchester University Press.

Kutolowski, J. (1965), 'The Effects of the Polish Insurrection of 1863 on American Civil War Diplomacy', *Historian* 27(4), 560–77.

Lakatos, Imre (1978), *The Methodology of Scientific Research Programmes*, John Worrall and Gregory Currie, eds., Cambridge: Cambridge University Press.

Lakoff, George and Mark Johnson (1999), *Philosophy in the Flesh: The Embodied Mind and Its Challenge to Western Thought*, London: Harper Collins Publishers.

Lakoff, George and Mark Johnson (2003) 2nd edn, *Metaphors We Live By*, Chicago: Chicago University Press,

Landau, Martin (1972), *Political theory and Political Science: Studies in the Methodology of Political Inquiry*, New York: Macmillan.

Lang, Daniel (1985), *Foreign Policy in the Early Republic: The Law of Nations and the Balance of Power*, Baton Rouge: Louisiana State University Press.

Larson, Deborah Welch (1985), *Origins of Containment: A Psychological Explanation*, Princeton: Princeton University Press.

Lasswell, Harold D. and Abraham Kaplan (1950), *Power and Society: A Framework for Political Inquiry*, New Haven: Yale University Press.

Lave, Charles A. and James G. March (1975), *An Introduction to Models in the Social Sciences*, New York: Harper & Row.

Layne, Christopher (1997), 'From Preponderance to Offshore Balancing: America's Future Grand Strategy', *International Security* 22(1), Summer, 86–124.

Layne, Christopher (2002), 'Offshore Balancing revisited', *The Washington Quarterly* 25(2), 233–48.

Layne, Christopher (2002/3), 'The "Poster Child for Offensive Realism": America as a Global Hegemon', *Security Studies* 12(2), 120–64.

Layne, Christopher (2006), *The Peace of Illusions: American Grand Strategy from 1940 to the Present*, Ithaca: Columbia University Press.

Leffler, Melvyn P. (1992), *A Preponderance of Power: National Security, the Truman Administration, and the Cold War*, Stanford, Calif.: Stanford University Press.

Levy, Jack S. (1994), 'The Theoretical Foundations of Paul W. Schroeder's International System', *International History Review* 14(4), 716–44.

Levy, Jack (2001a), 'Balances and Balancing: Concepts, Propositions and Research Design', in John A. Vasquez and Colin Elman, eds., *Realism and the Balancing of Power: A New Debate*, Upper Saddle River: Prentice Hall.

Levy, Jack (2001b), 'What do Great Powers Balance Against?,' in T. V. Paul, James J. Wirtz and Michel Fortmann, eds., *Balance Of Power: Theory and Practice in the 21st Century*, Stanford: Stanford University Press.

Levy, Jack S. (2004), 'What do Great Powers Balance Against and When?' in T. V. Paul, J. J. Wirtz and M. Fortmann, eds., *Balance of Power: Theory and Practice in the 21st Century*, Stanford: Stanford University Press.

Levy, Jack S. and William R. Thompson (2003), 'Balancing at Sea: Do States Coalesce around Leading Maritime Powers', Annual Meeting of the American Political Science Association Philadelphia.

Lieber, Keir A. and Gerard Alexander (2005), 'Waiting for Balancing: Why the World is Not Pushing Back', *International Security* 30(1), 109–39.

Liska, George (1962), *Nations in Alliance: The Limits of Interdependence*, Baltimore: John Hopkins University Press.

Liska, George (1977), *Quest for Equilibrium: America and the Balance of Power on Land and Sea*, Baltimore: John Hopkins University Press.

Little, Richard (1996), 'Friedrich Gentz, Rationalism and the Balance of Power', in Ian Clark and Iver B. Neumann, *Classical Theories of International Relations*, Houndmills: Macmillan.

Little, Richard (2003), 'The English School vs. American Realism: A Meeting of Minds or divided by a Common Language', *Review of International Studies* 29(3), 443–60.

Little, Richard (2007a), 'British Neutrality versus Offshore Balancing in the American Civil War: The English School Strikes Back', *Security Studies* 16(1): 68–95.

Little, Richard (2007b), 'Greek City States in the Fifth Century BCE: Persia and the Balance of Power', in Stuart J. Kaufman, Richard Little and William C. Wohlforth, eds., *The Balance of Power in World History*, London: Palgrave Macmillan.

Luke, Timothy W. (2004), 'Megametaphorics: Rereading Globalization and Virtualization as Rhetorics of World Politics', in Francis A. Beer and Christ'L De Landtsheer, eds. (2004a), *Metaphorical World Politics*, Lansing: Michigan State University Press.

Lukes, Steven (2004), *Power: A Radical View*, 2nd edn, Houndmills: Palgrave Macmillan.

Lukes, Steven (2005), 'Power and the Battle for Hearts and Minds', *Millennium* 33(3), 477–93.

Magee, Bryan (1999), *Confessions of a Philosopher: A Journey Through Western Philosophy*, London: Weidenfeld & Nicolson.

MacIver, R. M. (1947), *The Web of Government*, New York: Macmillan.

Mackinder, Halford J. (1904), 'The Geographical Pivot of History', *Geographical Journal* 13, 421–37.

McKinlay, Robert D. and Richard Little (1986), *Global Problems and World Order*, London: Frances Pinter.

Marks, Michael P. (2003), *The Prison as a Metaphor: Re-imagining International Relations*, New York: P. Lang.

Mattingly, Garrett (1962 [1955]), *Renaissance Diplomacy*, London: Cape.

Mearsheimer, John J. (2001), *The Tragedy of Great Power Politics*, New York: W. W. Norton and Co.

Mearsheimer, John J. (2006a), 'Conversations in *International Relations*: Interview with John J. Mearsheimer Part 1', in *International Relations* 20(1), 105–23.

Mearsheimer, John J. (2006b), 'Conversations in *International Relations*: Interview with John J. Mearsheimer Part 2', in *International Relations* 20(2), 231–43.

Medhurst, Martin J. (1997), ed., *Cold War Rhetoric: Strategy, Metaphor and Ideology*, Lansing: Michigan State University Press.

Merk, Frederick (1966), *The Monroe Doctrine and American Expansionism, 1843–1849*, New York: Knopf.

Merton, Robert K. (1957), ed., *Social Theory and Social Structure*, Glencoe Ill: The Free Press.

Merton, Robert K. (1993), *On the Shoulders of Giants: The Post-Italianate Edition*, Chicago: University of Chicago Press.

Miller, Eugene F. (1979), 'Metaphor and Political Knowledge', *The American Political Science Review* 73(1), 155–70.

Minter, Richard (2005), *Disinformation: 22 Media Myths that Undermine the War on Terror*, Washington: Regnery Publishing.

Molloy, Sean (2006) *The Hidden History of Realism*, London: Palgrave Macmillan.

Moore, F. C. T. (1982), 'On Taking Metaphors Literally', in David S. Maill, ed., *Metaphor: Problems and Perspectives*, Brighton: Harvester Press.

Morgan, Gareth (1997), *The Images of Organization*, 2nd edn, Thousand Oaks, Ca.: Sage Publications.

Morgenthau, Hans J. (1951), *American Foreign Policy: A Critical Examination* (published in the United States under the title *In Defense of National Interest*), London: Methuen.

Morgenthau, Hans J. (1971) 'The Perils of Empiricism', in his *Politics in the Twentieth Century*, Chicago: University of Chicago Press.

Morgenthau, Hans J. (1973), *Politics Among Nations: The Struggle for Power and Peace*, 5th edn, New York: Alfred A. Knopf.

Mosher, James S. (2003), 'Relative Gains Concerns when the Number of States in the International System Increases', *Journal of Conflict Resolution* 47(5), 642–68.

Murray, John Middleton (1931), *Countries of the Mind*, Oxford: J. M. Murray.

Musolff, Andreas (2004), *Metaphor and Political Discourse: Analogical Reasoning in Debates About Europe*, Houndmills: Palgrave Macmillan.

National Intelligence Council (2004), *Mapping the Global Future*, Report of the NIC's 2020 Project, www.cia.gov/nic/NIC_associates.html, last downloaded 7 December 2006.

Nelson, E. W. (1943), 'The Origins of Modern Balance-of-Power Politics', *Medievalia and Humanistica* 1, 124–42.

Niebuhr, Reinhold (1956), *An Interpretation of Christian Ethics*, New York: Meridian Living Age Books.

Nimmo, Dan and James C. Combs (1980), *Subliminal Politics, Myths and Mythmakers in America*, Englewood Cliffs: Prentice-Hall, Inc.

Nincovich, Frank (1998), 'No Post-Mortems for Postmodernism, Please: Review Essay', *Diplomatic History* 22(3), 451–66.

Nisbet, Robert A. (1969), *Social Change and History: Aspects of the Western Theory of Development*, London: Oxford University Press.

Noppen, J. P., van, (1985), *Metaphor: A Bibliography of Post-1970 Publications*, Amsterdam: John Benjamins.

Noppen, J. P., van and Edith Hols (1990), *Metaphor II: A Classified Bibliography of Publications from 1985 to 1990*, Amsterdam: John Benjamins.

Oakeshott, Michael (1962), 'The Voice of Poetry in the Conversation of Mankind', in *Rationalism in Politics and Other Essays*, London: Methuen.

Onuma, Yasuaki (2000), 'When was the Law of International Society Born? An Inquiry into the History of International Law from an Intercivilizational Perspective', *Journal of the History of International Law* 2, 1–66.

Osborn, Andrew (2005a), 'Uzbekistan told US to Close Down Air Base "After Gas Deal with Russia"', *The Independent*, 1 August, p. 22.

Osborn, Andrew (2005b), 'Russia and China Join Forces to challenge US Dominance', *The Independent*, 19 August, p. 27.

Osgood, Charles E. (1962), *An Alternative to War or Surrender*, Urbana: University of Illinois Press.

Osiander, Andreas (1994), *The States System of Europe, 1640–1990: Peacemaking and Conditions of International Stability*, Oxford: Oxford University Press.

Osiander, Andreas (2001), 'Before Sovereignty: Society and Politics in *Ancien Regime* Europe', *Review of International Studies* 27, Special Issue, December, 119–45.

Pape, Robert Anthony (2005), 'Soft Balancing Against the United States', *International Security* 30(1), 7–45.

Paul, T. V. (2004), 'Introduction: The Enduring Axioms of Balance of Power Theory and Their Contemporary Relevance', in T. V. Paul, James J. Wirtz and Michel Fortmann (2004), eds., *Balance Of Power: Theory and Practice in the 21st Century*, Stanford: Stanford University Press.

Paul, T. V. (2005), 'Soft Balancing in the Age of U.S. Primacy', *International Security* 30(1), 46–71.

Paul, T. V., James J. Wirtz and Michel Fortmann (2004), eds., *Balance Of Power: Theory and Practice in the 21st Century*, Stanford: Stanford University Press.

Pemberton, Jo-Anne (2001), *Global Metaphors: Modernity and the Quest for One World*, London: Pluto Press.

Pepper, Stephen C. (1972 [1942]), *World Hypotheses: A Study in Evidence*, Berkeley: University of California Press.

Phillips, Mark (1977), *Francesco Guicciardini: The Historian's Craft*, Manchester: Manchester University Press.

Pollard, A. F. (1922), 'The Balance of Power', in Edgar Algernon Robert Cecil, ed., *Essays on Liberalism*, London: W. Collins Sons & Co. Ltd.

Pollard, A. F. (1923), 'The Balance of Power', *Journal of British Institute of International Affairs* 2, 51–64.

Porter, Dale H. (1981), *The Emergence of the Past: A Theory of Historical Explanation*, Chicago: Chicago University Press.

Reis, A. (1978), 'The Churchill–Stalin Secret "Percentages" Agreement on the Balkans, Moscow, October 1944', *American Historical Review* 83, 368–87.

Reis, A. (1981), 'Spheres of Influence in Soviet Wartime Diplomacy', *Journal of Modern History* 53, 417–39.

Rendall, Matthew (2000), 'Russia, the Concert of Europe, and Greece, 1821–29: A Test of Hypotheses About the Vienna System', *Security Studies* 9(4), 55–96.

Rendall, Matthew (2002), 'Restraint or Self-Restraint of Russia: Nicholas I, the Treaty of Unkiar Skelassi, and the Vienna System, 1832–1841', *International History Review* 1, 37–63.

Rendall, Matthew (2006), 'Defensive Realism and the Concert of Europe', *Review of International Studies* 32(3), 523–40.

Reus-Smit, Christian (1999), *The Moral Purpose of the State: Culture, Social Identity and Institutional Rationality in International Relations*, Princeton: Princeton University Press.

Rice, Condoleezza (2005), 'The Promise of Democratic Peace', *Washington Post*, 11 December, p. B07 www.washingtonpost.com/wpdyn/content/article/2005/12/09/AR2005120901711.html, last downloaded 5 June 2006.

Richards, I. A. (1936), *The Philosophy of Rhetoric*, Oxford: Oxford University Press.

Ricoeur, Paul (1978), *The Rule of Metaphor: Multi-disciplinary Studies of the Creation of Meaning in Language*, trans. Robert Czerny, London: Routledge & Kegan Paul.

Rorty, Richard (1979), *Philosophy and the Mirror of Nature*, Princeton: Princeton University Press.

Rorty, Richard (1987), 'Hesse and Davidson on Metaphors', *Proceedings on the Aristotelian Society,* Supplementary volume 61, 283–96.

Rorty, Richard, ed. (1992), *The Linguistic Turn*, Chicago: University of Chicago Press.

Rose, Gideon (1998), 'Neoclassical realism and theories of foreign policy', *World Politics* 51(1), 144–72.

Rosecrance, Richard and Chih-Cheng Lo (1996), 'Balancing Stability and War: The Mysterious Case of the Napoleonic International System', *International Studies Quarterly* 40(4), 479–500.

Rosecrance, Richard (2002), 'War and Peace', *World Politics* 55, 137–66.

Rothbart, Daniel (1997), *Explaining the Growth of Scientific Knowledge: Metaphors, Models and Meaning*, Lewiston: Edwin Mellen Press.

Ruggie, John G. (1986), 'Continuity and Transformation in World Polity: Toward a Neorealist Synthesis', in Robert O. Keohane, ed., *Neorealism and Its Critics*, New York: Columbia University Press.

Ruggie, John G. (1998), *Constructing the World Polity*, London: Routledge.

Sarbin, Theodore R. (1964), 'Anxiety: The Reification of a Metaphor', *Archives of General Psychiatry* 10: 630–8.

Sarbin, Theodore R. (1972), 'Imagining as Muted Role-Taking: A Historical-Linguistic Analysis', in Peter W. Sheehan, ed., *The Function and Nature of Imagining*, New York: Academic Press.

Sarbin, Theodore R. (2003), 'The Metaphor-to-Myth Transformation with Special Reference to the "War on Terror"', *Peace and Conflict: Journal of Peace Psychology* 9(2), 149–57.

Sartori, Giovanni (1970), 'Concept Misformation in Comparative Politics', *International Political Science Review* 64(4), 1033–53.

Sayer, Andrew (2004), 'Seeking the Geographies of Power', *Economy and Society* 33(2), 255–70.

Schattschneider, E. E. (1960), *Semi Sovereign People: A Realist's View of Democracy in America*, New York, London: Holt, Rinehart and Winston.

Schmidt, Brian C. (1998), *The Political Discourse of Anarchy: A Disciplinary History of International Relations*, Albany, NY: State University of New York Press.

Schön, Donald A. (1963), *Displacement of Concepts*, London: Tavistock Publications.

Schön, Donald A. (1979), 'Generative Metaphor: A Perspective on Problem-Setting in Social Policy', in A. Ortony, ed., *Metaphor and Thought*, Cambridge: Cambridge University Press.

Schön, Donald A. and M. Rein (1994), *Frame Reflection*, New York: Basic Books.

Schroeder, Paul W. (1977a), 'Quantitative Studies in the Balance of Power: An Historian's Reaction', *The Journal of Conflict Resolution* 21(1), 3–22.

Schroeder, Paul W. (1977b), 'A Final Rejoinder', *The Journal of Conflict Resolution* 21(1), 57–74.

Schroeder, Paul W. (1989), 'The Nineteenth Century System: Balance of Power or Political Equilibrium', *Review of International Studies* 15, 135–53.

Schroeder, Paul W. (1992), 'Did the Vienna Settlement Rest on a Balance of Power?', *American History Review* 97, 683–706.

Schroeder, Paul W. (1994a), *The Transformation of European Politics: 1763–1848*, Oxford: Clarendon Press.

Schroeder, Paul W. (1994b), 'Historical Reality versus Neorealist Theory', *International Security* 19 (summer), 108–48.

Schroeder, Paul W. (2001), 'A. J. P. Taylor's International System', *International History Review* 23 (March), 3–27.

Schroeder, Paul W. (2003), 'Why Realism Does Not Work Well for International History (Whether or Not it Represents a Degenerate IR Research Strategy)', in John A. Vasquez and Colin Elman (2003), *Realism and the Balancing of Power: A New Debate*, Upper Saddle River: Prentice Hall.

Schuman, Frederick L. (1948), *International Politics: The Destiny of the Western State System*, New York: McGraw Hill.

Schweller, Randall L. (1993), 'Tripolarity and the Second World War', *International Studies Quarterly* 37, 73–103.

Schweller, Randall L. (1994), 'Bandwagoning for Profit: Bringing the Revisionist State Back In', *International Security* 19 (Summer), 72–107.

Schweller, Randall L. (1996), 'Neorealism's Status-Quo Bias: What Security Dilemma?', *Security Studies* 5 (Spring), 90–121.

Schweller, Randall L. (1998), *Deadly Imbalances: Tripolarity and Hitler's Strategy of World Conquest*, New York: Columbia University Press.

Schweller, Randall L. (2004), 'Unanswered Threats: A Neoclassical Realist Theory of Underbalancing', *International Security* 29(2), 159–201.

Schweller, Randall L. (2006), *Unanswered Threats: Political Constraints on the Balance of* Power, Princeton: Princeton University Press.

Schweller, Randall L. and David Priess (1997), 'A Tale of Two Realisms: Expanding the Institutions Debate', *Mershon International Studies Review* 41(1), 1–33.

Searle, John R. (1995), *The Construction of Social Reality*, London: Allan Lane.

Sellers, Charles (1966), *James K. Polk: Continentalist*, Princeton: Princeton University Press.

Shapiro, Michael J. (1986), 'Metaphor in the Philosophy of the Social Sciences', *Cultural Critique* 2, 191–214.

Sheehan, Michael (1989), 'The Place of the Balancer in Balance of Power Theory', *Review of International Studies* 15, 123–34.

Sheehan, Michael (1996), *The Balance of Power: History and Theory*, London and New York: Routledge.

Sherman, Chris (2005), *Google Power: Unleash the Full Potential of Google*, New York: McGraw-Hill Osborne Media.

Shibles, Warren (1971), *Metaphor: An Annotated Bibliography and History*, Whitewater, Wis.: Language Press.

Shimko, Keith L. (1994), 'Metaphors and Foreign Policy Decision Making', *Political Psychology* 15(4), 655–71.

Shimko, Keith L. (2004), 'The Power of Metaphors and the Metaphors of Power: The United States in the Cold War and After', in Francis A. Beer and Christ'L De Landtsheer, eds., *Metaphorical World Politics*, Lansing: Michigan State University Press.

Simmel, Georg (1955), *Conflict*, London: Collier-Macmillan.

Simpson, Gerry (2004), *Great Powers and Outlaw States: Unequal Sovereigns in the International Legal Order*, Cambridge: Cambridge University Press.

Singer, J. David, Stuart Bremer and John Stuckey (1972), 'Capability Distribution, Uncertainty and Major Power War, 1820–1965', in Bruce M. Russett, *Peace, War and Numbers*, Beverly Hills: Sage Publications.

Singer, J. David and Melvin Small (1966), 'The Composition and Status Ordering of the International System 1815–1940', *World Politics* 18(2), 236–82.

Slater, Jerome (1987), 'Dominoes in Central America: Will they Fall? Does It Matter?', *International Security* 12, 105.

Small, Melvin (1977), 'Doing Diplomatic History by Numbers', *The Journal of Conflict Resolution* 21(1), 23–34.

Smith, Rupert (2006), *The Utility of Force: The Art of War in the Modern World*, London: Penguin.

Snyder, Glenn H. (1997), *Alliance Politics*, Ithaca: Cornell University Press.

Snyder, Glenn H. (2002), 'Mearsheimer's World: Offensive Realism and the Struggle for Security', *International Security* 27(1), 149–73.

Sofka, James R. (2001), 'The Eighteenth Century International System: Parity or Primacy', *Review of International Studies* 27, Special Issue, December 147–64.

Spruyt, Hendrik (1994), *The Sovereign State and its Competitors*, Princeton: Princeton University Press.

Stamato, Linda (2000), 'Dispute Resolution and the Glass Ceiling: Ending Sexual Discrimination at the Top', *Dispute Resolution Journal*, February, policy.rutgers.edu/CNCR/0200drjarticle.html, last downloaded 6 December 2006.

Steele, Brent J. (2005), 'Ontological Security and the Power of Self-Identity: British Neutrality in the American Civil War', *Review of International Studies* 31(3), 519–40.

Steinberg, Philip E. (2000), *The Social Construction of Oceans*, Cambridge: Cambridge University Press.

Stevenson, David (2004), *1914–1918: The History of the First World War*, London: Allen Lane.

Steiner, George (1975), *After Babel: Aspects of Language and Translation*, London: Oxford University Press.

Strauss, Barry S. (1991), 'Of Balances, Bandwagons, and Ancient Greeks', in Richard Ned Lebow and Barry S. Strauss, eds., *Hegemonic Rivalry: From Thucydides to the Nuclear Age*, Boulder: Westview Press.

Stuart, Reginald C. (1988), *United States Expansionism and British North America 1775–1871*, Chapel Hill: University of North Carolina Press.

Suzuki, Shogo (2005), 'Japan's Socialisation into Janus-Faced European International Society', *European Journal of International Relations* 11(1), 137–64.

Tammen, Ronald L. (2000), *Power Transitions: Strategies for the 21st Century*, New York and London: Chatham House Publishers of Seven Bridges Press.

Taylor, A. J. P. (1954), *The Struggle for Mastery in Europe, 1848–1918*, Oxford: Clarendon Press.

Teschke, Benno (2003), *The Myth of 1648: Class, Geopolitics, and the Making of Modern International Relations*, London: Verso.

Theis, Cameron G. (2003), 'Sense and Sensibility in the Study of State Socialisation: a Reply to Kai Alderson', *Review of International Studies* 29(4), 543–50.

Thomas, David Hurst (2000), *Skull Wars: Kennewick Man, Archaeology, and the Battle for Native American Identity*, New York: Basic Books.

Thompson, William R. (1992), 'Dehio, Long Cycles, and the Geohistorical Context of Structural Transition', *World Politics* 45(1), 127–52.

Thompson, William R. (2006), 'Systemic Leadership, Evolutionary Processes, and International Relations Theory: The Unipolarity Question', *International Studies Review* 8(1), 1–22.

Tilly, Charles (1990), *Coercion, Capital and European States AD 990–1990*, Oxford: Basil Blackwell.

Toynbee, Arnold (1934), *A Study in History*, Vol. 3, Oxford: Oxford University Press.

Toynbee, Arnold (1939), *A Study in History*, Vol. 4, Oxford: Oxford University Press.

Trachtenberg, Marc (1999), *A Constructed Peace: The Making of a European Settlement, 1945–1963*, Princeton: Princeton University Press.

Tucker, R. W. (1952), 'Professor Morgenthau's Theory of Political Realism', *American Political Science Review* 46(2), 214–24.

Tudor, Henry (1972), *Political Myth*, London: Pall Mall.

Uzoigwe, G. N. (1988), 'The Results of the Berlin West Africa Conference: An Assessment', in Stig Förster, Wolfgang J. Mommsen and Ronald Robinson, *Bismarck, Europe, and Africa: The Berlin Africa Conference*

1884–1885 and the Onset of Partition, Oxford: Oxford University Press.

Vagts, Alfred (1948), 'The Balance of Power: Growth of an Idea', *World Politics* 1(1), 82–101.

Vagts, Alfred and Detlev F. Vagts (1979), 'The Balance of Power in International Law: A History of an Idea', *American Journal of International Law* 73(4), 555–80.

Vail, Jeff (2004), *A Theory of Power*, New York: iUniverse Inc.

Vail, Jeff (2005), 'The War is lost', www.jeffvail.net/index.html, last downloaded 10 October 2005.

Vasquez, John A. (1983), *The Power of Power Politics: A Critique*, London: Pinter Press.

Vasquez, John A. (1997), 'The Realist Paradigm and Degenerative Versus Progressive Research Programmes: An Appraisal of Neotraditional Research on Waltz's Balancing Proposition', *American Political Science Review* 91 (December), 899–912.

Vasquez, John A. and Colin Elman (2003), *Realism and the Balancing of Power: A New Debate*, Upper Saddle River: Prentice Hall.

Vigezzi, Brunello (2005), *The British Committee on the Theory of International Politics (1954–1985): The Rediscovery of History*, Milan: Edizioli Unicopoli.

Walt, Stephen M. (1987), *The Origins of Alliances*, Ithaca, NY: Cornell University Press.

Walt, Stephen M. (2005), *Taming American Power: The Global Response to US Primacy*, New York: W. W. Norton.

Waltz, Kenneth N. (1979), *Theory of International Politics*, Reading: Addison-Wesley.

Waltz, Kenneth N. (1981), 'The Spread of Nuclear Weapons: More May Be Better', *Adelphi Papers* No. 171.

Waltz, Kenneth N. (1986), 'A Response to My Critics', in Robert O. Keohane, *Neorealism and Its Critics*, 322–45, New York: Columbia University Press.

Waltz, Kenneth N. (1990), 'Realist Thought and Neorealist Theory', *Journal of International Affairs* 44(1), 21–37.

Waltz, Kenneth N. (1996), 'International Politics is Not Foreign Policy', *Security Studies* 6(1), autumn, 54–7.

Waltz, Kenneth N. (2000a), 'Globalization and American Power', *The National Interest* 59 (Spring): 46–56.

Waltz, Kenneth N. (2000b), 'Structural Realism After the Cold War', *International Security* 25(1), 5–41.

Watson, Adam (1992), *The Evolution of International Society: A Comparative Historical Analysis*, London: Routledge.

Watson, Adam (2007), *Hegemony and History*, London: Routledge.

Weber, Cynthia (2001), *International Relations Theory: A Critical Introduction*, London: Routledge.

Weldes, Jutta (1999), *Constructing National Interests: The United States and the Cuban Missile Crisis*, Minneapolis: University of Minnesota Press.

Wendt, Alexander (1992), 'Anarchy is what States Make of It', *International Organization* 46(2), 391–425.

Wendt, Alexander (1999), *Social Theory of International Politics*, Cambridge: Cambridge University Press.

Wesserling, H. L. (1988), 'The Berlin Conference and the Expansion of Europe: A Conclusion', in Stig Förster, Wolfgang J. Mommsen and Ronald Robinson, *Bismarck, Europe, and Africa: The Berlin Africa Conference 1884–1885 and the Onset of Partition*, Oxford: Oxford University Press.

Wheeler H. (1960), 'The Role of Myth Systems in American–Soviet Relations', *Journal of Conflict Resolution* 4, 179–84.

Wheelwright, Philip (1962), *Metaphor and Reality*, Bloomington: Indiana University Press.

Whitaker, Arthur Preston (1965), *The Western Hemisphere Idea: Its Rise and Decline*, Ithaca: Cornell University Press.

Whiteneck, Daniel J. (2001), 'Long-term Bandwagoning and short-term Balancing: The Lessons of Coalition Behaviour from 1792–1815', *Review of International Studies* 27(2), 151–68.

Wight, Martin (1966), 'The Balance of Power', in H. Butterfield and M. Wight, *Diplomatic Investigations: Essays in the Theory of International Politics*, London: Allen and Unwin.

Wight, Martin (1977), *Systems of States*, edited and introduced by Hedley Bull, Leicester: Leicester University Press.

Wight, Martin (1978), *Power Politics*, H. Bull and C. Holbraad eds., Leicester: Leicester University Press.

Williams, Michael (2005), *The Realist Tradition and the Limits of International Relations*, Cambridge: Cambridge University Press.

Williams, Michael (2006), *Culture and Security: Symbolic Power and the Politics of International Security*, London: Routledge.

Williamson, Oliver E. (1968), 'A dynamic theory of inter-firm behavior', in Bruce M. Russett, ed., *Economic Theories of International Politics*, Chicago: Markham.

Wittgenstein, Ludwig (1980), *Remarks on the Philosophy of Psychology*, Vol. 2, in G. H. von Wright and Heikki Nyman, trans. C. G. Luckhardt and M. A. E. Auwe, Oxford: Blackwell.

Wohlforth, William C. (1993), *The Elusive Balance of Power and Perceptions During the Cold War*, Ithaca: Cornell University Press.

Wohlforth, William C. (1999), 'The Stability of a Unipolar World', *International Security* 24(1), 5–41.

Wright, Moorhead (1975), *Theory and Practice of the Balance of Power 1486–1914: Selected European Writings*, London: Dent.

Zashin, Elliott and Phillip C. Chapman (1974), 'The Uses of Metaphor and Analogy: Toward a Renewal of Political language', *Journal of Politics* 36(2), 290–326.

Index